D0929991

Race,
colonialism
and the
city

By the same author

Key Problems of Sociological Theory
Discovering sociology

John Rex

Professor of Sociology
University of Warwick

Race, colonialism and the city

Routledge & Kegan Paul
London and Boston

First published 1973
by Routledge & Kegan Paul Ltd
Broadway House, 68–74 Carter Lane,
London EC4V 5EL and
9 Park Street,
Boston, Mass. 02108, U.S.A.
Printed in Great Britain by
Western Printing Services Ltd Bristol
© John Rex, 1973

ISBN 0 7100 7412 3

For Nelson Mandela and
all those of my fellow-countrymen
who lie in gaol

The folks with no titles in front of their names
All over the world today
Are raring up and talking back
To the folks called Mister

Langston Hughes,
'In explanation of our times',
Africa South, Cape Town,
vol. 1, no. 3, April 1957

Contents

Acknowledgments

The essays in this book have been organized into a coherent whole and reflect my movement of thought in a number of polemical contexts from reflections on race relations as a metropolitan urban problem to the much more important analysis of the exploitation of the Third World and its revolt against that exploitation. Chapter 1 is based on a paper read to an Anglo-French seminar on race relations at the Centre for the Study of Multi-Racial Societies, University of Sussex, September 1968. Chapter 2 was a working paper presented to my research team in Sparkbrook, Birmingham, in 1963. Chapters 3 and 21 were originally published in *Race*, and are reprinted by permission. Chapter 4 was a paper presented to the Summer School of the Town and Country Planning Association in Manchester in 1968. Chapter 5 was a contribution to a working group on planning education at the Centre for Environmental Studies in London, 1971. Chapters 6 to 11 (inclusive) were prepared as a contribution to a UNESCO symposium and are reprinted by permission. Chapter 12 originally appeared in the *Political Quarterly* in January 1968 and is reprinted by permission. Chapter 13 has appeared in the report of a Scandinavian Conference on Minorities published by the University of Lund. Chapter 14 was my presidential address to the Sociology Section of the British Association at Swansea in 1971. Chapter 15 was presented as a paper to a meeting of the British Society for Social Responsibility in Science, London, 1971. Chapter 16 is reproduced by permission from the *Journal for Bio-Social Science*, supplement 1, 1969. Chapter 17 is an entirely new version of a paper given to the British Sociological Association in 1969, an earlier version of which appeared in S. Zubaida (ed.), *Race and Racialism*, London, Tavistock, 1970. Chapter 18 is reproduced by permission from K. Richardson, D. Spears and M. Richards, *Race, Culture and Intelligence*,

Harmondsworth, Penguin, 1972. Chapter 19 originally appeared in the *British Journal of Sociology* in June 1959. Chapter 20 was presented as a paper to the Institute of Commonwealth Studies in 1968. The final chapter, which complements my book, *Race Relations in Sociological Theory*, London, Weidenfeld & Nicolson, 1970, is wholly new.

I wish to express my gratitude both to those who have stimulated me to deliver these papers and those who have allowed me to reprint chapters and articles.

On a more personal level I have to thank Pat Osborne and Lesley Crone for typing parts of the typescript; Lesley Crone for marshalling all my articles and seeing this book to press; and, last but not least, my colleague and former student, Ivan Oliver, who is a more scholarly man than I am and who nagged the life out of me till I got my footnotes nearly right.

A personal and biographical introduction

It is an interesting and important fact in the sociology of knowledge that the problem of race relations has occurred in sociology during the past twenty-five years in a variety of different forms. These reflect the changing political background of the times. In 1945, for example, the main area of concern was the danger of the recurrence of anti-semitism. In America there was a developing consciousness that the inferior status of the American negro could not be maintained after a war in defence of democracy and in a world in which the United States claimed to be the champion of the forces of the 'free world' against the threat of communist domination. But it is a good indication of how times have changed that in 1945 the National Association for the Advancement of Coloured People was regarded as a dangerously radical organization. So far as Southern Africa was concerned the problem of white supremacy and apartheid did not yet appear as a world problem, and it was generally believed that a statesman of world calibre, like Jan Christiaan Smuts, would find a gradualist solution to the problems of the Union. In Britain itself virtually no problem yet existed and it was not until the process of decolonization began that the incipient conflicts between native peoples and secondary colonialists broke out violently in countries like Malaysia and Guiana.

How different the situation is today. The problem of anti-semitism has been reduced to one of whether Jewish members should be admitted to élite golf clubs, while a new problem has emerged in the Zionist state of Israel, set upon maintaining by immigration a permanent Jewish majority in what was once the homeland of Palestine's Arabs. In the United States whole areas of cities have been set ablaze in what some see as an incipient negro revolution; a Marxist-Leninist party has been formed amongst black Americans; and a white Texan President has

been forced to declare that the programme of the non-violent
negro resistance is his own. In South Africa those who once
supported the South African equivalent of Hitler's stormtroopers,
the Ossewa Brandwag, now govern the country; every significant
African leader has been gaoled or subjected to some form of
confinement; while Africans see their own way forward as lying
in an armed struggle against the alliance of South Africa,
Rhodesia and Portugal. Britain has a population of West Indian
and Asian immigrants numbering about one million; there have
been race riots; and the psephologists have noted that playing the
race issue is one of the best ways of negating or reversing the
electoral swing. Most of the multi-racial former colonies have
had communal troubles; and all over the world there is a
growing consciousness of a revolution which is not simply the
class revolution of Karl Marx, but an uprising of coloured,
peasant and colonial peoples in a race war against their white
colonial and neo-colonial masters.

The contribution which professional sociologists have made
to the understanding of these problems is negligible. For many
years American sociologists were content to measure and monitor
the degrees of formal desegregation which had occurred and then,
suddenly, when the cities began to burn, their successors
wrongly diagnosed the problem simply as the problem of the
cities. In Britain, race relations theory remained on the elementary level of the so-called stranger hypothesis and the
colour-class hypothesis, the second of which perhaps gave some
small degree of illumination, but the former none at all. Then
faced with growing migration and growing racism the sociologists
were prepared to hand over the problem to the amateur gentle-
men of Oxford and the Home Office who moved sharply forward
in the mid-sixties to a rather weakened version of the positions
adopted by their American predecessors in 1939. No serious
centre for the study of the South African social system was
established, and such money as was devoted to race relations,
research in Britain's former overseas territories was frittered
away on a variety of ill-conceived and usually apolitical projects.
The most significant research undertaken in Britain or America
was that of comparative historians such as Eugene Genovese, and
theoretically-minded sociologists such as M. G. Smith, who
developed an interesting set of hypotheses about plural societies,

which fitted fairly well in territories such as the British West Indies before political tensions there became acute.

During this period I found myself at a South African university and became a sociologist. I lived in South Africa because my great-great-grandfather was some kind of royal bastard or semi-bastard who had been exiled there during the first British occupation, and lived on to produce two batches of bastard children who grew up in South Africa. My great-grandfather was an arch-reactionary on the Bantu frontier and he himself produced a line of jingoistic descendants. Other lines were those which derived from his brother, who is said to have married a black woman, and there is yet a third line which affiliated itself culturally to the Dutch and then the Afrikaners, producing amongst other things, at least one minister of the benighted Dutch Reformed Church of South Africa. I suppose it could be said, speaking loosely, that I had the desire to understand race relations better in my blood.

At university I was fortunate enough to find myself amongst a group of ex-servicemen of radical persuasion, and by the time I left I was convinced that the only respectable political choice lay between becoming a Communist or a Liberal, the freedom movement which later affiliated sympathetic whites having not yet come into existence. Intellectually my fellow-students and I were introduced to European social democratic thought and to the work of Park and his colleagues in Chicago by a great teacher, the late James Irving. With his aid we wrestled with the problem of defining and projecting the people's revolution in South Africa, and were engrossed as he told us of Park's study of Chicago, when the processes of invasion and succession which Park described seemed to be going on before our very eyes in Durban and in the near-by city of Port Elizabeth.

Towards the end of my stay at university my friends and I were watched, followed and harassed by the special branch of the South African police, and my own attempt to settle in Rhodesia was prevented as I was 'deemed undesirable because of information received from another government'. I had actually intended to write a thesis about the general strike amongst African workers in Bulawayo in 1948, but, as a result of my recall to South Africa, I received a new passport entitling me to travel to the United Kingdom, where I quickly came to terms with the fact that the only viable political party on the left, the Labour Party, was either not interested in racial questions, or committed to maintaining white supremacy through its manifold connections with white South African and Rhodesian trade unions and with what were commonly called 'kith and kin'. The main thing which I felt it necessary to do politically in the fifties was to help men such as Michael Scott and Trevor Huddleston to rouse British public opinion on the race question and particularly on the problems of mixed-race colonies in Africa. For a while, around 1960, it seemed that we had won. Britain embarked on a programme of rapid decolonization, and Harold Macmillan went to Cape Town to tell Dr Verwoerd of the wind of change now blowing. In rather more cynical retrospect one is now able to see that these winds emanated not from our campaigning so much as from the City of London, where those with financial interests in Africa saw that their profits in the former colonial territories of Africa could be as readily safeguarded by black as by white government.

Even this limited victory was qualified, however, when, in the wake of the civil war in the Congo, the Conservative and Labour parties alike drew back from any further steps towards democratization, and, though they might pay lip-service to some set of principles which should be involved in a constitutional settlement in Rhodesia, came to accept *de facto* the permanent maintenance of white supremacy in Southern Africa as a whole.

Meanwhile colonial immigration to Britain had begun. The plea *civis Britannicus sum*, which in the Conservative imperial consciousness had seemed to have some meaning, was now shown to be nothing but a hollow sham, and little children in what is ironically called Britain's Black Country began to chant 'If you want a nigger for your neighbour, vote Labour'. Not long after this a Conservative statesman of great intellectual repute began to formulate a new policy on immigration, which though it was based on quite different assumptions, struck a responsive chord in hard-core working-class areas, not merely in the Midlands, but in the East End of London. In response to Mr Powell's campaigning, the Labour and then the Conservative government conceded one after another of his points, even to the extent of refusing entry to British citizens from Kenya if they were of Indian descent.

How could a sociologist react to these events? In his role as citizen it was clear enough what he could do. If the South African government decreed that social mixing of the races was illegal or undesirable, he might immediately invite African and Indian friends to his house. If it threatened those who advocated one man one vote democracy with loss of livelihood and imprisonment, he could go on the streets and demand 'One man one vote'. If the Conservatives won the Smethwick seat on the basis of an implicitly racist programme, or if young thugs beat up the coloured residents of Notting Hill, he could help those coloured people to defend themselves from attack. And while a Labour prime minister of Britain cruised around Gibraltar with the white premier of Rhodesia, discussing terms for a settlement, he could help in cash or kind to provide arms for the guerillas on the Zambezi.

But *qua* sociologist he had other duties also. It was not sufficient to fight racism politically. The radical sociologist had the additional task of destroying the intellectual bases of racism and of providing in the struggle of the races a political sociology as sharp and as clear as that of Max Weber and as committed as that of Karl Marx.

My first reaction as a sociologist to the South African situation was that, as its political future was likely to be a revolutionary one, the kind of social book-keeping which had passed as sociology in Britain since the days of Booth, and had been introduced to the University of Cape Town, had little relevance. One had to know what questions to ask and that meant that one had to know something about sociological theory. Hence Talcott Parsons appeared more relevant and significant than Booth or any of his empiricist successors in Britain. On the other hand the Parsonian tradition had to be challenged in the name of conflict theory and revolutionary theory, so that my first tentative attempts to formulate a position in sociology took the form of an argument about the nature and scope of the subject. In a very real sense, therefore, my book *Key Problems of Sociological Theory*, as well as subsequent theoretical writings, have grown out of my engagement with the race problem.

In 1962, however, the construction of theoretical models of conflict on a general level had to be put on one side. I was in Birmingham, England, and the city had got itself into a state of near-hysteria over the problem of the so-called 'twilight zones'. I thought of Chicago and I thought of Durban as I went down to Sparkbrook to look at the British equivalent of Burgess's zone of transition, or of that seedy intermediate area in Durban where I had my one meeting with my ageing maternal grandfather, as he lay in bed smoking cheroots and cursing the Indians. It is interesting, too, to recall that at this time we held a demonstration in Birmingham, England, from which we despatched a telegram of greetings to Martin Luther King in gaol in Birmingham, Alabama.

The first chapters in this book arise from the Sparkbrook study. Their purpose was clear enough. They serve to show how factors in the urban environment serve to exacerbate racial tension. These problems were approached by the government of Great Britain between 1962 and 1970 by setting up interracial bodies to promote goodwill and by conniving at discrimination by local councils, employers and unions. Quite deliberately the papers deal in a microsociological way with the structured social encounters which take place on the ground in areas of immigrant settlement, and would serve to show, I hope, how irrelevant bodies like the Community Relations councils are.

Two developments which arise out of this type of work are, firstly, a discussion of the methodology and theory which underlie them and, secondly an interest in the urban process as such. On the first topic it seemed obvious to me that the trained incapacity of some of my more empiricist sociological colleagues was such that I had to set out in a rather dense and complex chapter what I meant by such concepts as 'housing class' and 'immigrant colony'. On the second I came into contact with the town-planning profession, where men of undoubted goodwill have developed a set of techniques of undoubted political impartiality for misunderstanding nearly every urban problem they encountered.

The British situation, however, could not be summed up in a series of urban studies. The conflict had moved to a political plane and, even if one did not concede that the actual process of discrimination and segregation had been arrested in any way, one had to say something additionally about the nature of racist theories, in terms of which men justify racial discrimination, but which, in fact, come to take on a life of their own. Chapters 6 to

12 in this volume, therefore, say something about the pattern of discrimination in Britain and the ideologies which supported it.

In my Sparkbrook study emphasis had, however, been on the urban variable, and I saw the need to correct it. My colleague and friend, Jamil Hilal, had already drawn my attention to the work of André Gundar Frank, but it was not until I went to Sweden that my students in the University of Lund persuaded me that Frank's theories were of overwhelming importance. I am sure that the general thesis, that the forms of so-called aid which the Third World receives from the affluent nations are, in fact, all forms of exploitation, has not yet been fully proved and documented. Indeed it may be only partially true. But it certainly provides an alternative ideal type for the analysis of international urban migration to be set against its opposite, which starts by assuming that the affluent countries are motivated by nothing but goodwill as they offer their aid. My notes on these problems in a Scandinavian context are set out in chapter 13 and lead to a revised statement of the problem in British cities in my Presidential Address to the British Association's Sociology Section in 1971.

While I was developing my theory of the interplay between colonial and urban factors in race relations a big new race relations industry had arisen in Britain. I was grateful for this, in that, without its initial backing, I would not have been able to start my Sparkbrook research. None the less, I became increasingly disillusioned as the general orientation of new race relations research became apparent. Basically the problem was one of the value of policy-oriented research, when policy makers were known to be unlikely to take any notice of what was being urged upon them. There was nothing in Britain quite parallel to the absorption of Daniel P. Moynihan and his report into the administration, but few of those writing had any idea of what sociological analysis was, and wrote as though the sole motivating factor in Her Britannic Majesty's government was the goodwill of all her subjects regardless of race. In order to explain this I have included in this book a paper on policy-oriented research, which I originally read to a meeting of the British Society for Social Responsibility in Science.

To say this is not to say that I was particularly enamoured of the kind of radical black power sociology which emerged at the other end of the political spectrum. In fact I was deeply distressed when I found that a majority of those in the Race Relations Group of the British Sociological Association's study group were not interested in a relatively objective and detached study of race relations problems in Britain and overseas, but, in the words of one of their officers, had decided to support 'The Black Cause'. Not being interested in more sloganeering I withdrew from the group to write. I made several attempts at formulating a general theoretical position and include two of them here. One was read to the Eugenics Society, the other to the annual conference of the British Association. Both include points of interest which were left out of my book *Race Relations in Sociological Theory* which was published in 1970.

My position at this time was best formulated in an argument with Professor Michael Banton. Banton had used a strict definition of racial theories, confining the term to those theories which made reference to genetic differences. I argued that it was an important sociological question whether, as a result of the discrediting of purely genetic theories, other kinds of theories might not fulfil a similar function. I still think this is so, but it is also the case that genetic and biological theories can, in a scientistic culture give a far firmer anchoring to racialist practice than any other. This is why the popularization of the theories of the Harvard psychologist Jensen, by the scientist turned politician Lord Snow and the psychometrician Hans Eysenck merit attention. I deal with this topic in chapter 18.

By the time I reached this position, however, I was moving towards a general sociological theory of race relations. I had joined in this debate as early as 1958 when the British Sociological Association devoted one of its study sessions to the plural society. This is an early formulation and is rather simplistic in a generally Marxist direction. I came to realize, however, that the plural society debate was important, because what the theorists of the plural society were doing was trying to find an alternative set of concepts for the analysis of colonial society to those offered either by orthodox stratification theory or by Marxism. This seemed to me to reflect political reality, for, just at this time, the theory of the Third World revolution was beginning to distinguish itself from European Marxism.

I have discussed elsewhere my views on the plural society

controversy. These are partly reflected in chapters 19 and 21. Much of what I say arises out of arguments which were opened up by M. G. Smith (1965). If my position differs markedly from his, it is simply because a man of such intellectual calibre is worth disagreeing with. I find all that he has written on the question of plural societies extraordinarily sharp and stimulating, and his latest volume of essays with Leo Kuper on pluralism in Africa is an essential text for anyone concerned with race relations (Smith and Kuper, 1969). More than that, I think the theoretical argument is central to the subject of sociology itself, much more so, certainly, than the Parsonian Utopia.

Two deeply pessimistic essays, chapters 20 and 21, deal again with the country of my birth, South Africa. As a sociologist, given the facts of the situation, I cannot offer anything either in the way of reformist hope or revolutionary optimism. I believe that Dr Vorster administers a system which has a historical distinctness in the way that North American slavery had. It is likely to remain viable as a system so long as white South Africans remain as united as they are, and while Britain and other countries have the economic ties of investment and trade which they do with South Africa. What one may perhaps do as a politically committed individual who is also a sociologist is to hope that the analysis of South African society presented will aid both the understanding and the liberation of Southern Africa. It may, therefore, be appropriate to end this introduction with a personal salute to those brave men who cross the Zambezi at night against hopeless odds to liberate their fellow countrymen, and, even more, to that greatest of my fellow-countrymen, Nelson Mandela, who posited in South Africa a society of equal men and women and ended his plea before sentence:

I hope to live to see these ideals realized, but for these ideals I am prepared to die.

Mandela did not die, and neither has the movement to which he belongs, and which stretches far beyond the boundaries of South Africa, to the jungles of Vietnam, to the rural and urban guerillas of Latin America, to members of Black Liberation movements in the United States, to the Arab peoples who struggle to find unity and liberation in a world in which what most other countries are interested in is their oil supply, and to the peoples of China, whose role in world affairs has yet to be decided. Increasingly it is to the conflicts and problems generated amongst these people and in their lands that sociologists will be looking for an understanding of the future, rather than perpetually reviewing that little range of local problems generated by Europe's industrial and political revolutions.

Race and the city

Part I

Inter-ethnic relations in an urban context

Inter-ethnic conflict never arises solely and simply because of perceived ethnic or physical difference. Such perceived differences may, it is true, be the basis on which individuals within any society are assigned to social positions, but the positions themselves already exist and, by virtue of having to fill them, members of differing ethnic groups find that the conflicts between their groups become exacerbated. In talking about inter-ethnic relations in the city, therefore, while I do not deny that there are various historical reasons why certain groups entering the social system of the city are likely to suffer discriminatory treatment at the hands of their hosts, what I want to do is to show those elements of the urban social structure and conflict system which contribute to sharpening or mitigating intergroup conflict.

There are two aspects of the urban social system which seem to me to be of the greatest importance in this respect. One is the differential distribution of housing opportunity which leads to the emergence of what I have called a system of housing class conflict. The other is the process whereby immigrants coming into the city are gradually socialized into the urban social system.

Differential distribution of housing opportunity would appear to follow from the model of the city as a system of ecologically and sociologically related community structures sketched by Burgess (see Park *et al.*, 1925) in his contribution to the original Chicago study of the city. So much of the discussion that has followed the publication of Burgess's essay seems to me to be irrelevant that it is perhaps important to insist that there are certain hints at least within it which are quite crucial to the theory of urban sociology. It matters very little indeed to us as sociologists whether the actual distribution of ecological zones is concentric or wedge-shaped. What matters is that communities are seen as being affected, in their internal structure, and in their relations with

3

one another, by the relationship which they have to landed property and, much more important, to property in buildings.

It is important also here to say a word about the relationship of the theory of housing classes to the work of Marx and Weber. Some Marxists, commenting on the study which Robert Moore and I made in Birmingham (Rex and Moore, 1967) have argued that we have discussed inter-ethnic relations purely in terms of a secondary variable. To this I would answer that while I believe that there is some relationship between a man's relationship to the means of housing and his relationship to the means of production, the former does also have a degree of independence from the latter; that the labour force tends to scatter for residential and community purposes after working hours; and that there are significant divisions opened up within the various classes, as a result of the conflicting interests which arise from their different housing situations. Hence I find it of interest and of value that Weber asks us to see any market situation as a potential class situation and that he specifically mentions (1967, p. 21) 'ownership of domestic property' as one possible basis of class formation. Another point of interest in Weber's approach to class formation is his emphasis upon the subjective element. He stresses that it is not merely the possession of property but also the meaning given to its possession which determines the behaviour of classes. The implication of this for us is that urban social systems may very well vary according to the culturally given values of the particular society, both with in respect of which housing situation is regarded as desirable, and with regard to the degree with which the system as a whole is regarded as legitimate.

With these theoretical positions stated, it is now possible to turn to the description of one housing class system which we observed in Birmingham, indicating as we go along the features of Birmingham's situation which we regard as unique and the features which we see as of more universal significance. One hopes that as a result of this contribution other sociologists will be stimulated to reconsider the evidence derived from urban societies in other material and cultural circumstances.

Birmingham, like many other cities which came to maturity in the nineteenth century Industrial Revolution, can be seen as going through three phases of housing development and, hence, three phases in the development of its system of housing class conflict. The first of these concerns the first emergence of the industrial community, the second the suburban migration, and the third the continuation of the outward movement coupled with the redevelopment of the inner ring.

The initial settlement saw the emergence of first two and then three housing classes, coupled with related life-styles typically associated with these classes. In the first place the owners of the new industries (the phrase 'captains of industry' is one which I find useful to indicate the extent to which their differentiation from society at large was more marked than that of those whom we today commonly call the 'middle classes') built their gracious town houses so as to enjoy proximity to important civic facilities, while at the same time being well placed in relation to the prevailing winds, so as to avoid the industrial dirt and smoke emanating from their factories. The working class on the other hand lived in the straight rows of red-brick cottages on the cheapest land where speculative builders of the eighteen-fifties built housing for industrial 'hands'. These two groups produced the two polar cultural types in the modern city, middle-class culture based upon family independence and property, and working-class culture based upon the class struggle and the struggle to make ends meet and stay alive.

By the end of the century the third cultural type emerged, as professional and white-collar workers, together with shop-keepers and a few fortunate skilled workers, bought or rented larger terraced properties where they could go some way towards imitating the life-style of the upper-middle classes. The servant bells in the attics and cellars of their surviving houses testify to this. And, this imitative pattern having been established, the ground was laid for the far more important fact of the move to suburbia which affected first these intermediate groups and then the great mass of the established lower-middle and working classes.

The game of leap-frog, which is the central fact of the socio-logical dynamics of urban growth, begins with the move of the upper-middle classes to large mansions in their own grounds in the inner suburbs. But what is far more significant is that shortly after the beginning of the twentieth century they are followed, first by the white-collar people and the skilled workers, and then by the great mass of the established working class.

Suburbia is basically a petit-bourgeois phenomenon. That is to say it aims at copying the independent life-style of the upper-middle classes, but is able to do so only with the help of the artificial aids which mortgage and credit facilities provide. Thus in Birmingham, as in other English cities, the typical suburban man is a man who is buying a three-bedroomed, semi-detached house with the aid of a mortgage loan repayable in twenty to twenty-five years. The security of his employment and his loan enable him to feel and act as an independent family man. Yet in English cities, privately owned and mortgaged petit-bourgeois suburbia quickly produces its working-class equivalent. One of the central political facts of the twentieth century is the capture of a measure of political control and hence of control of physical resources by the established and organized working classes. The consequence of this in the development of the city is the public provision of relatively high standard rented housing. The actual architectural styles adopted in these 'council houses', however, are ones which derive from petit-bourgeois suburbia, and the way of life which develops on the council estates is something of an amalgam of suburban and working-class styles.

For the vast majority of the population, a transition to either the private suburban or the council estates has been considered in England a desirable destiny, and one which contrasts favourably with the lot of those who remain behind or succeed them as residents of the inner ring. For unless or until a centripetal movement begins, as it sometimes does when office workers and unattached intellectuals begin actively to seek accommodation in the inner ring, those who live there are likely to be those who have failed in a competitive struggle for more highly desired types of housing. Amongst these, the most important groups are the owners of small old houses in the inner ring, whose relative status has declined both because of their increasing age and because of their relative lack of appeal when compared with suburban alternatives, the tenants of old slum property awaiting demolition, including some 'undesirable' tenants placed there by the local government, because they are thought unfit for tenancies of new houses, the new owners of the old white-collar terraces who most commonly live in a few rooms of a house which they let as lodgings to the newest immigrants and other

disadvantaged groups, and finally these new immigrants and disadvantaged groups themselves.

The existence of these varied types of housing, which give to
their inhabitants varying degrees of ownership, control and
security, means that, in the city as a whole, there is a class
conflict as well as a status order related to kinds of housing, and
that, at ward and neighbourhood level, the pattern of intergroup
relations will in part be influenced by the position which the
various groups of inhabitants occupy in relation to the housing
stock.

Since I wish to concentrate on the way in which housing class
situations affect immigrant ethnic groups, I propose to concentrate attention on one kind of neighbourhood, namely that in
which a good part of the total housing accommodation takes the
form of rooms let in lodgings. So far as the urban system as a
whole is concerned, I would only note that the people who live
in such areas are considered as occupying an inferior position,
albeit one which many people hold the inhabitants deserve.
They are at the opposite end on a scale of desirability of housing
from the inhabitants of both public and private suburbia. The
key to understanding this type of area, which Burgess called
the 'zone of transition', and which comes to be called in England
'the twilight zone', is to be found in the motivation of the landlords of the lodging-house. It is often thought that these are
ruthless capitalist exploiters, who are themselves rich, and cal-
lously disregard the welfare of their tenants. In some cases this
may be so, but when it is, this may well represent only the
advanced and rationalized form of a process which originally
takes another form. The crux of the matter is to understand this
other form of lodging-house proprietorship.

Very often, and perhaps more often than not, the entrepreneur
who provides housing in the lodging-house zone does so acci-
dentally, in the course of housing himself and solving his own
economic problems of survival. Commonly he is an immigrant
who fails to qualify for the sorts of financial and other aid which
are offered to some by building societies and to some by the local
government authority. Hence he is forced to other markets, and
finances house purchase in part with short-term loans from
banks or moneylenders, and in part by borrowing from friends.
It is inevitable that with the heavy repayment obligations which

such loans imply the purchaser must then turn his house into a money-earning asset. To do this means turning over part of one's house, not simply to one's own family or others to whom one feels a charitable obligation, but to those who can be regarded as financially exploitable. At the same time it means he will be quite prepared to take tenants who are willing to pay without asking too many questions about their non-financial qualifications.

The complement of the landlord's attitude is to be found in the attitudes of his tenants. For, after the various sorts of selection essential to the allocation of 'desirable housing' have occurred, there are bound to remain some who simply cannot qualify and are, therefore, in the desperate position of being willing to settle for precisely the sort of accommodation which the lodging-house landlord has to offer. Thus, while it is true that there is considerable conflict and tension between landlord and tenant, there is also symbiosis. Without intending to do so, they come to need each other.

The kind of housing to which this interlocking pattern of motivation gives rise is by common consent the worst housing in the city. It is not that the houses involved are old or, at the outset of their career as lodging-houses, physically decrepit. Since the houses which are most suitable for letting as lodgings are precisely those which were originally built to house the status-aspiring petit-bourgeoisie, they are inevitably structurally in better condition than the so-called slums. Yet at the very time when housing authorities are clearing the oldest and smallest cottages which are called slums, it is recognized that there is a kind of housing which is even less desirable than that which is officially condemned as a slum.

It follows from this that the most important conflicts in the twilight zone, or zone of transition, will be not between landlord and tenant in the lodging-houses, but between all the inhabitants of those houses, taken together, and their neighbours in the same urban ward. Of these the most important are the proprietors and tenants of the remaining non-slum houses, which are still in single-family occupation, and the tenants of slum houses. The former will see the spread of multiple occupation of houses as still further lowering the status of the streets in which they live, while the latter will see the lodging-house population as having unfairly obtained access to high standard housing and having misused it. The hostility of these two groups is likely to be reinforced by the fact that the local housing and health authorities, unable to provide an alternative form of housing for those who live in lodgings, must none the less act against the proprietors of a form of housing which is well below acceptable standards of health and amenity. The inhabitants of such houses, therefore, serve as a scapegoat for all those who are aware of the deficiencies of the city's housing system. It greatly facilitates this scape-goating process that many of those involved are both foreign and black.

What I have sought to do so far, then, is to show that the housing system of a modern English city is such that the new and poor immigrant who comes to live there does not find himself entering a social system in which there is either a system of equality or a system of legitimized and recognized inequality. What he finds is a system in which his own struggle to house himself places him in competition or conflict with all kinds of other groups and, as a first approximation to defining the position of ethnic groups newly entering the urban social system, we should say that they find themselves in a housing class situa-tion, and that their organizations will tend to take on the charac-teristics of trade unions on behalf of conflict groups.

Cross-cutting all this, however, is the process which I would call urban socialization. It is a process whereby men from rural, peasant, kin-based social systems must come to be effective role-players in an urban individualistic system based upon property on the one hand and bureaucracy on the other. We have now to see how the associational and community life of new immigrant groups is shaped by the functional demands of the colony, which acts as a staging post on his way towards sociali-zation as well as by the housing class system. Thus the West Indian or Pakistani may live in a mixed race lodging-house, but, for as much of his life as possible, he lives outside that lodging-house in the world of the immigrant colony. Again we may turn to the work of Max Weber (1958; 1961; 1968) for preliminary orientation to the study of this problem. Like Weber we need to distinguish three alternative forms of social order which occur as possibilities in the urbanizing process. The first of these is the social order of traditional society where effective and kin-based ties are strong, and rational calculation as a basis for behaviour is at its minimum. The second is a society of the market-place in which there is no overall social will and no human restraint on the level of exploitation. The third, the main object of Weber's interest and concern, was the kind of social order in which individualism and rational calculation operated within a framework or normative order.

The new immigrant with a minimal relationship to the host society would find himself in a position of the second type. He would have lost his ties with his fellow-countrymen, but his ties with the new society would be simply those of the 'callous cash nexus'. Not merely would he have purely contractual relations with his employer, but his only larder would be the grocer's shop, his only dining-room, a cheap café, and his only means of sexual and emotional fulfilment, the brothel. Those who have lived in the twilight zones will know that this ideal type is sometimes quite close to the reality which men experience. But it is also true that a life of this kind becomes unsustainable and that very few immigrants could live this way for long without the risk of mental breakdown or suicide. Thus most men new to the city seek out a group within which they can find emotional and moral support and social ties of a less rational-calculating kind.

The problem of what kind of group life men seek and hence of what types of groups are bound to exist in the zone of transition is an interesting one and of some importance to sociology. I believe that such groups must fulfil three major functions, each of which is closely related to the other. The first of these is the overcoming of social isolation. The second is the affirmation of values and beliefs. The third is the performance of some kind of pastoral or social-work function.

The connection between the first and second of these functions is obvious, as soon as we consider the paradox of urban loneliness. Why is it that, although the immigrant to the city finds more people there than he has ever seen simultaneously before, he is also more lonely than ever before. Obviously in part this is due to the fact that he can make no claim based upon kinship. But perhaps even more important than this, is the fact that he simply lacks the means to communicate his claim. For to overcome loneliness and social isolation means more than that we should have other people. People there may be in plenty. But, unless we have the shared language and culture to communicate with them, they might as well be stones or animals. The set of understandings, the shared culture and language necessary for communication, is provided for the immigrant by the colony of his fellow-countrymen. Anyone who shares that culture now becomes a kind of substitute kinsman. One has a claim on him as one does not have on other men one meets in the market-place. And with him one may let one's hair down, reveal something of oneself, and privately discuss the harsh world, within which workaday life must be lived without discussion.

There has been a good deal of debate consequent upon the work of Redfield (1947) and Oscar Lewis (1965) as to whether or not social relations amongst new immigrants to the city are more intense than they are in rural peasant communities. The answer is that they are very intense indeed, but that they are different. On the one hand the actual kinship network which sustains the society and culture back home is missing and the full home culture is not reproduced. But starting with the elements of that culture, men who discuss their new experiences privately with their fellow immigrants define new meanings, and create a new culture, which is specifically and peculiarly the culture of the urban immigrant colony.

A system of beliefs and values such as arises amongst immigrants not merely describes the world, it evaluates it, and imposes on those who share it the obligation to sustain or to change that world. Such a system is already given to some extent in the very structure of a language. But over and above this there are always new meanings to be defined and this various groups of immigrants will do. Undoubtedly, the process is facilitated when the group has a distinctive system of religious belief and practice. In the temple, the mosque, the church, or the chapel, the immigrant learns a moral orientation to his new world.

Almost inseparable from the groups to which a man turns for moral support and advice, however, are those who offer him help of a more material kind, and no group could survive long amongst immigrants which did not offer, along with its belief system and culture, some kind of help with the daily problems of housing, educating the young, getting work, communicating with those at home, or any of the other problems which the immigrant must solve if he is to survive. So, supplementing the bureaucratic services provided by the Welfare State, the immigrant finds that there are other services, which at worst act as a channel of communication with the formal services, but at best provide him with an additional and more direct source of aid.

What we may expect, therefore, amongst all new, under-privileged immigrant groups in the city, is that they will evolve some sort of colony structure, and that, although the actual physical dwelling place of an immigrant may be a room branching off a bleak corridor in a house where he neither knows nor cares about the other tenants, he will have some place to which he can go, to a church, to a restaurant or public house, to a shop, or simply out on to the pavement where he may be sure of meeting others like himself, others with whom he could feel at home.

The world of the colony is of course the springboard from which the immigrant will, unless the society is determined upon a policy of discrimination and segregation, enter the more individualistic society. He will gradually be less punctilious about his own religious observances. He will come to look outside the colony for friends and, when he is in need, he will go like any other citizen to claim his citizen's welfare rights. But to say that this is his long term destiny is in no sense to imply that the colony stands in the way of his making the transition. Far from this being the case, were it not for the colony, he would not have been able to survive long enough in the city to make even the first faltering steps towards assimilation. It would be misleading, however, to pretend that such a process of assimilation will be undergone by all immigrants to the city. The alternative is a system in which some ethnic groups deemed to be inferior are prevented by discrimination from leaving their colony base, so that the colony becomes a de facto ghetto. This by no means implies that those consigned to the ghetto will not adopt the culture of their hosts. They may well do so. But if they do suffer this fate of ghetto-ization their ultimate relationship with the city will come to depend upon the overall balance of political power, whether that in turn depends upon the ballot-box or upon street riots.

So far, however, we have been talking of ghettoes and colonies and conflict groups. It remains to be shown what relationship there is between these abstract sociological categories and the actual groups to which men belong.

The first thing to be said about this is that, whatever the overt purpose of the various organizations and groupings which exist, the likelihood is that they will continue to have a vigorous life, because they will be fulfilling the functions of a conflict organization or a colony as we have outlined them. Thus, whether we look at a church, a political, social or sporting club, an immigrant welfare association or the clientele of a public house or grocery, we may find that it may be pressed into service as a 'trade union', as a means of overcoming loneliness, as a value-affirming organization, or as a social-work agency. True, a church may specialize in one direction, a public house in another, but there is considerable overlap none the less, and the officers of these various organizations find themselves in much the same kind of business.

It would seem then that the struggle over housing rights and the urban socialization process dictate a certain pattern of community organization and structure, and that we should expect organizational forms of the kind mentioned to arise in areas of immigrant settlement. We should notice, however, that segregation and conflict are not the only possible patterns for the relations between these various groups. Indeed the most interesting feature of urban social dynamics is the way in which organizations based upon colonies and conflict groups become interlocked with one another, or give rise to wholly new, community-wide forms of organization.

In part this is due simply to the lack of fit between the organizational apparatus which a community inherits and its actual needs. Thus men cannot hope to find in England a church which exactly reflects in its gloss on the Christian or some other doctrine the picture of the world which has been worked out by members of an immigrant group or a sub-group within the host society. Nor is there a political party which exactly reflects the interests of each conflict group. It is true, of course, that for the sociologist the fascinating thing about the life of these and other organizations is how readily they become adapted to serve the new social situation created by inter-ethnic group contact. But, when this has been emphasized, it still remains the case, and an essential part of a full sociological description, that these organizations, having, as they do, commitments arising in other times and places, do represent an independent factor and a brake on the overall drive towards conflict. A Protestant church may be faced with an influx of confirmed members from another country asking for communion. A political party will be influenced by pressures of a more universalistic kind arising in other constituencies. And even a licensed public house might, out of regard to the terms of its licence, refrain from excluding strangers. Such movement between organizations as this produces may serve to create the sense that the organizational facilities of the community belong to all its members, rather than each organization being at the disposal of one group only. And this sense will be strengthened if the leaders of the various organizations come to recognize that some of their interests are shared. It may well be the case that, given the overall deterioration of the neighbourhood and the continual identification of the area in the public mind as a problem area, the leaders of different ethnic communities will unite, as it were against a common enemy, and pool the organizational resources to serve all ethnic groups at a higher level.

In my experience in Birmingham I felt bound to notice that, apart from the obvious tendencies towards conflict and segregation which were evident, the two processes which I have mentioned were at work. There were individual organizations which stretched a little beyond the bounds which group self-interest would have set for them. And there were additionally community-wide organizations of a federal character. But I would not want to over-emphasize their importance. They are the organizations which are commonly talked about by liberal-minded optimists, who are concerned at all cost to avoid conflict and judge the importance of different organizations somewhat wishfully. In my view they are at the moment merely braking mechanisms which serve to blur and check incipient conflict. Their existence by no means implies that the potentiality for conflict has been overcome. A sudden incident could polarize the situation, and, in any case, the overall effect of the urban encounter of the various ethnic groups has been to exacerbate whatever tendencies to conflict were present between them already.

In short I am arguing that unplanned urban migration, in which there is no regard paid to ensuring that those immigrants who want assimilation achieve it, can and should be planned with the aid of sociological knowledge.

2 Community and association amongst urban migrants

One of the oldest theoretical distinctions in the sociological analysis of systems of social relations is the distinction between 'community' and 'association'. This distinction derives from the work of Tönnies (1955) and distinguishes between spontaneous organizations which involve the whole life of an individual, and organizations, more formal and deliberately purposive in their structure, usually directed towards a clear and specific goal. I believe that some distinction along these lines has to be made in sociological analysis, but I also believe that it has to be made considerably more subtle if it is to capture the variety, and, still more, to explain the dynamics, of the situation in Sparkbrook. I draw a distinction, therefore, between what we call 'primary communities' and associations.

I use the term 'primary communities' to refer to those groups on which individuals depend to keep them out of a state of absolute social isolation. In primary communities men reveal more of themselves. They turn to their fellow-members in times of emergency. They tell secrets about themselves. They share their excitements and joys. They feel able to relax and to 'let their hair down'. In ordinary life outside they measure themselves against what they think other members of their primary group might think is proper behaviour. In stable societies most men find such a primary community amongst their immediate family and kin. But in a shifting urban environment they seek out some group to which they can commit themselves in an analogous way. They find their community in a lodging-house or in a small group of intimate friends with whom they spend a large part of their leisure.

It should not be thought that a man can live his whole life in such a primary community. Far from it. The economy, the political and social system in which urban men live is too complex for that. Men must participate in a much wider and more formally organized society to satisfy some of their most elementary needs and to realize their interests. Yet, for all this, primary communities are in some ways vital to existence. For it is not merely that men without them are lonely, true and important though this may be. What matters more is that without such group life they lack moral reference points and have no social mirror in which they can look at and know themselves. The lack of this kind of life leaves men in a state of anomie.

In Sparkbrook I was continually aware of the significance of primary groups of this sort and still more, perhaps, of the significance of their absence. One had only to sit for an hour or two in the headquarters of the Sparkbrook Association to be sure of meeting men and women for whom life was nearly insupportable, because they had no close group to whom they could appeal. They fed hungrily on the little warmth that they could find in the company of the Association's staff, but went away despairingly and reluctantly to attic rooms with no social meaning.

Perhaps more central to the Sparkbrook Association than any other person I met was an Estonian refugee, whom I met in the pubs or in the street or in the Association buildings night after night. According to his story he was the son of an Estonian farmer who, as the Russians approached, advised his son to go West. He went West and apparently 'found a job' for a while in the German army. As that army broke up he became a refugee again and eventually finished up with many other East European refugees working in the British mines. There were various sexual liaisons, but none became permanent and, gradually, as all the other Estonians left for Canada and the United States, he drifted alone into Birmingham. He says now that he doesn't go to Canada 'because you can't get a woman in Canada, but you can in Sparkbrook'. Yet he has no woman, even for a night, because, somewhere along the line, he was broken as a man, and lost the capacity for committed social interaction. Now there is work, and, after work, a pub where no one really wishes to know him, and, then, his attic. His life no longer has any significant social meaning for himself. He knows a person who bears his name, but he knows too that that name is at best a joke to people around him. No one needs him. And there is no prospect that anyone will. Even those who show any concern for his condition only wish that he would leave the area and not trouble their consciences any more.

Compare with this man, one of our West Indian friends. His conditions of life are, by any standards, difficult. He lives with his wife and five children in two rooms in a lodging-house. There is a cooker on the landing, and no bath. He has been in Birmingham five years and will soon go on the council house waiting list and then be considered for re-housing after another year. He had thought that he would get a house after five years, and he feels betrayed now that he knows he will not. Yet for all his suffering, his morale is high. He can tell his wife at night what he thinks of the council. He takes pride in his children. And in one of the two rooms which acts as a parlour he meets his friends with dignity. His is a whole life, because he has moral reference points. He has the spirit and the capacity to interact with other men and to organize with them to fight for his rights.

These are extreme cases. All the people who live in Sparkbrook do not either live in the total social void of our Estonian or enjoy the security of kinship which this West Indian has. For most there is a relatively inadequate home or circle of friends, and beyond that a world of more ephemeral contacts which may be leaned upon from time to time and in greater and lesser degree to solve problems and to give life meaning. They include the contacts of the street, the pub and the cafe. They include other members of formal organizations to which the particular individual may adhere. These contacts lack the depth and significance of contacts in a primary community and they have an importance of a different kind in the social structure. But they none the less help to contribute to the meaning of life in Sparkbrook.

The most superficial and empty contacts which we have with other human beings in the city are those with people whom we pass in the street. They remain very largely 'faces in the crowd'. At most we unconsciously classify them by the cultural badges they wear. And it is that kind of contact which men have at first when they go into pubs and cafes to spend an hour or two. But within the world of the pub some kind of social interaction begins and because we see in it the embryo of more formalized patterns of interaction, we wish to look at it analytically and in detail.

Let us take the case of an ex-soldier, whom our research team met in a pub, one of the many pathetic down-and-out people who crowd into slum pubs on a Saturday night, and whose life appeared to us to be one of continuous despair. He was a native Brummie and had served for many years in the army. His reference groups were his family and kin in the Ladypool Road, and the army, but both of these existed for him now only in memory. His mother and father had died and he, a bachelor, had failed to perpetuate the family line and so create a new role for himself. The army had discharged him, and, by so doing, no longer recognized his social existence. He could and did assert the importance of these groups in order to lay some claim to respect and dignity ('my mother was the finest person who ever lived'. 'I've had to fight all my life'). But the fact was that the people of Sparkbrook were no longer playing these roles. To associate with them he had to begin again.

His first encounter with the New Britain is in the Brewers' Arms. And the role which he enters there is one which is open to virtually anybody. It is that of a customer, and it is part of a role-system which also includes the roles of publican, publican's employees and fellow-customers. The characteristic of this role-system, however, is that it is based solely upon the 'callous cash nexus'. It is not a role-system in which, as Durkheim put it, 'the image of the one who completes me becomes inseparable from mine'. It is perhaps the special task of the sociologist to show precisely how relations of the second kind are established between people brought together by the first. Pubs and cafes are of particular importance here.

Of some interest, of course, is the role of alcohol. This helps to restructure a man's sensations and so to alter his world. It probably heightens his and others' capacity for social interaction by suppressing inhibitions. And it makes him susceptible to social and cultural impressions. Some such transformation of the world and of himself would be necessary in almost any social context to bring him into a new world of interaction.

As the alcoholic haze develops, things and activities about our ex-soldier, which at the beginning of the evening were meaningless, begin to take on social and communal meanings. In sitting round a table drinking with others, he finds himself in a very elementary familial situation. On the notice boards there is a notice about a collection for a bereaved customer, betokening the existence of an elementary mutual aid situation. And then people begin to sing. He does not know the words, but he sings as best he can. Someone buys him a drink, thus sharply re-defining the market situation, and, finally he, himself, may stand a round.

Difficulties arise with the songs, because they are the songs of Dublin and Galway rather than of the Ladypool Road. He starts by sharing only elementary musical notions and language with his fellow-drinkers. But very quickly he learns the words and after many visits he will build up quite a repertoire. It would, of course, be more difficult for a Pakistani, who starts by sharing neither the music nor the language. But the process whereby the outsider becomes incorporated into the system is essentially the same. On successively more significant levels he learns the language of social interaction and, by so doing, finds himself with a role to play, and internalizes the expectations of others.

Here we see the emergence of some kind of structured inter-action replacing the 'faces-in-the-crowd' experience of the city, albeit in a world set apart from daily life and aided by an alcoholic stimulus. We now wish to draw attention to certain elements in this situation, which are important, and which take a more definite form in more tightly structured types of association.

The first concerns the sharing of culture as a means of inter-action. We see here that the man concerned is not merely lonely in the sense of lacking other people about him. There is no lack of people in the city. What is lacking is a shared set of meanings, of norms governing interaction, and a set of beliefs about how the world is and should be. Some minimum shared culture of this kind is necessary, if significant interaction is to occur, and if people do not share it as a result of common education they must acquire it in other ways.

Social interaction presupposes some agreement on what the world is like. But this agreement rarely posits a world as seen by a detached objective scientist. It posits instead one in which objects, including other people, are charged with meaning. They become objects of fear, reverence and love. They are not merely objects to be manipulated at will. And group membership, therefore, depends upon the particular world-view, the particular set of spectacles one has for looking at the world. In Sparkbrook there were as many different groups as there were 'world-views' in this sense.

But a man's world-view depends not only on how he views objects. It may depend also on how he views himself. He may see the world as moving inevitably in some direction. Or he may see its movement in that direction as dependent upon his own performance. This is of very great importance, when we come to consider organizations of a more formal kind, and have to decide whether they imply an activist attitude to social change or not. We shall draw attention particularly to the difference between organizations which merely affirm beliefs and stop at this, and those which require action on the part of their members.

Another point to be noticed, however, is that the act of affirming and communicating beliefs may take place in circumstances set apart from daily life, and the implication of such acts are not always clear. In the case we have just mentioned our ex-soldier is drunk. How far does he carry over his new commitments to beliefs and values into his sober state. Equally, if we find a religious congregation affirming beliefs in sacred circumstances, are we to assume that these beliefs are carried over into daily life? Their effect may be purely cathartic. That is to say that, having had an opportunity to express their beliefs and hopes and aspirations in 'another world', they may better be able to accept the world as it is. My own belief is that very often the business of belief and value affirmation is purely cathartic, but that there are unusual circumstances in which the beliefs and norms of the sacred world may carry over into the profane world of daily life.

We have now passed beyond a consideration of primary communities to groups of individuals who are bound together, not by intimate personal ties, but through sharing a common set of cultural meanings, norms and beliefs, which structure the social forms within which they interact. But we have not yet considered groups which approach the associational type mentioned above. Obviously, groups of this kind are of considerable importance. Their main feature is that they have a clear purpose, and that their structure is related to this purpose.

A pure form of such an organization might sometimes be found in a trade union, a political party or an immigrant association. Such organizations might set themselves clear goals such as raising wages, getting voters or opposing discrimination, and their structure may be designed to facilitate these goals. But pure types like this exist only in theory. By virtue of their existence as social systems, such associations also fulfil other functions for their members. They may, for example, become belief and value affirming organizations and, in so far as this has a cathartic function for their members, the declared purpose of the organization might lose in importance. If we say that a political party has become rather like a church for its members, this is what we mean. Of course, it may equally be the case that a church, by adopting social goals, might become like a political party. But this is what we want to emphasize, namely, that looked at in terms of their functions, churches and political parties as well as other organizations may be serving the same function or competing in the same field.

Another common feature of organizations with a purposive character is that there is a distinction to be made between members and clients. Nearly all the organizations with which we shall be concerned do some kind of pastoral work, and such work implies (*a*) members who act on behalf of the organization and (*b*) clients who benefit from its services. At different times, however, the same individual may be both member and client.

Some organizations serve a wider clientele than others. In the welfare state the largest association is the state itself. Everyone is a member of this association and everyone may also be its client.

But the latter fact is so obvious that most people consider the state as alien to themselves, and see themselves solely as clients of this alien organization. Receiving services from the state is a quite different experience from receiving it from 'one's own organization', i.e. an organization of which one is both a member and a client.

None the less, there are some organizations in which the pastoral or welfare function is the predominant one, and in which the individual's contact with the organization is mainly in the client role. In the case of these organizations their effect on people's lives may be significant even if those individuals in no sense regard themselves as members. It may also be the case that these organizations could or do sub-contract welfare work for the state.

It is now possible to list the four major functions of associations

and to use these as a basis for distinguishing the various associational types with greater subtlety than the crude community-
association dichotomy enable us to do. The four functions are
(1) Overcoming social isolation, (2) Affirming cultural beliefs and
values, (3) Goal attainment, and (4) Pastoral work.

From the point of view of the individual the organization may
thus provide relief from loneliness, provide him with a set of
beliefs about the world and norms for interaction with members
and non-members, help him to attain his goals and provide him
with services as a client. Thus the fact that relatively few
individuals claim membership of an organization does not
necessarily mean that it is unimportant. The non-member may
subscribe to its aims, benefit from its success in achieving its
goals or use its services as a client.

With this background we may look at the functions which are
likely to be served by four major types of organization, namely,
political parties, churches, immigrant associations and the
community association. Such functions, of course, are not the
same as the declared purposes of the organization. These purposes
derive from history and there is a large element of accident in
which organizations have found a home in Sparkbrook. What we
are concerned with is their function in the here-and-now, and,
if we have learned any sociological lesson at all from our research,
it is that what might appear to be merely a sociological relic to
the outsider, turns out on analysis to be performing an important
function.

The political parties have as their goal the control of political
power in order to give a particular shape and direction to our
society. This they must do at both national and local level. Given
this, one might expect them to be concerned (a) with recruiting as
members all those who shared this ideal and (b) providing the
most effective organization for winning votes and capturing
political power. That is to say, one would expect the emphasis
here to be on the function of goal-attainment.

Of particular importance in political organizations, however, is
the mobilization of sanctions to enforce group demands upon the
society. Implicit in our notion of the community as composed of
conflicting interest groups is the notion of societies to realize
group interests. Overt violence is largely ruled out for the major
groupings but they may seek to enforce their interests through

the use of legitimate power. That is to say, they will seek to capture control of the city council and parliament, in order that legislation and administrative action may be taken to enforce the recognition of their own group-interests as against those of others. It is to the contest for control of legitimate political power that the activities of the party understood as a goal attainment organization are primarily directed. As a political party it seeks to attain its goals by indirect means by vote-winning. It is not a direct-action organization seeking immediate change through, for instance, welfare work or community organization. In our experience, however, the parties fulfilled all three of the other functions as well, apart from that of goal-attainment, and these functions seemed to their officers and members to be of equal importance to that of goal-attainment. The party affirmed a set of beliefs, a world view for its members. It provided a warm centre for social life. And it did a considerable amount of pastoral work. In other words, although these were political parties they were much else besides.

Affirmation of beliefs is clearly a very important function for political parties. One feature of this is the representation of the desired social future as inevitable. Thus Conservatives are apt to believe in the ineffectiveness of socialism and in the natural-ness of private enterprise. And socialists or supporters of the Labour Party are apt to believe in the inevitability of the triumph of the working class. To join an organization concerned with promoting free enterprise, or with the triumph of the working class, is to be brought into interaction with people who share the relevant world-view. But this may become an end in itself. Hearing the old beliefs reaffirmed may service to reassure the individual and actually prevent him from taking any effective action. Thus the Conservative may be reassured to find fellow-members who agree that Labour policy has led to an influx of immigrants living off National Assistance, and then do nothing about it. And the Labour supporter may find satisfaction in meeting others who denounce the landlords, but also do nothing about it. A world-view is affirmed and a cultural home created, but that is all.

Of course, it is not necessarily the case that this will happen. A party may not develop in this 'theological' direction. It could happen that the party remained militantly geared for action and that the belief-system fulfilled a purely subordinate function. Or it could be that from time to time the party cleared its decks for action as, for instance, at a general election, when the task of vote-getting assumed primary importance. What balance of functions there is in any particular constituency may vary. I wish here simply to draw attention to the fact that some such balance might exist and might be tilted in one way rather than the other.

Another point to be noted about the belief-affirmation function of the parties is that in this respect their influence reaches far beyond their members. Hundreds of people in Sparkbrook who were not themselves members of parties showed in their conversation that the political parties, before all other organizations, provided them with their beliefs and their faith. So far as the English at least were concerned, whether a man was Labour or Conservative was a more important question in most cases than whether he was an Anglican or a Baptist. Perhaps the only more important guide to his 'faith' was whether he read the *Daily Mirror* or the *Daily Express*.

The parties also provided a social home for their members. This was particularly true in the case of the Labour Party. For many the party meant before all else the club on a Saturday night with bingo, community singing and a sense of being with one's own kind. It was not easy to talk politics in the club for fear of disturbing the family atmosphere. Yet this organization was the base from which elections had to be organized, and it was a role in the club which helped to make several members into councillors. Political action, therefore, tended to become subordinate to the maintenance of a good and happy club.

Finally, the parties did pastoral work amongst members and non-members. The idea of a councillor or MP as a representative taking part in a political debate was foreign to most Sparkbrook people. He was seen instead as a welfare worker to whom one might go, as to a minister of religion or a social worker, to solve one's problem. But a client who chose to go to his councillor would probably do so because he was 'a chap you could trust' or 'on our side' (i.e. one who shared one's faith).

Thus the parties were by no means solely goal-attainment organizations acting on behalf of classes or other groups. They were deeply rooted in Sparkbrook and as part of Sparkbrook's associational organizations provided for many of the social and cultural needs of its people.

Affiliation to a particular church would seem at first sight to have implications remote from the immediate problems of Sparkbrook, and to show how a man stood on theological issues such as whether all or only some men can be saved. But, as Richard Niebuhr (1957) has shown, the sources of the Christian denominations are as much social as theological, and we were able to see a close relationship, not merely between theological positions and old class interests, but, in a lively and important way, between these positions and the existing conflicts of interest in Sparkbrook of 1965.

The social implications of religious belief derive from the fact that the salvation religions always have something to say about the relationship between the organization of the faithful and 'the world'. They may call on their members to renounce the world or ignore it. They may declare the Kingdom of Heaven to be 'not of this world' or seek to realize it in the here and now. They may see the world as divided into the elect and the damned, or they may not. But whichever they do say, they make a difference to men's attitudes towards ingroups and outgroups.

What we are saying here, in effect, is that just as the political parties start out as goal-attainment organizations but tend to become belief-affirming organizations, so the churches which start out as belief-affirming organizations tend to become goal-attainment organizations. The latter happens in so far as there is a connection between the beliefs affirmed and the interests of particular conflict-groups in the situation. One could, of course, easily overstate this case, but it is none the less important, when we are concerned with social function, to see the political element in religious organizations, just as we see the religious in the political.

Like the parties, the churches also provide a social home and do 'pastoral work' in the community, but in the latter respect there is an important distinction to be made. The parson's work, when he calls on a parishioner, may consist of what the local Catholic priest called 'talking about religious subjects', or it may be concerned with social welfare. It is only in the latter respect that the churches are competing in the same field as the councillors and social workers. But it must be said that the ministers of religion in Sparkbrook found this distinction difficult to draw.

In fact, the churches, like other associations, tended to help in solving the material problems of those who shared their faith. And they were more or less active in the community at large according to whether or not they were exclusive in defining their membership. The Anglican Church claiming pastoral responsibility for the community as a whole was at one extreme, and some of the non-conformist denominations at the other. In a special category was the Roman Catholic Church, which was largely Irish in composition, and, like the mosque and the Sikh temple, concerned with the spiritual welfare and pastoral care of an immigrant group.

The organizations to which we have already referred mostly have long histories and are reasonably clear as to their objectives. This is far from being true of immigrant organizations and we find it difficult to know where to begin in describing their functions. Perhaps, though, it is best to see them first as goal-attainment organizations, if only because other organizations do not give any special priority to the needs and interests of immigrants.

One could posit an ideal type of immigrant organization of this kind. It would have as its goal the prevention of discrimination, and it would seek, through contact with the agents of the state and other communities, and, through mobilizing what sanctions the immigrants possess, to ensure that they received their rights. Such an organization would involve an effective organization of committee offices, and good contact between the office-bearers and their clientele, on the one hand, and between office-bearers and the larger community, on the other. In fact, however, we find none of these things, which would suggest that the organizations serve other functions.

Most important perhaps is pastoral work. Each individual immigrant arrives in a new country with a load of problems. The immigrant associations will be called in, even while discrimination exists, to offer solutions for them. They must help to find jobs, to solve passport difficulties, to help their members to understand and deal with the law as it exists, to find lodgings and to solve many other problems. And the individual immigrant who knows that there is a man of his own background who has skill in dealing with these problems, will go straight to him, rather than to a well-meaning stranger, whom he does not know he can trust.

But, as one talks to immigrant leaders about the social work which they do, it becomes clear that this includes not only the solution of problems of the kind we have mentioned, but problems far more of the spiritual welfare kind which present themselves to the churches. They will be concerned about the moral welfare of the younger immigrants facing the temptations of city life. They will want to help people to maintain food taboos in difficult circumstances. They will be concerned to maintain religious observances and to keep their fellows in touch with home. In all these respects, the leaders of the Pakistani and the Irish Catholic community, in particular, face similar problems. The Irish Catholics go to mass in a local ballroom. The Pakistanis collect money for a mosque. Both find a tremendous need for a moral centre for an immigrant community.

Whether or not there is this concern with the spiritual problems of the immigrant, however, there will at least be a problem of maintaining the group's culture. Faced with the welter of conflicting cultural meanings of the city, the immigrant, at least until he knows his way round, needs a cultural retreat, where he knows the rules, and knows that other people accept the rules. For a while, therefore, he must live 'in the colony'. The colony may grow around a church or a mosque. It may be found in an ethnically segregated pub-clientele. Or it may be found within the context of Saturday night parties. But, for a while at least, such a set of reference points is essential for the immigrant, even though its existence does not mean that he is set against assimilation.

A central problem facing the immigrants, however, is that their small numbers relative to the population of the city make them weak and ineffective. We referred above to the mobilization of such sanctions as the immigrants possess. But what are these sanctions? In the case of larger groups, quite obviously there was the possibility of capturing legitimate political power through elections. But this was not open to smaller ethnic minorities.

The nearest to effective political action was taken by the more established members of the Irish community. They were sufficiently numerous amongst the working class to be able to influence all of its activities. The Labour Club, in fact, was predominantly Irish in its culture. The songs and the jokes at its Saturday night concert were Irish, and, even those who were not themselves Irish in origin, shared in them. Moreover, one of the three Labour councillors was an Irish immigrant of many years standing, and distinguished himself on all public occasions by defending the reputation of the Irish immigrant, even, in fact, of the Tinkers.

But this alternative was not open to the colonial immigrants. The only political alternative was, other than that of seeking some consideration for their interests by other groups, was the formation of their own political organization to put up its own candidate for election. This was tried by some members of the Pakistani community with some small success, because it was clear that the candidate had 500 votes to bargain with in future elections.

Much more, however, the ethnic minorities saw themselves as on the defensive. They directed their activities to establishing the best possible relations with the representatives of authority, particularly with the Public Health Department, and with generally improving the image and the stereotype of their community. Such activities, however, since they were based upon the avoidance of conflict, were always coupled with some pressure on their own members to conform with demands made upon them. The Commonwealth Property Owners' Association and the Commonwealth Welfare Association, one Pakistani and one West Indian, were the principal organizations of this kind.

The other kind of association which we have to discuss apart from the political parties, the churches and the immigrant organizations is of the type represented by the Sparkbrook Association, and the two important questions here are 'Whom does it represent?' and 'What functions does it perform?'

We have assumed in our discussion of all other organizations that they are to a very large extent the organizations of various conflict groups. We should, however, wish to qualify this now by saying that there are various reasons why, in the process of living together, some slight degree of consensus does arise. Firstly, the various organizations are to some extent influenced by their 'manifest functions', i.e. by the purposes for which they claim to exist. Thus a non-conformist church does feel compelled to proclaim the Christian gospel, even though it may proclaim it in a peculiar form which appeals especially to particular interest groups. Or again, the Labour Party can be challenged to work in terms of its declared belief in international class solidarity. Secondly, there is bound to be at least some marginal overlapping of membership, so that the lines of intergroup conflict become blurred. Thirdly, there does arise in such a situation a group of office-holders, who find themselves having to contain potential conflicts within limits, and who come to develop an interest in maintaining minimum norms of group interaction. And fourthly, there continues in existence a norm of middle-class respectability to which some members of all groups in practice try to adhere.

The existence of norms of this kind coupled with the manifest deterioration of the moral and material environment inevitably gives rise to a relatively incoherent demand that 'something should be done'. In part this comes from the political representatives of the ward. In part it comes from the professional people such as doctors, ministers of religion and social workers. In part it comes from the old residents. Probably each of these groups see the situation differently, diagnose its causes differently, and would wish to propose different remedies. But what they lack is the organizational means. It is a situation in which if someone calls a meeting there will be a response and a community organization will be formed.

In the case of Sparkbrook, this initiative was taken by a councillor who called a meeting of the electorate, thus producing a representative body of people of a new kind. Hitherto, the electorate had not been a coherent body and had acted purely as individuals casting their votes. Corporate action of any kind had been confined to the parties and their supporters. Now, for the first time, there was a non-party and non-sectarian organization on a community-wide basis.

But the community meeting was necessarily an ephemeral kind of organization. Power to act on its behalf and in its name passed quickly to a committee, and, from the committee, to a full-time officer and one or two more active committee members. Moreover, the committee also had a responsibility to another electorate, namely, those interested in social reform outside the area. It was bound to be governed in its actions by the norms of this group rather than by those of the local electorate.

Two possibilities are excluded from this kind of organization. It cannot rely upon continuous and coherent support from the local community. Nor can it, as a church or political party can, relate itself to a national organization with staff and resources.

It must therefore depend in part on its own resources, and on those of people of goodwill outside, and in part on the support of the local authority. In so far as it does the latter, it finds itself subcontracting the welfare work of the local authority. This work, however, differs in two respects from that which the local authority might otherwise have done. Firstly there is more of it, and, secondly, it is influenced by the norms of voluntary agencies and of the local community.

The community association so formed has four possible functions. It alters the social structure and creates new groupings of people through the group-work which it promotes. It does 'pastoral' work among those who present themselves as clients. It acts as a tension-management system serving to give expression to, but also to channel and manage, the conflicts of interests which do occur. And it is a body which may act as a political pressure group on behalf of the community as a whole.

If the community association develops as a community centre, in which there is participation by the general public, it can become the basis for a new type of community, in which ethnic and other divisions disappear. But this is unlikely so long as men's identifications are with class and ethnic groups. In these circumstances most people are likely to see themselves as clients rather than as members of the association. There is, however, an intermediate stage in which participation in one of the group organizations promoted by the association produces a partial identification with its work, and in Sparkbrook there appeared to be a number of individuals in this category, in part clients, in part 'helpers' of the association.

It is important to notice, however, that the association will have an important function in making the legal and welfare rights of citizens more accessible. These rights, which are of the utmost importance in helping men to adapt to and to find a foothold in urban society, remain purely theoretical unless there is some centre through which they can be publicized and unless there are agents to see to it that they are granted and enforced. The association will therefore, be a means of admitting men not merely to its own membership but to that of the larger urban and national society.

The fact that the organization of the association is based upon a relatively incoherent platform of 'something must be done' involves both advantages and disadvantages from the point of view of promoting communal solidarity. The advantage lies in the fact that all groups may be attracted to joining. The disadvantage is that, once together, the groups may not be able to formulate common aims. Yet there is also the possibility that the statement of aims and grievances by groups in the association, rather than outside it, may result in the tensions between groups being managed and understood. Thus, when a representative of the old residents complains about the Pakistanis, several things will happen. First, the complaints themselves may be more reasonably stated in the presence of a Pakistani representative, and the Pakistani representative will be able to explain, and sometimes to reformulate, the aims of his group.

Given that such tensions are managed, the possibility emerges that there are some goals, e.g. improving street lighting or pavements or providing more play space, which are common to all groups. These goals might go even further and lead to demands for comprehensive redevelopment of the area. Effective action on any of these issues will enhance the feeling of solidarity within the association. Again, however, it should be noticed that the pull towards expressing the special goals of interest groups is strong and that there is a permanent problem of preventing individuals from trying to forward group aims in the name of the association as such. But this itself is a tribute to the association. In so far as its good name is sought as a means of legitimation, it has begun to provide some kind of focus for a developing community consensus.

We have now reviewed the kind of associational framework within which life is lived in a community in the zone of transition. Community there means the casual contact on the street or shop and the rather less casual contact in the pub and café. It includes the organizations which provide escape from loneliness, which offer alternative sets of meanings and values, and which afford the organizational means of attaining group goals. It includes the organizations through which men as clients have their cases attended to and their welfare rights guaranteed. It includes conflict and the means of managing conflict. The outcome of all this is not determinate. A balance between competing interests may be struck, but it may quite suddenly change.

3   The concept of housing class and the sociology of race relations

Race relations is an area of interdisciplinary study and it is to be expected that students from different disciplines will have sometimes complementary, sometimes conflicting, insights into particular problems. None the less this does not mean that there are no distinct disciplinary ways of posing and looking at problems. Still less does it mean that complex concepts can be elucidated, or theories tested and refuted, by simplistic and sub-disciplinary survey methods. It was with this in mind, that I introduced into an empirical study of race relations in the urban zone of transition in Birmingham, the sociological concept of 'housing classes'.

I take sociology to be concerned with the ways in which the behaviour of individuals is affected by their participation in more or less fixed, and more or less fluid and changing, structures of social relations. It is concerned with those influences on behaviour arising from 'outside' the individual, rather than those which arise 'internally', 'in his head' or 'from the personality system'. Thus, while psychologists may be interested in the question of whether a certain kind of personality system is associated with racially prejudiced beliefs and behaviour, the sociologist will be concerned with whether such beliefs and behaviour are meaningfully, and perhaps causally, connected with being involved in a network of social relations and expectancies.

The word causal in the above paragraph merits some discussion. It should not be taken to mean that it is the goal of the sociologist simply to establish correlations between specific types of behaviour, quantitatively measured, and some index of social participation. Such explanations may be offered, but in sociology they cry out for further explanation in terms of meaning. Thus, for example, if there is a correlation between delinquency and being the child of a broken home, the sociologist would go on to show what sort of meaningful connection existed between the perception of social relations of a boy from a broken home, and the commission of a delinquent act. The truly sociological interest lies in the model of social relations, which is posited at this stage, and which may subsequently be tested against these empirical data.

It is perhaps worth noting that the two great founders of sociology as a subject, Max Weber and Emile Durkheim, both insisted on the close relationship in sociology between the explanation of behaviour in terms of normative, meaningful and external influences, and statistical proof. Thus Durkheim (1938, especially chap. 1) began by studying legal and moral codes, but then went on to consider whether statistical trends were not indicative of underlying and more fluid patterns of behaviour. Weber, on the other hand, suggested that the plausible stories which we might give about the meaning of behaviour, including the degree to which it was influenced by belief in a legitimate order, should be supplemented by reference to 'the existence of a probability that action in fact normally takes this course which has been held to be meaningful'. (Weber, 1968, vol. I, chap. 1.) Thus the real problem in sociology is to discover the fluid pattern of social relations, interaction and expectancy which is reflected in observable rates for any type of behaviour, and this involves problems of a complex epistemological kind. What we want to talk about are the 'social relations' which influence any individual's conduct. But the very notion of social relations is complex in two ways. On the one hand when we say of any individual (whom we may refer to as A) that he perceives or is influenced by social relations, we mean that he makes some kind of mental construct of the mental construct he believes that one other individual or set of individuals, B, is making of the behaviour of another individual or set of individuals, C.[1] On the other hand, since the sociologist cannot actually get into A's

[1] Actually when we speak of B making a construct of C's behaviour we are oversimplifying what happens. B does make such a construct. C also makes a construct of B's behaviour and B's expectations of himself. He may then comply or not comply with these expectations. A's belief that a social relation exists, rests upon his own model or construct of this whole pattern of interaction.

head, his concept of A's world of social relations involves a construct of A's construct.

Even then, however, we have not stated the full complexity of the sociologist's analytical task. For when he makes a construct of any particular social relation which may be operating in A's world, he does so, as does any scientist who makes constructs of processes, with an implicit *ceteris paribus* clause. Thus, to say that an individual's behaviour is influenced by his involvement in a 'housing class', is by no means to say that this is the sole pattern of social relations influencing him. What one is doing is offering an ideal type which may help to illuminate the complex world of social reality.

The actual social behaviour of people in the twilight zone is, of course, the product of many interwoven social patterns of varying degrees of importance. One of the most important of these is the fact that the people who meet there have either themselves had encounters or understand their experience in terms of images of past encounters between colonial workers and peasants, and colonizing settlers, soldiers and administrators. Furthermore, it is obvious that relations within and between communities will be affected by the fact that there exists in the society a specific pattern of social relations of production, and a resulting pattern of class conflict and stratification.

While it is obvious that factors such as these, and no doubt others such as the reaction of groups of people of differing cultural and religious backgrounds to one another, are important, it is still worth while asking whether there are not certain factors, arising specifically from an urban situation, which structure the world of social relations in which immigrants and their hosts, and different racial and ethnic groups, encounter one another. It seemed to me that there were, and that they were underrated in two types of sociological writing. One was that which claimed that there was no such thing as urban sociology. The other was the kind of Marxism which insisted that all other conflicts were ultimately traceable to and explicable in terms of the conflict between capital and labour in industry. The concept of housing classes was intended to pose questions and point the way towards a more precise delineation of the social structure and conflicts of the city.

The model suggested in *Race, Community and Conflict* (Rex

and Moore, 1967) and in my later essay 'The Sociology of the Urban Zone of Transition' (1968) was, of course, a simplistic one. Like all such models it had, in the first place, to oversimplify. I therefore posited a variety of relationships to the 'means of residence' and a tendency to conflict, analogous to the 'relationships to the means of production' and consequent industrial conflicts of Marxist sociology.

As in Marxist sociology, the notion of a housing class leads one to ask whether class-interests or 'objective class position' lead or do not lead to the formation of classes for themselves, i.e. collectivities having some degree or organization, some degree of subjective class identification by members, some common values, and an orientation to conflict with other classes.

Specifying such a model for any practical urban context would, it was further suggested, depend upon the kinds of housing available, the kinds of tenure legally recognized, and the form of housing allocation (i.e. whether through a free or practically free housing market or through bureaucratic allocation). In the situation in Birmingham, England, it seemed useful, as a starting point, to suggest some six or seven types of housing situation arising from these factors. Of special importance were the observations that there was a larger bureaucratically allocated section than in most countries, that 'discrimination' could operate in this sector as well as in the free market sector, and that there were certain forms of tenure, especially those of the resident lodging-house landlord and the lodging-house tenant, which were to be differentiated from that of the owner-occupier and the tenant of a whole privately-owned house, in that tenures of this kind were the most insecure of all. These were specific hypotheses offered *ad hoc* to illuminate the Birmingham situation. Naturally, before they can be thought to have any kind of generalizable quality, they would have to be tested elsewhere. Moreover it is by no means suggested that other cities in England and elsewhere do not have other histories, other forms of housing stock and tenure, and other groups in a state of conflict.

Marxists, of course, are familiar with the notion that the existence of differences of ownership and of market interests do not lead automatically and immediately to specific forms of groups consciousness or preparedness for action. The same problem area is to be found in Weber's sociology. The question which the 'housing class' concept poses, therefore, is that of the other forms of consciousness in terms of which participants may conceptualize their situation than that of conscious participation in a housing class conflict group. Two such forms of consciousness (in terms of the Marxist analogy 'false consciousness') were suggested.

On the one hand the point was made, again by analogy with Marxist theory, that a situation of potential class conflict might be understood by participants as a graded system of status groups, and that those who were conscious of having both a weak market position and a low position in the status order, might aspire to stronger, higher positions. Such a system of status grading of the ways of life of various neighbourhoods would, of course, like any status system, be regarded with varying degrees of respect, fatalistic acceptance, cynicism or contempt by the participants; but this fact did not make it impossible in principle to ask people what the status order of the neighbourhood was (i.e. asking people in effect not 'What do you think is the status rank order of Edgbaston or Sparkbrook?' but 'What do you think that other people think?').

More fundamentally, however, it was recognized that at the level of this formation of 'housing-classes-for-themselves' the whole process of class formation might be overlaid and distorted by another fundamental process, in which immigrants to the city form colonies, which might provide the means to partial temporary pluralistic integration, but which might also act as a springboard from which immigrants might launch themselves into the city and its social and cultural order. Naturally this ideal-type also might be elaborated and refined in many ways—and the arguments surrounding the work of Wirth, Redfield and Oscar Lewis suggest that its main lines are by no means agreed. But what is important here is to note that the concrete formation of a class-for-itself might be impossible because the organizational means had been pre-empted by colony-like structures.

Given this basic outline of the housing class conflict model for the analysis of urban and race relations problems, an infinite amount of refinement is possible. Unfortunately the model has been subject to a certain amount of criticism based either (a) on the notion that it was claimed that it served solely and by itself to explain racial conflict in the city or (b) that it would explain the whole of racial tension without leaving any unexplained residue or (c) that what was being suggested was a simple empirical hypothesis about the correlates of racial prejudice which could be refuted by a simple survey. Let it be emphasized therefore that what is being suggested here is that (a) conflict of housing resources is one, and only one, of a number of factors helping to determine the character of racial encounters in the city, (b) such conflict escalates and intensifies other pre-existing conflicts, and (c) it was never my intention to suggest a one-to-one correlation between housing class position and racial attitudes.

The most important comment upon and criticism of the concept which I have seen is that of John Lambert and Camilla Filkin (1971). This is to the effect that the model assumes a unitary value system in the city and that such a value system never exists in practice. To this I would reply on three levels. Firstly it must be clear that in positing a conflict model, I was explicitly rejecting any kind of functionalist consensualism. Secondly, as pointed out earlier, it is possible even while recognizing the possibility of conflicting value scales to posit that one such scale is dominant and recognized as being dominant even by those who do not accept it. (It was suggested in *Race, Community and Conflict* (Rex and Moore, 1967) that the suburban migration involved a dominant value pattern of this kind.) But third, and perhaps most important, it can be conceded that multiple value systems do exist, and that more complex models can and should be built, using that of *Race, Community and Conflict* simply as a starting point. The value of the Lambert and Filkin criticism is that it shows just how complex a sociological model such as this must be.

A different and less acceptable type of criticism is that which seeks to refute certain specific aspects of the housing class model with the aid of empirical evidence regarding the attitudes and behaviour of immigrant lodging-house landlords. Thus my colleague and I were criticized for arguing that such landlords were forced into their position by the lack of available alternatives (Davies and Taylor, 1970), when survey evidence suggested that they had chosen it. The problem with this kind of conclusion is simply that we can never know what significance to attach to replies to questionnaires about housing preference. It is well known by now that, even amongst the English working class, certain preferences are not expressed simply because they are unrealistic. What is less commonly recognized is that further constraints are placed upon an individual's choice by his culturally determined perception of the situation. To be sure, there is an intimate relationship between cultural perception and cultural values here, and it may be argued that differences of culturally determined values are precisely what questions about choice are seeking to discover. None the less there are also constraints placed on choice at the level of knowledge and perceptions. Thus we do not prove anything at all decisive when we learn from a survey that a certain percentage of Pakistani immigrants did not 'want' council houses. What we do learn is that they gave a particular answer to a questionnaire.

This particular problem may, of course, partly be solved by depth interviewing, but only partly, because, in the last analysis, many of the choices which we would put to them would be hypothetical. What we have to do is to give an account of the constraints which we, as sociologists, know to exist in the world, and an account of the immigrant's perception of the world, before going on to discover what 'choices' are made. Unfortunately sociologists have a fatal fascination with the study of individual preferences, because these are easily amenable to investigation by survey. This produces a kind of 'trained incapacity' which prevents them looking at such obvious sources of data about the social world as statements of local authority policy.

The description of constraints of this kind is what has led on occasions to a distinction being made between objective interests and false consciousness. I would not myself want to suggest that there was a distinction here which had any ontological validity. It is worthwhile however to distinguish between patterns of social relations which sociologists know to exist in a society, the way in which these same patterns are subjectively understood by participant actors, and thirdly what these participant actors propose to do about their social world. This third element brings us to the stage of true class-formation, the stage which the Marxist tradition calls that of the formation of a class-for-itself. This is the most important area of investigation which the concept of housing classes suggests, and the understanding of its nature is quite crucial to the formulation of research problems.

The Marxist tradition has never adequately clarified what is involved, sociologically speaking, in the formation of a class-for-itself. Minimally, however, it must involve the development of organizational means, the affiliation of individuals to organizations as officers, members, clients and supporters, the development of social norms, values and sentiments shared between members of the class, and a degree of consciousness of kind. The Marxist tradition also emphasizes the distinction between true revolutionary consciousness and false consciousness. This is a distinction which raises important epistemological difficulties, and I do not, therefore, wish to accept it in its entirety. What I do wish to accept, however, is the insight that the formation of a 'class-for-itself' is a highly contingent process and that, even though the social constraints imposed on the class by its situation serve to drive it in particular directions, the other structures of social relations within which people find themselves are likely to deflect them from this simple direction. What happens is that the actual organizations which members join, their character and function, and the norms and meanings which they formulate are the resultant of conflicting pressures. This includes the possibility that, since social phenomena cannot yield a simple arithmetical compromise when they are brought into conflict the actual development of organizations will be confused, conflicting and internally contradictory.

The area in which one would begin to look for a partial development of housing classes so that they become classes-for-themselves is in the study of the organizations, norms, values, beliefs and sentiments of the associations, which exist in great profusion in the city. Integral to the argument of *Race, Community and Conflict* was a chapter originally entitled 'The Functions of Associations' which emphasized the great importance of associations for the understanding of the sociology, both of the city and of race relations. Unfortunately this chapter had to be greatly reduced in scope and its argument was only partially repeated in my later essay (included here as chap. 2). It may, therefore, be useful to recall the main points which were made there.

The actual associations which are to be found in the city are churches, political parties, social, drinking, and sports clubs, café and pub clienteles, friendly and charitable societies, and a number of other types. What I suggested, however, was that these associations could not be understood only in terms of their overt purpose or, as Malinowski would have said, their 'charters'. They could be much better understood as the agencies either of incipient housing-classes-for-themselves or of immigrant colonies. All of them, it was suggested, performed in varying degrees the functions of overcoming social isolation, of acting as 'trade unions' on behalf of an interest group, of doing pastoral or social work amongst their members and a wider clientele and of elaborating new meanings, norms and belief systems. The first and third of these functions are probably best understood in terms of the notion of a colony structure in the city. The second is the expression in associational terms of the class-for-itself idea. The fourth is the most problematic since it is relevant both to the development of the colony and to the development of interest groups and classes.

The true importance of associations and the meaning and norms which are expressed through them, however, only becomes apparent when one contrasts what one finds through their study with what is revealed or concealed by surveys of attitudes (see Richmond, 1970). The commonly recognized difficulty with the latter type of study is that there is always uncertainty about the degree to which expressed attitude has a pay-off in actual behaviour. What is less frequently recognized however is that what the sociologist is interested in are not isolated observations of behaviour, but a network of interaction, expectancies and social relations, and that, for the study of these, neither the study of attitudes, nor of 'behaviour' in an uninterpreted form, is particularly revealing.

What is important to the sociologist of race relations is the sociology of knowledge, values and belief systems as they occur within the context of associational life and in the flux of social interaction as it occurs in changing urban conditions. If one assumes that the task of the sociologist is to study social relations and interaction, then the first assumption which must be made in his descriptive interpretation of the social world is that the actors whom he observed have a shared inter-subjective world. This depends upon the language that actors use and the way they use it. It depends upon what they agree to be the case, what is 'out there', how it is to be evaluated, whether it is to be regarded as good or bad, alterable or unalterable, sacred or profane, and how what is observed at one particular time is connected in its meaning with things observed at another time. All this is far too complex to be captured in a measured attitude and it is not sufficient to reply that at least it is possible to speak unambiguously about attitudes, for such apparent clarity is achieved only at the cost of making one's research irrelevant to the subject which one set out to study.

The sociology of knowledge, however, can go beyond saying merely that language is in an infinite state of flux and, therefore, incapable of being captured by scientific concepts. For some languages, some interpretations of the world, are more important than others, and what one is seeking in the study of social structure and conflict are especially those interpretations which have some authority and influence, those in fact which determine the pattern of social relations. Thus, for example, what matters far more than a recurrent prejudice, observed in the beliefs and behaviour of masses of people, is the sanctioning of such beliefs and behaviour by those in authority. Thus if a respected politician begins to introduce 'racist' material into his speeches, or if the mass media begin to construe the news in a racist way, there is a real sense in which we should say that society had changed.

What concerns us here, however, is the concept of housing classes and the sorts of evidence which should be sought to verify statements about such classes. The relevance of what has been said above to this question is simply that mere evidence of individual attitudes, crudely measured, does not refute the sort of hypotheses offered in *Race, Community and Conflct*. It might be relevant, it is true, if the measurement of attitudes is reasonably sophisticated. But far more relevant are the interpretations of the world, of what is there, of how it is to be evaluated, and what should be, which are reflected in the belief systems, the symbols and the simple policies of the associations which arise in the city.

I would not claim, in conclusion, that the concept of housing classes, as I developed it in the course of my study with Robert Moore in Sparkbrook, is in any sense a final truth. But it does help, I believe, to throw light on a Labour Group on the council keeping the council estates white and confining the immigrants to the twilight zones. It does help to explain the activities of the immigrant landlords' organizations, supported by landlords and tenants. And it helps when one hears the ladies in one of the Nonconformist churches singing,

> Saviour, if of Zion's City
> I through grace a member am

to know that the strength of their convictions has something to do with the fact that their once-genteel homes are now threatened by the tide of multi-occupation. But there is more to the establishment of a connection between such associations and their beliefs and housing situations than the crude empirical techniques of the most professionalized sociologist will allow. Perhaps this defence and explication of the concept of housing class might serve to show what the problem areas for the researcher really are.

Finally let it be emphasized once again that the structures of patterns of social relations, or norms and beliefs by housing class is one and only one part of the total explanation of racial conflict. For my own part, as I have shown elsewhere (Rex, 1970; Zubaida, 1970), race relations even in metropolitan countries are heavily and crucially influenced by colonialism, both past and present, but in an urban situation I suggest housing-class situation gives new meaning to pre-existing racial tension. *Race, Community and Conflict* set out to explore this phase of escalating racial tension at a crucial time and place, namely Birmingham, England, just before the introduction of immigration control.

4   Images of community

The nature of community

The cities of Britain and of other advanced industrial societies grew up without the intervention of town planners. The consequence was congestion and inefficiency, and in the long run planning proved necessary to enable them to function as economic and social units at all. Now, however, planning has entered a new phase. We are not merely asking what can be done to eliminate the obvious frustrations and contradictions which arise out of existing patterns of land use. What we find ourselves doing is deciding what kinds of community life should or should not be promoted and encouraged during the next hundred years. For better or for ill, many decisions of this kind have been taken since 1945 and, no doubt, many more will be taken in the future without any real sociological understanding of the nature of community. What I want to discuss is the possibility of making some kind of evaluative assessment of what we are doing in sociological and community terms.[1]

I am quite aware that many sociologists shy away from any discussion of these issues and that most planners would not be

[1] What sociologists are frequently called upon to do by planners is to offer value judgements based upon scientific research. Quite rightly they refuse, insisting properly that no sociological research can tell us what we should do. It is none the less the case that sociology has always been accompanied by a moral discussion, a discussion about our image of man, of what he is and what he could be. What I wish to suggest is that if planners want to learn something about what they should do from sociologists, they will find it in this literature. But they should not think that they will be able to get out of the responsibility of making moral judgements themselves by basing themselves on scientific 'truth'. What I am doing in this chapter is to invite planners to reconsider their goals in the light of one of the most important images of man in society, that offered by Emile Durkheim.

43

prepared to listen to naïve talk from sociologists about creating a community spirit. But the fact is that the mainstream of the European sociological tradition does have something to say on these matters, and that planners would do well to acquaint themselves with this tradition, instead of simply listening to, and then rejecting, the political and sociological romanticism of what may perhaps best be called vulgar garden-cityism.

To make the negative point first, when I write, as I shall, about a morally significant experience of community life, I do not have in mind a situation in which all men love their next-door neighbours, or even one in which they are actively concerned in their neighbours' affairs. For modern man to live in this way would seem to me to be childish and definitely (in a literal sense of the term) 'suburban'. Yet I do not mean that I think the urban condition implies total individualism. Our problem therefore is simply this: to define those kinds of community life which are compatible with the intellectual and moral enrichment which we have the right to expect from an urban civilization.

The main source of the ideas which I wish to put forward is a great book by one of sociology's founding fathers: Emile Durkheim's *The Division of Labor in Society* (1933). This was an attempt to enunciate an ideal for an advanced differentiated and complex civilization, in opposition to the individualism of Herbert Spencer. What I wish to do is to apply some of Durkheim's concepts to the sociology of the city and of town planning.

Durkheim did not believe that the sort of industrial society which Herbert Spencer had envisaged could be based upon sheer unadulterated economic individualism. Yet, equally, he saw that it was mischievous to suggest that morality required a return to the undifferentiated social unity of primitive, or rural, or agricultural society. Hence, he went on to say, one had to set out the principles of a new type of social solidarity, distinctively different from that of the primitive world. He called the primitive form of social solidarity 'mechanical', and the advanced form 'organic'.

Durkheim saw organic solidarity as arising from the division of labour, a concept which he used to include the differentiation of social as well as economic tasks. Because people are different in their capacities, their goals and their aspirations, this did not mean that they were not dependent upon one another. Indeed the opposite was the case. Precisely when social differentiation occurred, men became more dependent upon one another, and in becoming dependent, were morally enriched, for they could now do their own specialized tasks more efficiently, and at the same time share in what was in effect a collective social labour. At best they would be conscious of this larger social unity; but the point of consciousness is not in fact the crucial one, for very often the very taking of other people's services for granted might be said to raise the moral level of life beyond that of individualism.

Surely it is possible to make sense of the moral aspirations of urban man in these terms. On the surface the city may appear to us as nothing more than a machine for producing individualistic economic men. The most urbanized man appears as suburban man, secure in the possession of his property and (literally as well as metaphorically) minding his own garden. Undoubtedly if we did some market research on him we could find him to be totally lacking in community spirit, and the critics and the defenders of suburban life would draw their own conclusions. If, however, we were to make a less restricted analysis of the system of social relations, which our suburbanite takes for granted, while he is completing his questionnaire, we might find that what appears to be a lack of community spirit is really an indication of the fact that he is a mature social man living in modern industrial conditions, rather than a primitive or a child. He plays a role in a differentiated system of social labour and that system of social labour is, as Durkheim pointed out, not merely a matter of convenience, but a moral fact.

Social form and unity

In order to understand the nature of urban social unity, however, it is as well to begin with the simpler social form represented by a small and industrially homogeneous settlement, which is the urban equivalent of Durkheim's mechanical solidarity. In such a settlement the residential community of neighbours consists of families whose heads also work together. This residential community may be stratified and may even have an upper-class residential area, or it may be that the owners of the means of production are absentees who leave to the workers the residential community adjacent to their works. In the former case there emerges a paternalistic but close-knit community best typified by predominantly agricultural settlements and by small company towns. In the latter one finds the intense sense of social solidarity represented by an English mining community.

This type of settlement may undergo several types of development according to the manner of its articulation with the larger society. One, to which we shall return later, is the linking together in a larger cultural unity of many similar industrially homogeneous units without any of them undergoing internal change or beginning to perform a specialized function for the whole group. It is most clearly seen in mining areas. But, for the moment, the one which we need to notice is that which occurs through industrial differentiation and which leads to city development.

The major differences between the social systems of a city and of the kind of settlement we have just described are that its citizens follow diverse occupations, that the residential and work communities are not identical, and that there is a conscious separation of the world of work on the one hand and of the world of home and of leisure on the other.

The meaningfulness of urban existence

Those who are concerned with planning and with architecture in modern urban residential settlements are often frustrated by the triviality of the interests and the social activities which are carried on on a ward and neighbourhood basis, and, unable to understand what is going on, they tend to blame their clients, and to urge upon them the desirability of some kind of community activity. Similarly, parsons dealing with their parishioners, in what has come to be called the suburban captivity of the churches, find themselves demasculinized as they busy themselves helping mothers to bring up their children.

One can readily understand this frustration, and, as a sociologist, one sees its connection with what Robert Nisbet (1964) has called the 'alienation' of suburban man. According to his analysis, a bureaucratically organized mass society has now succeeded in solving the major problems of existence: the activities and decisions which are left to the individual man are the trivial and unimportant ones. One joins a company as an employee; one gets one's house with the aid of a building society or of the local council; one insures against the risks of life. But there is an absence of what Nisbet calls 'hard property' and the sense of responsibility which goes with it. The individual tends his garden, plays with his children, visits the neighbours for coffee and checks on the relative standards of their furniture and his own. But his participation in a larger world is confined to his role as a televiewer.

There is a great deal in the critique of Nisbet and other similar writers with which one cannot but agree, and it may well be that in the future we may be forced to find ways of making suburban existence more significant and meaningful. It is also true, however, and this is a truth to which planners should address themselves, that suburban man looks as socially and culturally impoverished as he does in the literature of romantic sociology and town planning simply because we have failed to look at his life as a whole. The really important aspects of his life may perhaps be describable in terms of the answers he would have given to the questions we left off our questionnaire.

Urban relationships

In order to explain more clearly what I mean here I think it is perhaps useful to look closely and critically at the notions of impersonality, anonymity, and privacy and the way in which they have been used in analysing what Wirth called 'urbanism as a way of life'. It is, of course, perfectly true as Simmel (1950), Wirth (1964) and Park (1925) have all pointed out, that it is characteristic of urban life that one interacts with most people most of the time on an apparently superficial level. But one should not go on from this to conclude (as none of these writers did) that people who live this way are necessarily deprived. Far from it. In fact, the lack of depth of human relations is an enormous boon. One could not possibly enter fully and completely into all the relations which are on offer in the city without getting a kind of social indigestion. One can, however, savour them, and in so doing enjoy the riches of urban life.

That controversial writer, Jane Jacobs (1965) has, I think, grasped the importance of this point in her account of what we may expect culturally and socially from living in a city street.

Certainly not that one should be in and out of the neighbours' houses all the time, and still less that they should be in and out of ours. What matters is that with our individual security and privacy guaranteed, so long as that is the way we want it, we should none the less be able to walk down the street and interact there with significant other people. There is no need for us to fall in love with them, to save their souls or to get them to join the party. Let them make love, worship and politicize as they please. They may none the less matter to us. They are still more than mere rustic props and the texture of social life may certainly be enriched by having social relations like these along with more intimate ones.

Devotees of that most sophisticated and urbane of comedians, Mort Sahl, may remember a story he tells of the capture of a Russian spy in Greenwich Village. The witnesses at the case were asked how they knew that the accused was in fact a Russian spy. They said that they had asked him and that he had told them. When asked what was said in response to this confession they reported that people had merely said 'Ah, well that's the Village!'. The richness of urban life lies precisely in the possibility of experiences of this kind. The suburbanite, in fact, by no means always confines himself to living at home with his or her family. Or at least we should say that other possibilities are open to him if he chooses to use them. Quite clearly there is more chance in a city that men and women may find others to share their interests, and the attraction of city life for many lies precisely in this. It is possible to provide far more by way of specialized and advanced educational amenities for a city population than for a village one, and this too is an obvious reason for choosing a city life. But the ultimate attraction of the city cannot I believe be summed up under any of these heads. It lies simply in the diversity of un-planned social and cultural experience which takes a man a little beyond himself and makes him more than what he was.

Immigrants

One very important factor to be taken account of in this regard is the role of the new immigrants to the city. Of course it is true that such immigrants live in conditions of overcrowding, squalor and social disorganization, and it is true that for them the urban experience means getting out of their present situation to the nice, genteel conditions of the suburbs. Every decent Irish family should make this progression in three generations. What is often overlooked, however, is that, both because of their reaffirmation of the values of collective solidarity, and because of their cultural distinctiveness, they add an element of great interest to the city. Indeed it may not be too much to say that the presence of some kind of immigrant colony area, some kind of Latin Quarter, is the defining feature of any true city.

Among other things, of course, the areas of immigrant settlement and so-called vice areas are also often the areas of intellectual creativity. Students live here, as do unmarried couples and deviants of all sorts. These are the people who can think the thoughts and do the things which are not available to suburban man. Yet, precisely because they are not available to him, he needs to live symbiotically with those to whom they are. Thus I do not think that a student of mine was far wrong when he upbraided me, in the course of a tutorial on urban sociology, for being too much concerned with suburbia and its residents and asked why we do not think more in terms of planning cities which would meet the needs of what he called 'the down-town intellectual'.

Anomie

So far what I might appear to have been doing is simply to state the case for living in large internally-differentiated cities instead of small homogeneous communities. What I want to now emphasize, however, is that the Durkheimian perspective which I have been adopting does not imply that the kind of social, cultural and moral enrichment which I have been discussing follows as a matter of course from mere growth and differentiation. For, as Durkheim puts it, the social division of labour may occur without the new apportionment of tasks being in any way co-ordinated. Thus, instead of particular social positions being seen as contributing to a larger social and cultural unity, they are divorced from the larger context and leave the individual incumbents of such positions with a sense of purposelessness. This is the state of affairs which Durkheim describes as one of anomie or 'normlessness'.

Now many a planner, reading Durkheim's book for the first time would no doubt claim that it was precisely the role of the planner to see to it that the kind of co-ordination of divided efforts to which he refers was achieved, and that it was precisely the growth of cities as the result of unplanned competition for land use which had led, if not to anomie, then to anarchy. This, however, seems to me to be disputable. What I wish to argue is that planning based upon too narrow a perspective and too individualistic a sociology has, in fact, created a sense of purposelessness and normlessness and anomie, far worse than anything which existed in industrial cities which had reached maturity.

The planners' criteria

What appals the sociologist, when he meets those who are concerned with the planning of urban areas, is how naïve are the criteria of what human beings need for their existence and happiness. Most usually they seem to be based upon some kind of estimate of future consumer demand. Thus, and here I am parodying only a little the discussion about future provision which one hears in the north-east of England, if there are at the moment X per cent of the population in the income group earning above £2,000 per year, and a high proportion of these have country cottages and go ski-ing, then we must calculate what the percentage in this income group will be in the future, and provide the appropriate number of country cottages, ski-slopes, and ski-cupboards under the stairs. The point here is that the individual is here considered simply as an individual consumer who has no relationships with his fellows and whose needs can be measured in isolation from his fellows.

Many who would agree with me about the fatuousness of this kind of planning would perhaps find my next point too radical. Yet I insist upon it. This is that to take one residential part of the city out of its context is as disastrous as taking the single individual out of his context of social relations. And this is what the mainstream tradition behind the town and country planning movement in Britain has done. The suburb at its best was, in fact, a great achievement. It did provide more space; it gave the family privacy and, by freeing the individual from the encumbrance of intense social relations with his immediate neighbours, it made possible his interaction with chosen fellowmen on a city-wide basis. What the garden city movement did was to put him back near his work, and at the same time to take away most of the advantages of living in a large choice-providing community. In divorcing the suburb from its necessary urban context, it idealized all that was worst in suburbia. A unit which made sense within the organic context of the city was now torn from that context and made meaningless for those who had to live their lives within it.

At this stage I expect many of my readers to accuse me of simply being negative or of standing for the old unplanned urban anarchy. I hasten, therfore, to say that I wish to be far from negative. What I want to do is to urge that we take the city seriously as a social and cultural unit and that we make provision, not merely for suburban lawns and houses, but for downtown streets, not merely for isolated conjugal families in the suburbs, but for all those other people who help to keep the social life of the city going. If we don't make such provision, and if we see the problem of planning as one of simply providing an indefinite number of houses with schools and shopping facilities cut off by parks and by roads from the nasty business of industrial production, we shall not of course prevent urban people living an urban way of life. They will simply find a way of using appropriate buildings for their own purposes.

The mould of uniformity

Much of the most exciting research in urban sociology has, in fact, been concerned with the way in which buildings are made over to new uses as one population succeeds another in the city's zone of transition. Perhaps it is exciting simply because here people have problems so acute that they cannot fit themselves into the moulds which local authorities present to them as the only possible ones for urban men. Instead they present *themselves* to the city and in so doing bring into being a way of life to which the buildings have to be adapted.

The reaction of local authorities to this situation is to see such people as dangerous, deviant and problematic. They are brought before the courts for offences against housing and public health regulations; they are accused of neglecting their children and of having improper sexual and family lives. The aim of the authorities then becomes one of replacing such people with others of a more acceptable sort. Confronted with the squalid lodging-houses of the twilight zones, the planners suggest that the whole lot should be bulldozed away, that new schools and houses be built and a better sort of person imported into the area. Similarly, local authorities and housing associations propose replacing the existing buildings with new houses and flats to be occupied by carefully selected and responsible tenants. Thus, suburbia, which is dependent upon the inner ring for its spiritual life's blood, spreads into the inner ring itself, destroying all that was vital in the community life there. This is called urban renewal.

Of course, there are limits to the extent to which suburbia can be established so close to the city centre. Land is too expensive for one thing, and the city cannot afford to house so few people where high densities used to prevail. Since, however, a large part of the problem is falsely diagnosed as one of lack of green spaces, the problem can very readily be solved by building high blocks of flats and actually saving space on the ground for the planting of more grass. Thus we get, not something which adequately and worthily replaces cosmopolitanism, the variety and the cultural richness of the inner ring, but a kind of flatted suburbia, which unfortunately has not even the advantages of privacy and easy access to play space for the children. In some places children fall out of the windows; certainly there is a tremendous sense of social isolation among the women who live their lives in their flats and in the lifts; and sometimes when, as happened recently in London, the buildings themselves prove unsafe, there is a real danger of riots.

What I am criticizing, however, is not the inadequacy of the windows or of the women's tea-clubs or of the building materials, but the anomie of it all. Starting with a complex and differentiated social organism, the authorities end up by creating a mass of uniform individual families between whom no sort of complementarity and no sort of co-ordination exists. Instead of planning becoming the means of overcoming anomie, it has become its instrument.

Fortunately, urban man is a resilient animal. He triumphed over the redbrick terraces in which the speculative builders of the mid-nineteenth century put him to live, and he produced the richness of working-class culture and society. Perhaps he may yet be able to triumph over his new environment, to use improved transport to flee from the garden city to the fullness of city life, and somehow to keep the pace of downtown life going even among the bare green open spaces and the high and meaningless towers. How he does this may be the subject of urban sociology in the twenty-first century, as much as the zone of transition was in the twentieth.

Planning for decline

So far, however, we have been considering only one line of development, and we have been looking at what planning means in a situation of economic growth and of urban growth and renewal. I now want to look at an entirely different situation which we face in the North East of England and which is no less central in its importance for planners. I want to discuss the situation which exists in mining and in other kinds of old industrial area, which does not necessarily result in the development of cities at all, and which, whatever its present form, is faced with catastrophic economic decline, and the consequent need for reorganizing both its physical and social structure. A great many planners are working in this kind of area today and it is perhaps time that we recognized that planning in conditions of economic decline is as normal as planning in conditions of economic expansion.

We may characterize the small villages of towns which constitute the units of this older kind of society by saying (*i*) that they are occupationally homogeneous; (*ii*) that social relations in the place of residence overlap with and reinforce those at work; (*iii*) that although the individual family exists and is a primary focus of loyalty it is none the less swallowed up in a larger social unit, whether of the extended kin group or of those in the same neighbourhood; and (*iv*) that the community sees itself as cut off from a larger society either because of the physical uniqueness of its work, or because of the uniqueness of the social position of the community members or both. In short this is a small community, but one which means everything emotionally for those who must live within it.

Occupational homogeneity is a peculiar feature of mining

communities. Location of the community is subject here to a set of determinants quite different from those which determine the location of other towns and villages. If the seam follows a particular course, villages must be located along that course, whatever the economic geography of the territory above ground. Thus there is no need for mining villages to be closely related to conurbations. If they happen to be so related, it will be largely a matter of accident.

Given that this is the case, community life for the miner is quite unlike that for men in other occupations. He is not continually thrown together with men from other jobs, as an urban man must be. Quite commonly he walks to work; but even if he has to travel due to the exhaustion of a seam, or, as they say, works in a travelling pit, the men with whom he travels are likely to be his fellow miners. Men from other occupations are seen as outsiders, less close to the real centre of things than miners themselves are, and will almost always be looked upon with suspicion.

Occasionally, of course, a pit village may be engulfed in a conurbation and there are also other communities in heavy industries (e.g. steel production and ship-building) which produce a considerable degree of occupational homogeneity among those who constitute the residential community. In these cases the community of workmates and their families may exist within a city and yet have little social intercourse with other sub-communities. Such an industrially based town or suburb within the conurbation is, therefore, likely to be quite unlike the suburbs we were discussing earlier. They belong to a differently structured type of society.

Inevitably, leisure time activity in a community of this kind is not as differentiated and specialized as that in the city. Since the work is hard, it is likely to take the form of social relaxation which gets as far as possible away from the world of work in its content, even though those who are companions in recreation are those who share the same kind of need. The central institution, therefore, is likely to be the social club or, in its absence, a suitable pub. It is in the club that men meet to talk about work, about trade union affairs and about their hobbies and the sports which they watch. It is, of course, largely a male world, but one which also provides an occasional night out for wives and outings and excursions for children and old people. There is no institution or grouping quite like this in a differentiated and specialized urban society.

One is very easily misunderstood if one says that in this intensely communal atmosphere, the family performs a different role from that which it does in large cities. The family in the pit village is a tremendously important focus in everyone's life. It provides the background to all other activities which go on, and members of the community would explain that it is because it is so strong a unit that it can be taken for granted. When someone speaks of a son or a daughter a brother or a sister as 'our Harry' or 'our Mary' it is clear that reference is to a group charged with profound emotional significance. None the less the family is not the sole focus of loyalty in such communities and its strength perhaps lies in the way in which it is embedded within other groups. Lack of mobility means that there is likely to be a considerably extended kinship network surrounding the family, and, kin apart, there is a significant community of neighbours, workmates and club members. It may be perhaps because ties with these extra-familial groups are so strong that it becomes necessary to specify reference to one's brother Harry as 'our'. In a larger community there would be very few Harrys apart from one's kin with whom one was on first name terms.

Another feature of the relationship between family and the larger community which has been noted is the relationship between role differentiation within the family and the intensity of relations in the social networks available to the marital partners. Because the family is so embedded in a community context, it becomes possible for the husband to turn to a world of workmates and clubmates, for the wife to turn to her kin and neighbours, and for each to make a very large emotional investment outside the family without being suspected of disloyalty. The world of the husband and the world of the wife as distinct worlds are easily recognized. Their existence does not betoken either coldness or cruelty, as urban middle-class people think. Those who live in communities like this are not precariously dependent upon their families in the way a suburban man is. They manage their personal relations without the help of psychiatrists, and manage them perfectly well.

The final feature of the internal life of these occupationally homogeneous communities which we must notice is the solidarity felt by the community because of a shared common labour, because of shared physical danger, or because of the social struggle by means of which they defend themselves against other human beings who threaten them.

Those who merely pass through pit villages and occupationally homogeneous industrial towns see their squalor without seeing their grandeur. True the workers here suffer what industrial sociology, adapting Marx's term, nowadays calls alienation. They have little actual control of their work, but in one sense of the term 'alienation', they certainly do not suffer as the ordinary city worker does. They do not see their work as meaningless. They are not mere cogs in a machine, whose ultimate purpose is beyond their ken. The pit is quite evidently *there*. So, in the early villages of Yorkshire's and Lancashire's industrial revolution, was the mill. And so, perhaps surpassing all other examples in its splendour, is the ship which grows daily on the riverbank at the bottom of the street.

This meaningfulness of communal labour and of local history is, of course, something that no planner can hope to create. It is something which must simply be seized and used when, happily, it presents itself. Nor can one create the worker's solidarity which years of class struggle and experience of danger and disaster have brought. One can only respect them and see that they are not mischievously destroyed.

Social growth points

This simple society then, is at the opposite pole to the organic solidarity of cities. It is not simply Durkheim's mechanical solidarity. It would be too much of an oversimplification to say that social and moral unity here arose from the fact that all people were the same, or that they possessed an undifferentiated collective conscience. None the less it is true that along the axis of differentiation this is, relatively speaking, an undifferentiated community.

Now, however, I come to the main point about these communities. Durkheim did not discuss 'mechanical solidarity' in order to sneer at it, or to point to it simply as an outmoded social form. Nor should we do this in our discussion of the occupationally homogeneous community. For us, as for Durkheim, the importance of discussing this kind of community at all is to see it as morally significant, to see that it stands along with a developed urban society, and, in contrast to the meaninglessness of anomie, as one of the two types of significant and self-fulfilling community available to man.

One can perhaps put this another way by suggesting the idea of social growth points. Just as it has been recognized that piecemeal industrial development, now here, now there, according to where the workers are, does not lead to economic growth, so we should recognize that not all forms of community development produce that sort of overlapping, interlocking or complementarity of social ties which makes for the growth of a satisfying community. One successful line of development here has been an urban and civic one. The other has been that of the small, occupationally homogeneous community.

I have discussed this social type primarily in relation to mining communities because they provide an excellent example. It is, however, worth drawing attention to two related forms of development. One is that in agricultural settlements; the other in towns where dissociation of homelife and worklife has not proceeded very far. Agricultural communities, of course, have many of the characteristics which I have been describing. Certainly they are occupationally homogeneous; certainly there is an overlapping of social ties and a sense of a wider group context within which family life becomes embedded; and certainly there is that same peculiar sense of the reality and significance of the work and absence of alienation. The main difference at first would seem simply to be that of scale.

In principle this is so, and one could imagine a society in which there was in fact a close similarity of structure between communities of this kind and the industrial communities we have been discussing. Perhaps the similarity is evident in countries where land reform has brought true peasant communities into existence. The crucial difference from a sociological point of view between mining and agricultural communities in Britain is simply this: in agriculture stratification is an evident part of community structure, because those who own the means of production and give orders to others at work, also live on the spot and dictate the terms, albeit paternalistically, and even acceptably, on which community life should be conducted.

It is true, of course, that the agricultural village has the same degree of self-containedness as the mining village. But its people do not have the same kind of social and cultural autonomy. So far as the miners are concerned, however the bosses may see the industry as a whole, they have their own way of doing so. They have their own unions and they have, in a very striking form, their own festivals, at which the cultural unity of all the villages taken together can find expression. Thus whereas the residually feudal institutions of the agricultural community prevent the full participation of all the people in a wider society, in the case of the mining community, class homogeneity, independence and corporateness finally set the seal on the intensity of community life.

The question arises, however, whether the advantages and satisfactions of this kind of community life could not be perpetuated in urban conditions. Could we not have cities based upon industrially homogeneous suburbs, each of which has its own internal integrity, yet which shared a civic life with other kinds of community? Perhaps this is a concept which has been insufficiently explored. I imagine that in conditions of advanced industrial society it would not be pressed too far, since it would not be compatible with the degree of mobility which such a society needs. None the less there might be possibilities of not assigning every group of industrial workers in the city to occupational anonymity within the suburbs, but rather of allowing some sub-communities who have their own mystery, their own integrity and their own dignity to go on existing within the city.

Possible ideals

I conclude this discussion of types of community, therefore, by suggesting that there are two or perhaps three worthwhile ideals regarding community life-styles which might inform our thinking, as we take decisions which could perpetuate or destroy the communities we have known in the past in Britain. At one extreme is the urban ideal, based upon the ideas of differentiation and complementarity. This divides up not merely the different occupations, but different sectors of a man's life. Yet it leaves him the opportunity of finding a whole life by taking in, in varying depths, as much as he chooses of the variety of experience which the city has to offer. At the other extreme is the idea of industrial and social homogeneity, where the fulness of life lies in the strength of overlapping social ties which give such communities, not merely a kind of snugness, but also a vigour which urban society can rarely recapture.

Thirdly, however, there is the possibility of a mixed type, which would enable us to get the best of both worlds. If I admit this, however, I would not want it to be used as the sociological justification of nearly everything that goes off at half-cock. What I am thinking of, when I raise this possibility, is that once the concept of a rich and diverse life has been agreed, there may yet be some scope within that for the creation of social and cultural enclaves built around industrial suburbs and townships. Moreover it might well be that a small and occupationally homogeneous community is so situated that it can benefit from its relationship to a city's facilities, without being wholly swallowed up as just another suburb. Such variations can serve to make urban life even richer than it would otherwise be. As one moved around the city one would have a diversity of experience in at least three respects. The experience would vary in content. It would vary in the depths in which one chose or was expected to take it in. And it would vary in the extent to which it was segregated from other experiences.

The stop-go cycle

So far I have been talking about the variety of community experience. I have yet to talk explicitly about the effect of change of growth and decline upon it. This is what I now want to do by way of conclusion. And what I want to say in summary is this: that economic and industrial change in Britain since town planning started has taken the form of violent cycles of stop-go, and that social and community change has tagged along behind, doing what it could to meet the exigencies which arise from day to day, yet basically imposing on the country a dreary and ill-considered uniformity.

In our cities the stop-go cycle takes the form of largely uncontrolled economic expansion followed by a consciousness of congestion and overcrowding. The authorities then begin digging up the city centre to make way for the extra traffic; there is a demand for more and more land at the periphery for overspill; and usually, a racialist panic, as those least able to defend themselves become the scapegoat of urban failure.

In heavy industrial areas the cycle takes a different form. As people become aware of the decline of the old industries, plans are worked out for a controlled rundown. Some pits, shipyards and steelworks are scheduled for closure, but others, the public is assured, can not only survive, but become even more efficient. So the first limited plans for closure are accepted, and a programme of social and economic investment is embarked upon in the surviving enterprises. From time to time, however, an unscheduled closure occurs, and the powers-that-be argue that we must be toughminded if we are to achieve economic efficiency. Then it suddenly appears that the closure programme is to be even more extensive than has been thought. Pits and factories and shipyards which had been included in the development programme are now scheduled for closure, together with their hundreds of thousands invested in new equipment.

In these circumstances, of course, the planner has no basis to work from. No one knows at the outset how large the conurbations are to be or how many villages and towns can be expected to survive. So the planner himself takes the decision. He will create a new town to accommodate hypothetical overspill or schedule a certain number of villages for eventual disappearance. And, if he is imbued with sufficient local patrotism and has the skills of a successful confidence trickster, he will try to upgrade his area in the development stakes, planning new towns or the incorporation of neighbouring villages, when the economic forecast dictates planning for shrinkage. This is perhaps the most interesting morally grey area in the society of planning today.[1]

Inevitably, then, without any clear conception of what sort of economic possibilities we are planning for, we reduce the problem of planning residential communities to its lowest common denominator. There is no point in thinking in terms of a city with specialized areas and differentiated populations and no point in planning a long-term future for a community in the

[1] Each of the developments suggested in somewhat exaggerated form in this paragraph and the preceding one has been exemplified in my experience in the Midlands and north-east England.

heavy industrial areas. All we can do is to go on repetitively declaring redevelopment areas, or planning little garden cities, all of which are supposed to have the simple function of raising everyone's morale and encouraging industry to settle. And the people in the new areas are always thought of as nice respectable people, with no complicating urban relationships and no aspirations, other than those connected with living in suburbia.

It may be, of course, that these trends are functionally inevitable in a mass society. The desocialization of man in a universal suburbia may perhaps be what is necessary for a society in which powerful élites permanently manipulate public opinion and engineer consent to their policies, but I am not as pessimistic as this. I believe that our failure to produce adequate types of community life is the consequence of our failure to develop an adequate sociology of planning. If we were to develop such a sociology, living in cities and in other kinds of settlement would cease to be definable in terms of living in houses of particular standards and particular densities. It would become an experience which men would value for its own sake. And valuing it in this way, they would be less available to manipulation by political élites.

Metasociological assumptions

The assumption which I make in all this is, of course, not simply a sociological one, because I do not believe that sociology can of itself tell us what we should do. There is, however, a kind of metasociology which starts with an image of what man is, and what can become, and it is from this kind of metasociology that planners will inevitably draw their inspiration.

What I have been trying to say here is simply that the metasociological assumptions which the planners I meet seem to draw on are so trivial that they appear to be nothing more than rationalizations of what they are forced to do by their masters, or what they do simply for reasons of expediency. What I ask instead is that, faced with the inevitable necessity of taking decisions about the future of our community life as some areas grow and others go into decline, we should turn to the great tradition of sociology and see what it has to say about the nature of community.

The concept of man and his community which I have suggested to you is, of course, not the only one which is possible. Another, deriving from Marx, would suggest that communal ideals cannot be achieved without a transformation of the social relations of production and that, given that transformation, they would be achieved automatically by the new men whom the revolution would create. And there is also the tradition of nineteenth-century utilitarianism leading, along one path, to the sociology of Herbert Spencer, and along another, to the municipal socialism of the Fabians.

Myself, I find these two traditions of metasociological thought inadequate as a basis for the sociology of planning, because the first is too vague about how the post-revolutionary transformation of community life is to occur, and the second, whether in its Spencerian or its Fabian form, treats man as an individual and sees no moral value in the social relations which he forms. I do not pretend that the Durkheimian theory of man and community which I have put before you is entirely adequate either. But it does have the merit of its complexity. It reminds us of the moral importance of the small community, which nineteenth-century utilitarianism thought of as transcended by a free market society. But it also has something of compelling importance to say about the nature of that free society in itself. The simple society achieves its moral strength, through the overlapping and inter-locking of social ties, the civic community by the integration of differentiated but complementary individual roles.

I may be told that Aristotle said all that was to be said on this matter long ago; that when he spoke of man as a creature destined by nature to live in the polis, he was enunciating exactly the same notion as Durkheim did when he spoke of organic solidarity. Perhaps this is true, up to a point, but even the smallest community with which we have to deal today is as big as Aristotle's polis, and what we have to do is to recognize the possibility of a larger and yet morally meaningful unit, against which the polis appears as the oikos did against the Aristotelian polis.

But I would not want to end by suggesting that one ideal and one ideal alone will work in contemporary planning. Far from it. In fact I would want to say that the attempt to find a single universal ideal is precisely what has led us astray. In some circumstances what we should be trying to do is to preserve the socially valuable small-scale communities which reflect Durkheim's mechanical solidarity. In other cases we should be concerned to see how such communities can be welded together into larger, more differentiated units. And there will be not one, but many types of urban society, through which organic solidarity might be achieved. It is the task of the planner and the sociologist to work out what kinds of community the economic circumstances will allow in each particular case and, having done this, to provide for the kind of physical facilities which will make it possible.

5

Some theses on sociology and planning

The limits of sociological theory in the field of planning

1   The basic problem which sociologists face in their relations with planners is this. The planners expect them to predict patterns of social relations which are likely to exist in a future community, when in fact such patterns of social relations are inherently unpredictable for two reasons. The first reason is that patterns of social relations are subject to rapid change and that there are no laws, proven in past research, which can certainly be held to apply to the future. The second is that patterns of social relations are, to some extent at least, a matter of choice, and that to pretend otherwise is simply to give legitimacy on pseudo-scientific grounds to the imposition of social patterns by one lot of people on another.

2   The one thing which sociologists clearly can do is to make *ex post facto* studies. These are far more useful to and important for planning than is commonly supposed. Not only can we learn in a general sense from past mistakes, but there is a pattern of sociological analysis which is highly suitable for the analysis of planned situations. The essence of this type of analysis, which derives from Malinowski, is that the *charter* of an institution or organized form of social life (i.e. what the institution is officially said to be for) is contrasted with its *function* (how it actually affects people, social structures and social groups). Thus, in studying a New Town we can look at its declared goals, which are often even quantifiable; we can study the deviation of what actually happens from what was intended to happen; and we can ask why this deviation occurs. In answering the last question we discover what functional relationship really holds between the New Town and the larger society. One of the main achievements of urban sociology in the future may lie in discovering what social functions different forms of settlement are actually serving

as distinct from the functions that planners think they are serving.

3 The reason why there is such variance between what planners achieve and what they say they are trying to achieve is not simply that they are frauds and hypocrites. It is that social goals are not the only ones which they set themselves. They have real physical problems to deal with, and there is naturally a temptation to try to prove that what is physically convenient is also socially desirable.

4 The actual *social* goals which planners and other decision-makers set themselves are not, however, to be dismissed as mere ideological top-dressing. At their best they describe concrete social structures which are held to be desirable. What the sociologist can and should do is to look at these goals carefully, spell out their sociological meaning, and subject these to criticism by developing alternative ideal forms. Thus, for example, there is some sociologically described content in the garden city ideal, more can be made explicit, and the whole concept can be illuminated and criticized by comparing it to other related ideals. Giving a sociological description of a social ideal presupposes a knowledge of sociological concepts and theories and methods of social research. The development of an ability to state social ideals in terms of a precise sociological language could be a prime objective of planning education.

5 Two main fallacies which underly the expectations which some planners have of sociologists are (*a*) that there can be in the modern world fairly large residential units which function as some kind of consensus-based community and (*b*) that the way to find out what people want is to ask them through market research type surveys. One of the growing themes in urban sociology is that there is no such thing as an urban or even a village consensus, that differently placed people (in a social and economic sense) will have different and conflicting goals even though they live together, and that the sense of belonging together which we seek, can only be achieved in the sense of belonging to the same conflict situation, albeit on different sides.

6 The fact that there is no consensus does not mean that no generalizations are possible. Sociological research has begun to reveal some of the typical patterns of conflict which may be expected in an urban situation. The inner-city area or twilight

zone on the one hand and the commuter village on the other have been most carefully studied, but more studies of this type are needed with the goal of establishing a morphology of community types, which could also be a morphology of conflict types.

7 One major set of problems for the urban sociologist is that of the relations between the 'laws of nature' which underly urban development and the interventions of decision makers. The original Chicago School assumed a Social Darwinist position, and explained the mechanism which underlay urban growth and development to be one of unfettered competition for land-use. Thus urban sociology seemed to be possible only in conditions of laissez faire. There could be no urban sociology if there was planning. But this conclusion only followed if it was assumed that the decisions of the planners were arbitrary or random. In fact the decisions of planners and of other decision-makers in the urban process are far from being random. The principal focus of urban sociology therefore should be the study of factors affecting the decisions of decision-makers whether these decision-makers are planners, estage agents, private developers, builders, councillors or housing officers.

8 There is no such thing as a science of unexperienced futures. To a limited extent it is possible to extrapolate existing trends in quantifiable indices and thereby have relatively reliable figures to work with. Even simple estimates of future population, however, are proved wrong when new factors intervene, and when the technique of statistical extrapolation is extended to provide a basis for planning such factors as the provision of leisure facilities, planning itself becomes absurd. What sociologists can do is to describe a developing community conflict situation, and make intelligent guesses at what might happen as things develop. They might also make intelligent guesses or judgements about what would have to be done to divert a given situation in some desired direction.

9 The view of urban sociology expounded here is not based on the notion of the city or some larger unit as a system. Such approaches, exemplified by Parson's concept of a self-equilibrating social order which develops mechanisms for goal-attainment, adaptation, integration and 'pattern-maintenance' and tension management, always seem to assume a consciously or unconsciously held goal which pertains not to particular groups of

individuals but to the urban system as a whole. We take the view that the urban order rests upon a balance of power which is continually changing.

10 There is a kind of sociology, slightly different from this which is advocated, for instance by Amitai Etzioni (1968). According to him, we should look on the social world neither as disordered chaos or as a law-like order which we can understand but not alter, but rather by analogy with a motor-car which we are driving. Such a sociology has practical applications and draws attention to the various mechanisms whereby information is gathered, sifted and reflected upon and whereby decisions, having been made, are implemented. Such a sociology might commend itself to planners. It should be noted, however, that social models of this kind which emphasize words like 'information', 'cybernetic', 'feed-back' and 'decision-making', tend to underplay or ignore entirely the question of where the values come from in terms of which decisions are made.

11 The systems approach to urban sociology regards the question of the distribution of power as unproblematic. Power is simply a 'resource' of the system. Our view of the city is that it includes many different groups of people whose goals conflict with one another, and our view of power is that it is a means which these different groups use to impose their will on one another. It may be, of course, that a particular balance of power might lead to the emergence, at least temporarily, of some level of agreed values, and that these will give the planner something to work with. But the extent to which the welfare state consensus fails to satisfy minority groups in our society at present should serve as a warning as to the relativity of such standards.

12 It should be clear that what sociology aims at is not simply to become one amongst a number of specialisms used in planning. Rather the sociologist claims a kind of understanding of urban processes which should enable judgements about the structure of co-operation and conflict which lies before us in our cities. It is the sort of understanding which can be of great practical use to the planner, once the planner is clear which of the many possible urban sides he is on.

Politics as an urban variable

1   From what has been said above, it is clear that we cannot simply extrapolate some kind of political trend into the future. The approach suggested is fundamentally opposed to the extension of the technique of extrapolation in general. The sphere of politics is the sphere in which it has least applicability, because politics is about the changing balance of power, and because politics is about value choice.

2   People in cities are differentially placed with regard to the control of residential property and other related facilities. Some own houses outright. A great many more occupy houses which they have mortgaged and a third large group are rent-paying tenants. It was possible during a study of conflict over housing in Birmingham to distinguish at least seven different housing-class situations. These were those of:

1   The outright owners of large houses in desirable areas;
2   Mortgage payers who 'own' whole houses in desirable areas;
3   Council tenants in council-built houses;
4   Council tenants in slum houses awaiting demolition;
5   Tenants of whole houses owned by private landlords;
6   Owners of houses bought with short-term loans who are compelled to let rooms to meet their repayment obligations;
7   Tenants of rooms in a lodging-house.

In other cities other classes may be found depending upon the kind of housing-stock available and also what constraints and value-choices affect what is 'desirable'.

3   Pahl (1970) suggested that the population of commuter villages, small though these villages may be, involve a variety of groups with different goals and are subject to different constraints. So one finds in Hertfordshire villages any or all of the following:

1   Large property owners;
2   Salaried immigrants with capital who choose a village style of life;
3   Spiralists, i.e. those who work for large organizations

and who must find a home in a district for a stage in
their careers;

4 Those with limited income and little capital who are
forced into the villages because urban housing is too
expensive;

5 The retired;

6 Council house tenants;

6 Tied cottages and other tenants;

8 Local tradesmen.

4 In these two cases, and no doubt in others, the various
groups have conflicting interests and will strive to defend those
interests against others. They do this either overtly by forming
political parties, or by forming associations to defend their
interests against local government. The conflict is less acute than
it would otherwise be because some of the groups in paragraph 2,
especially groups (4), (5) and (7), themselves aspire to move into
other group situations, especially (2) and (3), and some of the
groups in paragraph 3 may wish to leave the area altogether.
Uncertainty about their own position may make them less
resentful of the privileges of others. The basic conflicts are,
therefore, between relatively few groups.

5 The introduction of party politics into local government
means that the Labour, Liberal and Conservative Parties orient
themselves to serving the interests of some of the groups mentioned above: specifically the Labour Party seeks the support of
the council house tenants and the aspirant council house tenantry, while the Conservative Party seeks the support of 'home-
owners' and aspirant home-owners. One party expresses the
cause of the 'welfare state', the other that of the 'property-owning
democracy'.

6 A number of sociologists have noticed that in the advanced
industrial societies a balance is struck between these two groups
of interests, and that a relative consensus arises, which combines
the values of the welfare state with those of the property-owning
democracy. In terms of urban sociology this means that both or all
parties must allow for a private and a public housing sector.
Most planners, subject as they are to changing political masters,
work within this relatively unstable consensus.

7 The consensus, *is*, however, unstable and it is also note-

worthy that it does not meet the needs of all groups. In fact the urban political system is normally managed by one or more privileged groups in their own interests. They continually discriminate against other groups, leaving them whatever accommodation is least desired. In trying to serve the interests of these groups or even ensuring that their conditions are up to minimum public health and physical planning standards, social workers, planners and others may find themselves in conflict with the more privileged groups. At this point they may seek to set up minimum professional standards which are the condition of their collaboration with their political masters.

8   The basic pattern which we have assumed in paragraphs 5, 6 and 7 is that which exists in large industrial cities in England. But as has been pointed out elsewhere:

> ... Considerable variations in this pattern of housing-class conflict would follow from differences in the economic, political and cultural situation in different industrial countries. The model we have posited assumes the existence of a socialist movement in relation to housing amongst the native working classes, an inability to exercise political power on their own behalf by disadvantaged groups, and an aspiration to relatively detached family life in a suburban condition amongst all groups. Where these assumptions do not hold other conflict and status patterns may emerge. (Rex, 1968a, pp. 211–31).

This was written specifically with the comparison between Britain and America in mind. But it may well be asked whether we can assume that all these factors will continue to hold in the future in Britain itself and whether the electors in, say, the metropolitan fringe will continue to feel that their interests are adequately articulated by the existing political parties.

9   For the planner these notes on 'the political variable' would appear to hold these lessons:

1   The sense of representing consensual values which many planners have may be illusory;
2   The planner will continually find himself drawing attention to interests which lack representation;
3   The planner may increasingly find himself mediating

between interests and trying to propose new consensual values which permit some kind of truce between the different sides.

10   It is not possible for these issues to become a part of the planning education curriculum without causing controversy. There is no reason, however, why they should not be treated in a detailed and non-partisan way. Objectivity in sociology is not attained by pretending that differences of interest do not exist. It results from bringing these into the open and confronting one with the other.

Colonial migration to Britain 1945-70

Part II

6

The colonial background of migration

Racial discrimination and racial prejudice are phenomena of colonialism. It was as a result of the conquest of poor and relatively underdeveloped countries by the technologically advanced nations during the nineteenth century, that new kinds of economy, new forms of social relations of production involving both conqueror and conquered, were brought into being. The inequalities between men of different nations, ethnic groups or religions, or between men with different skin colours, which resulted, were often justified in biological racist theories or some functional equivalent.

The political scene in these underdeveloped countries today is marked by a revolt of the newly independent nations or by the underprivileged within those nations against their former colonial masters and those, who, in neo-colonial or post-colonial society, continue to represent them. The colonial revolt has many names and indeed it has many varieties, but as often as not, this revolt of the poor peasant, or the man who queues at the labour exchange in colonial capitals, or of the descendant of a slave family still living in something like plantation conditions, comes to be understood by the revolutionary himself as a revolt of the black or the yellow man against the white. The main theme of the history of our times is the revolution of these who see themselves as oppressed races, in some kind of race war against those who oppress them.

The conflict which has occurred in this post-colonial epoch has been evident primarily in the former colonial countries them- selves. Sometimes it has taken the direct form of a war of independence; sometimes there has been a continuing conflict after independence against the newly-established native ruling class. Sometimes the colonial revolt has become caught up in the conflict between the great powers and has become another theatre for the cold war. Sometimes workers have struck or farmers refused to deliver crops in order to redefine the terms of the economic relationship between native and colonialist or native and settler.

But the conflict between colonial people and the colonizing powers is by no means confined to the colonial territories themselves. For, as the age of colonialism has passed, and the plantations, the peasant production, the mining operations of the former colonial territories, have ceased to be profitable, colonial people have left their own countries to seek work in the rich urban industrial societies of the metropolitan countries themselves. Thus there is a confrontation between workers from colonial economic contexts and the free and organized working class of the metropolitan countries. The confrontation takes place in marginal areas of employment where jobs must be filled, yet cannot be filled from the metropolitan working-class population. For many certainly, however, it takes place in *urban* conditions, so that the descendants of the colonial people find themselves disadvantaged in their search for housing, and compelled to live in *de facto* conditions of segregation from normal urban community and society.

Along with the crisis of post-colonial society, therefore, a central feature of modern societies in north-west Europe and America is the crisis of race relations in the advanced metropolitan countries themselves. It is a crisis which presents itself in some countries as a crisis of urban deterioration and of racial discrimination. In others it takes the form of a violent revolt of the underprivileged in these cities. Thus in North America negro rioters have burnt down whole quarters of cities. By so doing they have spotlighted the crisis of these cities, which is a crisis of the poor and the underprivileged, but which is above all a crisis of race relations.

Colonial and metropolitan factors affecting race relations

The encounter of negroes and non-white immigrants, on the one hand, and the white population of metropolitan cities, on the other, is compounded of several different elements. In the main, however, these may be reduced to two. On the one hand there is the fact that those who now meet as fellow-workers, as fellow-citizens, as employers and employees, as politicians and voters, meet within the institutional framework of advanced industrial social systems, whereas some of them had previously met in the context of colonial society, a fact which places an initial strain on the relationships which develop in metropolitan cities and places of employment. But, on the other hand, the structure of the metropolitan society itself is such that to live within it is to live within a complex system of social conflict. Thus a relationship, which in any case has the potential for conflict within it, is further strained by the context within which it occurs.

The economic and political institutions of colonialism

The peoples of Europe have long been accustomed to the fact that colonial societies involve roles which could not exist in their own societies. Particularly this is true of the actual colonizing powers, Great Britain, France, Portugal, Spain, Belgium and Holland. But an awareness of these roles, and the contrast between them and the acceptable roles of European society, is shared with other countries as well. Thus, whereas the industrial worker in the European countries would be unlikely to tolerate for long a situation in which his own position was not protected by a right to trade union bargaining and to a minimum of welfare, he will be aware that in the colonial territories, workers and peasants rarely have anything like the same kind of security and freedom. He knows that there is a difference between the position of a free worker like himself and the unfree colonial worker.

The central reference point here is that of the institution of slavery and the plantation system of production. For what trade unionism means, and what welfare benefits as-of-right mean, is that the worker is a free worker. He can dispose of his labour freely and is not his employer's property. The slave, on the other hand, is someone else's property, and is unfree, and those who are slaves are suspect, both because the existence of slave status makes the free worker's status less secure and because the free worker may have learned to accept the racialist justification of slavery, *viz.*, that a man is a slave because he, is in some sense, an inferior being.

The question involved here is not simply a psychological

question of attitudes. It is one in the sociology of knowledge. The conception of being a worker or being an employee, in the sense in which the terms are used in advanced industrial societies, is a popular conception of a sociological character. It has meaning only in terms of a set of typifications of work situations which the participants in that society have learned. Thus to know what the term free worker means is to know what its polar opposite—slavery—means. Between these two types are, of course, many intermediate stages.

Thus, for example, many agricultural, mining and industrial activities in colonial contexts have been staffed by labour, indentured for a term of years. In the mining industries of Africa, workers have been required to live in compounds, cut off from their families for a term of nine months or more. And, in many places, at many times, varying degrees of political and military power have been used to recruit a labour force. All these types of labour help to define what free labour is not. Another dimension to the negation of free-labour also exists, however.

This is that, whereas the free wage worker enters the labour market directly in order to sell his labour and thereby to finance his own household and family, there is another possibility. This is that a man should be a part of his employer's or master's household. This is above all the situation of the domestic servant who stands at one remove from the calculation of market opportunity which, as Weber saw, was the essence of modern society. It is the domestic servant's master who calculates market opportunity. The fortunes of the servant depend as do those of children on the fortunes of the paterfamilias.

Just as there are degrees of unfreedom culminating in slavery, however, so there are degrees of exclusion from participation in the labour market, degrees to which the individual participates in the budgetary system of his master's oikos. Typically, in situations where labour and land are abundant, farmers may incorporate the domestic budgets of their farm-servants in their own, providing them with what are called in England 'tied cottages' (i.e. cottages whose tenancy depends upon continued employment), providing them with part of their income in kind, demanding that all purchases by them be made at the farm store or providing educational and other facilities for the farm-servants' children.

Peasants, similarly, may or may not have direct access to the market, although in their case the market is one through which crops or produce rather than labour are sold. The situation in which he sells his product directly to an ultimate consumer, haggling with his buyer and threatening to sell to another, are rare. In most colonial situations he is dependent upon some kind of marketing agency, which, although in some ideal cases it may simply 'charge for its services', will exploit the advantages of its situation to the degree that that situation is marked by a power differential.

Another alternative restriction of the workers' access to the market is share-cropping, a system under which the tenant is able to dispose directly of only a part of his crop. The other part is disposed of by his master. This is a situation in which direct access to the market is combined with participation in the internal economy of the master's household.

But a further possibility confronts the peasant. This is that he may stay out, opt out or be left out of the social system based upon market relations. This alternative may, it is true, be freely chosen, and there is much evidence that the colonial authorities have at times had to devote much energy to persuading peasants to leave the subsistence sector and join the market sector of the economy. None the less, land shortage, as well as the relative deprivation to which the peasant is subject, as the process of modernization gets under way, do make existence outside the market economy increasingly irksome to many, and younger and better-educated men from peasant societies may well seek to move both from subsistence agriculture and from agriculture itself to wage-earning industrial employment. There will, therefore, be a continual movement out of the area of what, in British colonial territories, was called 'indirect rule', to colonial towns and indeed to the metropolitan industrial countries themselves. Of some sociological interest here is the colonial town which may act as a kind of filter through which young men of peasant origin got the taste of urban industrial society. Thus, although many colonial towns are not towns in the same sense as then to be found in urban industrial society, they do none the less have some sociological relation to them, as well as to the peasant world from which they recruit their population.

All the economic roles which we have mentioned so far—

those of slave, the indentured worker, the migrant worker in the compound, the domestic or farm servant, the peasant or share-cropper on a semi-feudal estate, the peasant living by subsistence —presuppose the existence of a specific political situation in which there is inequality of power between the colonialist and the colonized. The history of the countries, therefore, will be one, in which, quite frequently, there is a memory of military conquest or of military action against a rebellion. Failing this, there is always a disparity of technological levels between the colonizing and colonized peoples, which renders the latter dependent on the former. Thus it is implicit, in all that has been said about colonial economic roles, that the colonial nation is seen as defeated and educationally and technologically backward. Such a view tends to be stabilized by the development of racist theories in the metropolitan countries and amongst settlers in the colonial country.

Paternalistic versions of such theories may indeed be developed and it may be argued that the colonizing power has a mission to raise the standards of the colonial nation and to work for this benefit, but this does not alter the basic perception of inequality (see for example Bolt, 1971).

Many of the race-relations problems which exist in the world today are, in fact, colonial problems. If we are to use our terminology strictly, of course, a colonial problem only becomes a race-relations problem if and in so far as there is both discrimination against individuals on the basis of perceived characteristics, and the justification of this discrimination in terms of some biological or related theory. None the less, it is clear that this has been the case in countries which have seen considerable white settlement, as in the case of the Union of South Africa, and in those cases where there is coexistence between different populations playing different roles on the economic system. Examples of the latter are relations between East Indians and negroes in Africa, the Caribbean and Latin America or the relation between American Indians and other peoples in Latin America. In all these cases we have what may be called plural societies. Relations between groups of differing national and ethnic origin within them include many subtle features, but they include none the less, at their best, an element of power, including both economic and military power.

7

The perception of the immigrant in metropolitan society

It is not our task here to review the full range of situations arising from colonial economies, which take on a 'racial' character. What concerns us is the fact that problems arise when people from colonial economies and, more generally, black people, find their way to the cities of metropolitan countries, and seek to enter the roles of industrial worker and citizen which are available to them.

The type case of such a situation is presented in the cities of Great Britain, France, Holland, Belgium and Portugal, where immigrants have migrated from former colonial territories. But it may not be stretching our theoretical framework too far, to suggest that similar problems arise in the United States, when the descendants of negro slaves, who worked originally on Southern plantations, have settled in 'the North' and in the urban economy and society. There is also some similarity between this situation and that in settler societies, when metropolitan-type cities have been built in the colonial territories and become targets of immigration for colonial nations. Thus a city like Johannesburg is quite different from one like Freetown, sociologically speaking. The former is a metropolitan industrial city in its own right. The latter is a filter between colonial and metropolitan society of a kind we have discussed earlier. Thus, it is possible to envisage a frame of reference for the study of inter-racial contact in an urban industrial context, which includes Chicago and Johannesburg, as much as it does London, Birmingham or Paris. But we must now turn to the problems of the social structures of metropolitan societies themselves, to see the way in which there is a complex interplay between processes arising from the colonial countries, and processes arising from the metropolitan economy and society.

The first point to be noted about these countries is the relative stability of their political institutions, and the fact that, for better or for worse, they have succeeded, despite war and economic crises, in avoiding a cataclysmic class conflict through which their political institutions might be overthrown. Thus Lipset has maintained that the Western capitalist democracies have solved their major political problems through the 'incorporation' of the working class into the society on the basis of a welfare and trade union bargain (see Lipset, 1959) while Bell and others have spoken on the end of ideology, i.e. the end of political conflict about the goals and basic shape of the society (see Bell, 1960). However arguable these theses may be in general terms it is clear that, *relative to colonial societies*, there is substantial truth in their assertions.

One fact to which Lipset and Bell draw insufficient attention, however, is the existence in the advanced capitalist countries of a new problem of poverty and underprivilege. True, those who suffer this poverty and underprivilege may lack the numbers and the organization to form the truly revolutionary kind of organization which Lipset and Bell have in mind as constituting a real threat to the social order. But they are none the less a permanent part of the new social order and any attempt to understand the dynamics of race relations in these countries must take their existences into account.

The new poor and underprivileged are in part the product of uneven economic and social development in the advanced countries. They include the elderly, those employed in less affluent sectors of the economy, the sick and the unemployed. In some cases they may still be in a state of absolute poverty, but it would be generally admitted by most students of the subject, that the crux of the problem is that of relative deprivation. By the standards of the interwar period many of those concerned might be held to be relatively well-off. But in relation to the acceptable standards which have resulted from increased productivity, from welfare measures and from trade union bargaining, they remain clearly an underprivileged and politically underpresented group.

Differing situations exist in different countries according to whether or not there is a high level of unemployment. In the United States the unemployed and the under-employed loom large amongst the poor. In Great Britain with its relatively high level of employment in the sixties the problem has been of a different kind.

One important variable is the degree to which the revolution of automation has been carried through. Thus, in contemporary Britain, there are a number of jobs which are unacceptable to the majority of the population not because of their wage level taken by itself, but because the conditions in the hours of employment are thought to be intolerable. Thus, *incomes apart*, those who are to be found in these jobs are thought to be underprivileged.

Again, even in the advanced sections of industry, because the level of production is variable, there will be a considerable number of marginal jobs which, though they pay well when they exist, are exceptionally vulnerable to economic fluctuations. Thus those who, for whatever reason, are regarded as being destined for the earliest redundancy can also be counted as amongst the underprivileged.

Clearly jobs of the kinds mentioned above are likely to be filled, if at all, by those whose market position is weakest, either because they lack the necessary skills for an advanced society, or because they are discriminated against. A more efficient industry would simply adapt to the labour shortage by further mechanization and automation.[1]

The disappearance of marginal types of employment, and the necessary level of education and skill required for any job at all, can lead to the emergence of a pool of permanently unemployed individuals. But even when there is no absolute educational or skill difference between the employable and the employed, the number of jobs might be too small and the group most vulnerable to discrimination will be the one which is permanently unemployed. It is perhaps also worth noticing that, even in the situation mentioned in the previous paragraph, in which there are inferior and menial jobs available, they may be spurned by the native metropolitan working class, and, since some of them who came from this class lack the skills or education necessary to do other work, there emerges a phenomenon functionally equivalent to 'poor-Whiteism' in South Africa and the Southern United States. Whether there is actual unemployment or not, however,

[1] In some cases, however, a more advanced technology may produce conditions of work unacceptable to the native working class. See Deakin *et al.*, 1970, chapter 8.

situations of underprivilege may exist. Indeed, since many rights in the modern welfare state are no longer related to employment and income, two men in the same situation in terms of employment and income may none the less find themselves to all intents and purposes in different class situations, because of their differential access to welfare or other rights.

The most important of the other rights is, in fact, housing, for the fact is that a man's housing situation in modern society no longer depends solely and simply upon his ability to pay. On the one hand, there will be some groups who are enabled to enjoy a position of advantage over and above their market situation, because of their political power. On the other, there is the fact that other groups will be discriminated against, regardless of income and ability to pay for housing. Hence the city, as a social and ecological system, is *not* solely and simply the product of market competition, as Park *et al.* (1925) seemed in part of their writings to suggest. It provides men with differential housing opportunities on criteria which are not related to economic factors only, but depend also on political criteria.

Thus we see that there are a number of situations of poverty and underprivilege, which are built into the structures of urban industrial society. Despite affluence, we find that there are sometimes insufficient jobs to go around. Because of automation and the consequent need for higher skill levels, there may emerge a class of individuals too inadequately educated to obtain employment at all. In the industrially backward areas, or in areas of industry vulnerable to unemployment, there may be actual jobs which are disadvantageously placed. Independently of all these factors moreover, there is a question of relative access to welfare benefits and to housing. Retired people may be insufficiently well-organized to maintain or increase the level of their pensions. Sick benefits may not maintain their relation to earnings. And the housing system will be in part politically organized so that the underprivileged in housing may be added to, or exist independently of, the underprivileged in employment.

Finally and crucially, in this section on the poor and the underprivileged in advanced industrial societies, we should notice the role of education. For educational disadvantage serves not merely to reinforce the disadvantages already mentioned: it makes them transmissible from one generation to another. Schooling is linked to housing. If the underprivileged live together in the same segrated neighbourhood, their children will go to the same schools—and they will be slum schools for the underprivileged. Proposals for the dispersal of school children from their home neighbourhoods, moreover, only serve to make the situation worse. For to declare that a child has to be moved to another school helps to emphasize, either that he is a problem, or that his neighbourhood is a problem, thus drawing attention strongly to his inferior status.

Perception of the coloured colonial worker in metropolitan society

The existence of underprivileged situations and roles is thus built into the social structure. They do not depend upon the existence of coloured or colonial people in that society. But we now have to see how it is that coloured and colonial people are incorporated into this system of differential power and privilege. We shall show how the situation of being colonial and coloured, and that of being of the new poor, serve to reinforce and to exacerbate one another. The coloured immigrant or his descendents fail to pass through privately or publicly controlled gateways to privilege and, having failed to do so, find that they are even more under-privileged than others who fail to get through the gates. Moreover the degree of underprivilege and suspicion which accrue to them as colonials increases, because their 'new poor' position serves to confirm suspicion of their inadequacy. This is a form of rein-forcement which adds to what Myrdal (1968) has written about the cumulative cycle of racial discrimination and prejudice. The question of the admission of immigrant labour into metropolitan countries is one of the first importance to organized labour in those countries. The memory, and sometimes the actual ex-perience, of prolonged unemployment, together with the clear understanding of the inferior position of the colonial, can only mean that labour will resist uncontrolled immigration. Moreover, even if a code of fair practice is worked out which guarantees that immigrant labour will not be used to undermine standards, and which guarantees that immigrant labour will suffer redundancy first, there will still be a fear that in less definite ways the immi-grant worker might be more docile and compliant.

Moreover, the welfare bargain as well as the trade union bargain of organized labour is threatened by immigration. If there are limited housing, education and health resources, the appearance of immigrants, even if their arrival is accompanied by equivalent emigration, will seem to lessen the chances of the metropolitan native worker enjoying these benefits. It may be expected, therefore, that these workers will wish to limit any access which the immigrant might have to the welfare pool.

To make the points which have been made in the last two paragraphs is in no sense to be taken to *justify* racial discrimination. The point which we are making is a structural one, namely, that it is in the nature of the free unionized labour that it will seek to strengthen, or at least to avoid weakening, its market position and that this will inevitably lead it to adopt an anti-immigrant posture.

It must now be pointed out, however, that the actual behaviour of the metropolitan working class under these conditions is rarely determined solely by its perception in a rational calculating fashion of its own market situation. Many other factors are involved, some of them due to a simple carry-over of learned beliefs and attitudes derived from colonial experience, some of them arising from a concern with status as a matter distinct from social class, and some of them fulfilling a personality need for specific personality types.

The relationship between status beliefs and attitudes to colonial and coloured workers is particularly important. Whatever his class-orientation in market-negotiations over the price of his labour, the metropolitan worker is at least aware of the differential evaluation of occupations in terms of their status, and, if his own occupation has a low status, whether or not he thinks the evaluation right, he will be aware of it. He may wish that the status be enhanced and will do what he can to enhance it by associating it with favourable stereotypes. The sterotypes of the coloured colonial, however, suggest the lowest status of all. More than that, it suggests ignorance, incapacity and evil—indeed in its more extreme forms it suggests sub-humanity. Inevitably, therefore, part of the 'public relations' system which must operate if the individual is to ensure high status for his occupation, or for that matter, for his neighbourhood, must be concerned with dissociating the stereotype of his occupation from that of the coloured and colonial.

It has already been pointed out that the image of the coloured colonial truly reflects his historical role. The problem of status-evaluations is, therefore, doubly an economic one. On the one hand, it relates to the relative esteem in which occupational roles are held. On the other, it relates to actual historical socio-economic structures. We can none the less ask, however, whether stereotypes of the coloured colonial are not subject to change.

The question here is really one of the agencies or the ex-periences through which stereotypes are acquired. We may divide them into (a) reports deriving from a family member or close friend, (b) reports spoken or written by those who have visited the territories concerned, (c) statements about colonial peoples made by political leaders and other influentials and (d) representation of the colonial coloured worker in the mass media.

Family experience of contact with colonial peoples is a very important source of information or of stereotypes for most individuals in in metropolitan countries. It is not true to say that such experience can only be gained by harking back to a remote past. All the major colonial powers and the United States have known military involvement in the Third World since 1945, and even the non-colonial powers have been involved in policing duties on behalf of the United Nations. This means that there are few families in which reference to events in the Third World is not interpreted through association with the experiences of a family member who has been involved in military service in the former colonial world. *Prima facie* it would hardly appear likely that this would be a favourable source of stereotype, since soldiers have usually actually been trained to regard the colonial as in some senses an enemy.

Apart from soldiers, missionaries and travellers have been a main source of information. Stereotypes from this source, it is true, do change, but during the great period of Christian missions, the representation of the African or Asian as a heathen living in benighted darkness could not but produce an unfavourable stereotype. Indeed the whole process of evangelism could be, and was often thought of as, one of making the African or Asiatic into a kind of White Man. On the other hand an apparently more liberal attitude which allowed for the existence of differences between men, often did so with an assumption of the inferiority of the black man (see Bolt, 1971). Thus, a European monarch or politician who allowed himself to be entertained by 'heathen' tribal dancing, helped to reinforce derogatory stereotypes, even though appearing more liberal in his attitudes to native customs than the missionary.

The media of mass-communication also play their role in inculcating stereotypes. They are both sources of information in themselves and the means of sorting out, classifying, stabilizing and defining experiences derived from other sources: what effect these media have, of course, depends upon who owns them and what the owners interest in the matter is. Given the scale of the task represented by any attempt to establish a stereotype of the colonial worker as equal, however, it can hardly be expected that even the most liberal newspaper or television broadcast will do much, however good its intentions. In fact Myrdal (1962) has suggested that even the most liberal newspapers in the United States start by making assumptions which are unfair to the negro.

Some would question whether the problems of class and status thus far discussed are the sole source of unfavourable stereotypes. In particular the suggestion is made that strangeness of religions or customs or language creates suspicion of itself, and that there is some sort of natural repugnance to racial miscegenation. There is no space to review all the arguments for the relative primacy of such factors here: it must suffice to say that strangeness could be an exciting and stimulating factor, leading to exploration and discovery rather than repugnance, and that the so-called fear of miscegenation is found predominantly amongst ruling groups, and then only in certain contexts (e.g. legal marriage as opposed to concubinage).

To undervalue these factors as *primary* causes of discrimination and prejudice, however, by no means implies that we deny their causal influence. For, even though a bar to intermarriage may at first be a crude means of keeping class-lines clear, by the second generation when children have been brought up to believe that intermarriage is a primary evil a whole pattern of taboos on contact and etiquette governing interracial meeting arises.

Much of what has been said in the last few pages could be taken as referring to psychological entities called attitudes, and the problem of changing the situations outlined would then be a problem of bringing about a personality change or of the re-educating of individuals. What we wish to suggest here, however, is that the problem is also one in the sociology of knowledge; that is to say we are concerned with an analysis and understanding of the stock of typifications, which are shared by individuals in any metropolitan society, and the sharing of which makes an inter-subjective world possible for them (see Berger and Luckmann, 1967).

Social interaction, out of which societies are built, is only possible if individuals are capable, in Mead's term, of taking the role of another (see Mead, 1934) and for this to occur the two partners to the relationship must be able to believe that their action takes place in a common inter-subjective world: such a world is created when experiences are interpreted in terms of a shared language, a shared set of meanings. It is in this context that we must look at what happens when coloured colonial immigrants enter metropolitan urban industrial society.

As we suggested earlier, one of the shared concepts in terms of which north-west Europeans and Americans interpret their world is the concept of free labour. This concept is taken to have a specific relationship of contrast and opposition to a whole set of other concepts such as slave, servant and serf. At the same time, men with black skins and natives of colonial countries have usually been perceived as being related to one of these other concepts. Thus learning to accept, say, a negro or Indian migrant worker, as a fellow-worker in a metropolitan urban industrial context means, in effect, learning a new social language, or learning to read the social world in a new way.

The easiest way of dealing with this problem is to avoid it. That is to say it may be expected that when such a situation arises there will be affirmations made that the social structure has not or should not change. Either the coloured man must return to that social place to which the belief system assigns him, or if he does stay it must be in an inferior place within the metropolitan social system. Nor will their affirmations be confined to stereotypes, i.e. to assertions about what the black man is like. They will also involve the elaboration of theories as to how the world is and why it is as it is.

The belief systems which arose during the period of colonialism were not, however, unambiguous. Along with the theory of the colonial man as being an ignorant evil heathen enemy, went the theory of the supreme justice of the colonial system. Thus, if only out of cynical hypocrisy, the colonial powers encouraged their imperial subjects to believe that to say *civis Romanus sum* actually meant something, and that they had a claim to recognition in the metropolitan society. Such a belief was bound to be a factor in situations when racist affirmations were made in justification of a policy of discrimination. Racism in an established metropolitan society would, therefore, never have a completely clear run.

Apart, however, from imperialist ideologies, the belief systems of liberal democracy and of the socialist labour movement expressed universalistic values. True, these belief systems had been fashioned to meet the internal needs of European society, and the burghers of the South African towns of Swellendam and Graaf-Rienet who adopted the slogans of 'Liberty, Equality and Fraternity' in 1789 were quite right in their assumption that these values were not intended to cover the case of colonial natives (see de Kiewet, 1941), but none the less there are hundreds of institutional contexts in which discrimination can be halted or made less systematic because of the existence of such values.

Discrimination against the coloured colonial worker in metropolitan society

We have now arrived at a position where we can assess the likely consequences of the arrival of colonial native immigrants in metropolitan society. Colonialism has its history, and these metropolitan societies have their history. Together their two histories, and the economic sociology which they imply, provide us with the starting point for the study of race relations in our modern cities.

The first set of facts to be noted has to do with immigration control. In this matter there is considerable variation between the advanced urban societies. Thus Australia has for many years pursued a White Australia policy, which excludes coloured colonials from neighbouring territories from seeking employment in Australia or taking up permanent residence in her cities. Great Britain, having reached a total coloured population of about 800,000 by 1969, reduced further immigration from the Commonwealth to a mere trickle (HMSO, 1965b). France, however, continued to give unrestricted access to French citizens including the natives of Guadelope and Martinique as she had done previously to her citizens in Algeria.

South Africa dealt with its internal problem of migration to the cities by ever more severe pass-laws and influx control, which made entry to her cities for a native African as difficult as entry into a foreign country. The United States, on the other hand, never attempted any similar policy to prevent a steady migration of negroes to her cities and particularly to her northern cities.

For those immigrants who did arrive, however, the problem was one of classifying them and of assigning them to roles in the host society, or alternatively of setting up a system of gates through which they had to pass: the easiest way of resolving the dilemma of recognizing a colonial coloured man as a fellow-worker was simply to assign him to an inferior role in the metro-politan society. Thus, although some went through the gates, the majority were assigned to membership of the new poor and underprivileged of metropolitan society.

What this has meant has been that the colonial worker has been accepted into the inferior and marginal industrial roles which we mentioned earlier. When there have not been enough jobs, he has taken more than his fair share of unemployment, and, so far as his housing is concerned, he has been assigned to whatever form of accommodation, and whatever part of the city was least attractive in terms of the particular country's values.

There is a great deal of variability between different countries in these matters. In some countries, while coloured men have inferior jobs and inferior incomes, there is no social barrier to the enjoyment of resources and privileges for those who can pay. In others, even those few who can earn enough can still be under-privileged, because they are prevented from using their wealth to buy social position. In some countries the level of employment overall is high, but coloured workers do menial work only and are discriminated against further in this sphere of housing. In other countries the employment level is low and the ghetto population is largely unemployed. Different urban societies differ vastly in the degree to which they value suburban and central city life. They differ in the extent to which both the economy and land and building use in the cities are planned. And they differ in the extent to which the immigrants and their descendants can constitute a viable political force.

No single essay can at this stage in the history of race relations sum up the importance of this urban race relations crisis in all societies. This could only be achieved after prolonged comparative work. What is intended here is that we should take the history of race relations in one country, Great Britain, note what has actually occurred, and what factors are incipient there, and then, by considering what is unique about the British situation, make suggestions as to what may happen in other circumstances.

8

Immigration control and employment

Control of immigration

Great Britain has throughout the period of its industrial growth been a country of immigration as well as of emigration. As many of her citizens went overseas to find employment in the White Commonwealth countries of Canada, Australia and New Zealand, settler societies such as South Africa, Rhodesia and Kenya, and less permanently in other colonial territories, so they were replaced by immigrants arriving primarily from Europe and from Ireland.

Immigration from foreign countries to Great Britain was restricted in 1904, and has since been the subject of continuous control. Immigration into Britain and into her colonies by citizens from Commonwealth countries was, however, not restricted before 1962. Thus an unknown number of Commonwealth citizens entered Great Britain before 1962 and considerable numbers of Asiatic Commonwealth citizens exercised their right to settle in British colonial territories in Africa and elsewhere. Ireland, although an independent country, has no form of immigration or emigration control system covering travel to and from the United Kingdom and no certain estimates of the numbers of Irish entering the United Kingdom is, therefore, possible.

The immigration of aliens undoubtedly presented problems at first (Foot, 1966; Garrard, 1971). By and large, however, it could be said that the absorption of limited numbers of white aliens presented no great difficulty, despite the fact that in the first generation they spoke little English.

What did appear as problematic to the British people, their journalists, their politicians, and, finally, their government, was the immigration between 1950 and 1962 of considerable numbers of non-white immigrants first from the Caribbean and then from

India and Pakistan. No statistics were kept covering this immigration until 1962, but Table 1, showing net inward immigration
(Davison, 1966), summarizes the estimates made by the Home
Office of net inward immigration from the 'Tropical Commonwealth' (including Cyprus) during the period 1955–62. The
figures show that throughout the period the West Indians remained the largest single group of coloured immigrants from
the Commonwealth, that there was a quite astonishing increase
in the numbers coming in from all countries between 1959 and
1962, and that, in 1961, the number of Indians increased sharply
and the number of Pakistanis increased ten-fold.

Table 1   *Immigration from the tropical Commonwealth 1955–62*

Origin	1955	1956	1957	1958	1959	1960	1961	1962 (first six months)
West Indies	27,550	29,800	23,020	15,020	16,390	49,670	66,290	31,800
India	5,800	5,600	6,620	6,200	2,920	23,750	23,750	19,050
Pakistan	1,850	2,050	5,170	4,690	860	2,500	25,080	25,090
Total	42,700	46,850	42,400	29,900	21,600	57,700	136,400	94,890

Those who argue for immigration control maintain that these
figures show that an immigration of unpredictable proportions
was beginning in 1961, while those who oppose controls argue
that it was precisely fear that controls might be introduced which
led to a panic amongst those who would otherwise have post-
poned their immigration for some years. The Leader of the Opposition, Mr Hugh Gaitskell, argued, in opposing control, that West
Indian immigration was already self-controlled, and that this was
shown by the fact that there was a relationship between the rate
of immigration and the level of employment in Britain.[1]

Certainly, however, there can be little doubt that the arrival of
coloured immigrants in such large numbers appeared as a threat
to some sections of the British population. Riots in Notting Hill
and Nottingham occurred in the late fifties and were followed by
sustained complaints in the correspondence columns, particularly
of local newspapers, alleging that immigrants were making the
housing shortage worse, were persistently unemployed and living
off public assistance, and that they were turning the houses in

[1] See *Hansard*, House of Commons, 5.12.61, cols 1172–3.

which they lived into slums. Allegations such as these were usually demonstrably false, but this alone could not prevent the weight of protest from having some effect.

The facts of the immigrant situation were that they did suffer a higher rate of unemployment than native-born whites, that they did settle in areas where the housing shortage was acute and that, particularly because of the phenomenon of multiple-occupation of houses by coloured households, they did cause these houses to deteriorate. But it was also the case that coloured people suffered discrimination in employment and housing, that the areas where they settled were areas which were actually losing population and needed immigrants to man industries, and that housing deterioration followed from the closure of normal housing opportunities to coloured people.

In 1962 the Conservative government introduced control of immigration from the Commonwealth; net immigration figures for the following two and a half years are shown in Table 2 (HMSO, 1965b).

Table 2 *Commonwealth Immigration 1963–5*

Origin	1963	1964	1965 (Jan.–June)
Canada, Australia and New Zealand	8,951	13,382	15,714
Other Commonwealth Countries and Dependent Territories	59,049	62,117	33,383

Under the new scheme all workers coming to settle were required to obtain work-vouchers. The number of vouchers issued for the white Commonwealth countries in 1964 was 817 and the number for the other Commonwealth countries was 13,888. Figures for dependents arriving to settle in 1964 were: white Commonwealth, 2,243; other Commonwealth, 38,952. This degree of immigration control was, however, still thought to be inadequate and the Labour government's White Paper on Immigration in 1965 argued (HMSO, 1965b):

it must be recognized that the presence in this country of nearly one million immigrants from the Commonweath with different social and cultural backgrounds raises a number of problems and creates various social tensions in those areas where they have concentrated.

It was, therefore, decided to restrict the issue of vouchers to those with special skills and those who had jobs to come to, and to restrict the total number to 8,500 of whom 1,000 would have to be Maltese. Since special skills were defined in terms of higher or further education, the total number of working class immigrants from the colonial Commonwealth was likely to be at most about 3–4,000. In fact it was substantially less than this. Since moreover, the number to be permitted entry from any one country was to be not more than 15 per cent of the total, the total number of Indian, Pakistani or Jamaican workers who could enter the country legally could not now rise above a few hundred per year.

Subsequent to the passing of the 1965 Act which followed the White Paper, the figures for voucher holders and dependants entering Britain were as shown in Table 3 (HMSO, 1962, 1967, 1968). Despite immigration control, the yearly inflow of depen-

Table 3 *Immigration of voucher holders and dependants from the Commonwealth 1965–7*

		1965	*1966*	*1967*
White Commonwealth	Voucher holders	755	320	262
	Dependants	1,986	2,896	2,730
Other Commonwealth	Voucher holders	12,125	5,141	4,716
	Dependants	39,228	42,026	50,083

dants from the coloured Commonwealth was increasing. This, together with the problem of illegal entry and the problem of other categories of immigrants who fell outside the scope of the Act altogether, now became the main focus of political activity for those who still saw coloured immigration as a threat.

The problem of illegal entry led to intense police activity on the southern and eastern English coasts to detect secret landings, and to concentration by immigration officers on the detection of forgeries, whereby new immigrants sought to be classified as dependants. The right of entry to British citizens of Asian origin living in East Africa remained, but the number who were allowed to enter in any one year after 1968 was to be restricted to a total of 1,500.

Those who regarded *any* coloured immigration as undesirable now concentrated on two points: (1) the possibility of voluntary repatriation of those immigrants already in the country and (2) the cessation of immigration by dependants. These policies, originally advocated by an alliance of extreme right-wing political organizations called the National Front, were given a new importance in March 1968, when they were advocated by Conservative politicians such as Mr Enoch Powell.

In fact, on both these points, many of those who opposed immigration by coloured immigrants exaggerated the degree of growth of the coloured British population. The striking feature of immigration from the coloured Commonwealth to Britain compared with other immigrations was the degree to which it was accompanied by an outflow of returning migrants and a careful analysis of the dependants' problem, based upon the most cautious assumptions, was that the total number of available dependants for those immigrants who had arrived by December 1967 was 236,000 and the total coloured population together with all dependants legally entitled and likely to enter Britain in the next few years after 1969 was 1,406,000 (Eversley and Sukdeo, 1969, p. 56).

The important point for our analysis to be derived from this whole discussion about immigration control is that, despite the smallness of scale of the problem, the possibility of continuing coloured immigration was seen as endangering British society, either, on the one hand, because of the likely behaviour of the immigrants themselves, or because it was believed that the presence of too large numbers might give rise to racial strife. Another possible explanation of a more sociological kind is that the social system was threatened by the merging of the metropolitan and colonial labour-systems and that immigration control was a means of keeping them and thus maintaining the relative integrity of the metropolitan system. Clearly a limited number of colonial workers could be accommodated in marginal roles in industry. Mass immigration, however, would bring into question more fundamental features of the labour system.[1]

[1] Further legislation was introduced by the Conservative government of 1971 designed to put Commonwealth and alien immigrants in a similar position.

Employment of coloured immigrants

The striking fact about the employment of coloured Commonwealth immigrants is not that there was discrimination against
them, although this, as we shall see below, there certainly was.
What is really surprising is the extent to which coloured immigrants were accepted as workers in certain kinds of employment,
without any alarm being raised. The nature of this acceptance has
been very well analysed by Peach in his study of the distribution
of West Indian immigrants in British industry (1968).

Peach's conclusion was that immigrants were attracted to those
regions which were growing rapidly or which were static, provided that there was no rapid inward migration of white immigrants
from other regions. That is to say that coloured settlement
occurred in London, where there was a high degree of economic
growth but a net loss of population, through migration in the
Midlands, where there was a moderate degree of economic
growth coupled with only moderate inward migration, and in the
East and West Ridings where there was moderate economic
growth coupled with outward migration.

Peach considers two hypotheses, one that these figures show
that coloured immigrants are acting as replacement labour and
the other that their arrival is the cause of white departures. He
concludes that the sociological evidence and the evidence of the
industry tables of the 1961 census support the former hypothesis.
Thus it appears that although the proportions of all West Indian
workers employed in expanding industries was almost the same
as that of the total working population, they were strongly over-
represented in the declining industries. This evidence is further
supported by the fact that West Indians have settled in larger and
declining towns, compared with small but growing towns.

What this would seem to show is that the kind of role which we
suggested earlier might be assigned to colonial workers was the
role which had been assigned to West Indians. On the one hand,
we find them to a surprising degree filling jobs unwanted by
white men. On the other, we find them playing a part in the
growth industries where they might well be marginal employees
most vulnerable to unemployment.

Davison (1966) has pointed out an important difference in the
occupational structures of West Indian and Asiatic immigrants.

According to the 1961 census the relative percentages for various immigrant groups and for English workers who were in the top groups of occupations (i.e. professional, employers and managers, foremen, skilled manual, working on own account or non-manual) were as follows:

Indian	76	Cypriot	53
English	71	Irish	48
Polish	71	Other Caribbean	45
Pakistani	54	Jamaican	44

Two points might perhaps be made about these figures. One is that there is in fact a considerable migration of Asiatic professional men, especially doctors, and the Asiatic migration also services itself to a higher degree than the West Indian. The other is that the major influx of Indian and Pakistani workers occurred after the 1961 census. Hence what we may now expect to find is the existence of considerable numbers of Asiatic workers in replacement manual employment, coupled with fair numbers in the professional groups, either servicing their own people, or filling gaps which have arisen in middle-class occupations (e.g. the rather low-paid and not much sought-after position of hospital doctor).

In so far as the thesis regarding replacement labour is correct, it may perhaps seem a little unnecessary for the research team employed by Political and Economic Planning (1968) to have concerned itself with seeking to discover the level of discrimination at all levels of employment. In fact, many of the areas of employment to which they applied job-testing techniques or in relation to which they interviewed 'those in a position to discriminate' were not areas which coloured workers ever sought to enter. Not surprisingly they found that coloured workers tended to under-report discrimination. The PEP study is none the less extremely important, since, although the fact is that there is some tendency for certain areas of employment to be open to replacement labour, this means neither that coloured workers do not seek to enter other areas nor that there is no discrimination within the relatively open areas. The social frontier of colour discrimination (i.e. the barrier which the ex-colonial worker must cross in order to win equality with the metropolitan population) is a shifting one. Conflict occurs over where it actually lies. The PEP survey gives a map of where it lay in late 1967. It is the only systematic quantitative study of its kind in Britain.

The survey produced three basic sorts of evidence: (*a*) a survey of the experience of coloured people in seeking employment, as that experience appeared to them, (*b*) the evidence of 'job-testers' of varying cultural backgrounds and colour derived from their experience of applying for work and (*c*) the response to questioning of 'those in a position to discriminate', these being taken to include employers and trade unions at a national and local level, labour exchanges of the Department of Labour and private employment bureaux.

The sample of immigrants who were questioned included West Indians, Pakistanis, Indians and Cypriots. The percentages of each group claiming varying degrees of discrimination experience are shown in Table 4 (PEP, 1968, p. 20*a*).

Table 4   *Immigrant experience of discrimination in employment*

	West Indian	Pakistani	Indian	Cypriot	Total
Personal experience claimed, evidence provided	45	34	35	6	36
No exposure through applying where immigrant known to be employed, or applying for only few jobs	17	12	19	7	15
Avoided discrimination through personal or racial characteristics or 'luck'	16	6	9	18	11
Belief in discrimination through knowledge of experience of others. No reason given for self having avoided it	9	6	10	7	10
Uncertain about existence of discrimination	8	24	12	34	16
No belief in discrimination	5	18	15	28	12
	100	100	100	100	100

Two points stand out in this table. First, it is clear that the Cypriots, who are commonly thought of as white and who come from one of Britain's former strategic colonies have far less experience of or belief in the existence of discrimination than the West Indians, Pakistanis and Indians. Second, there seems to be a stronger belief in its existence amongst West Indians than among the two groups of Asiatic immigrants. Though this could in principle be due to the possibility that Asiatic labour suffered less discrimination, regional variations show that it was where Asiatic labour was acceptable in a replacement role, as, for example, in the West Riding of Yorkshire, that less experience of discrimination was reported (see also Butterworth, 1967; Patterson, 1968; Wright, 1968).

What we are dealing with here, it must be remembered, is perceived experience of discrimination, not the actual extent of it. Thus the figures could be too low as an estimate of the latter, simply because those who were studied had insufficient information. This appears to be the case from the fact that claims to have experienced discrimination were highest amongst those immigrants who spoke English. On the other hand it is somewhat difficult to assess the variable of the immigrant education, in that, while having English trade qualifications is associated with a high level of claims to have experienced discrimination, so also are having indigenous trade qualifications or degrees. While the first association is in all probability due to the actual discrimination, the second could be due to the lack of comparability of qualification or lack of means of assessing these qualifications by employers.

Applications by English, Hungarian, West Indian and Indian and Pakistani job-testers were made to forty firms cited as discriminatory by immigrants. In only one case was a job actually offered to a coloured immigrant while the English and Hungarian testers had fifteen and ten offers respectively. This seems to suggest that discrimination was at least as widespread as was claimed by coloured immigrants. The authors of the report, in fact, go even further and conclude from this that discrimination was under-reported by immigrants. The survey of 'those in a position to discriminate' serves to confirm this, since this reveals attitudes to the possible employment of coloured workers in jobs for which they would not normally apply. It would appear from these results that any serious attempt to press their claims further by coloured immigrants would be met by determined resistance.

Certain of the conclusions in this section are important. These include findings (a) that national employers see no difficulty about employing coloured workers in manual work, but are convinced that coloured men are not suitable for entry into the executive positions which they control, while local employers do see difficulties in the sphere of manual work, particularly from the native white workers; (b) that there is a complete distinction in the minds of national employers between executive roles requiring personal characteristics not thought to be possessed by coloured immigrants, and technical roles, depending upon qualifications and skill which coloured immigrants might have; (c) thirty-seven out of one hundred and fifty companies at local level admitted that they did not employ coloured workers either as a matter of principle (in four cases) or because they would only do so as a last resort; (d) the firms most frequently refusing to employ, or avoiding employing, coloured labour were in the retail and service sector; (e) the attitudes of local workers were often cited by employers as a reason for not employing coloured labour, while the trade unions at national and local level denied discriminatory practice, though complaining that coloured immigrants were slow to appreciate the benefits of trades unions.

From this evidence, it would appear that the most important gatekeepers in the metropolitan society are the local employers. National employers control entry into executive and technical positions, but the crucial decisions as to which areas of manual work should be open are left to the local branches and their managers. The latter do, in fact, discriminate, even in the sphere of unskilled manual work, but much more in other spheres. The principal reasons given for this discrimination could be grouped under three headings as (i) problems of language, qualifications and lack of mobility of immigrant workers, (ii) customer resistance to the employment of immigrants and (iii) employee resistance.

These reasons for opposing the employment of immigrants were given to some extent by employers, trade unionists, labour exchanges and employment bureaux. It would seem, however, from the evidence that is implicit in the answers of trade unionists and employment agencies, that they ultimately do not control the situation. The trade unionist may decide to fight or not to fight an individual case, and goverment-run labour exchanges may bring pressure to bear upon discriminating firms, but employment policy is settled by the firms themselves. The decision, therefore, as to how far the coloured immigrant could become a full member of the metropolitan society rested with local managers, their personnel managers and foremen. What was the upshot of their decisions? From the PEP report and from other sources we may conclude (1) that there were some industries in which labour of any kind was so scarce that employers were glad to have coloured and non-English speaking workers, (2) that sometimes a high percentage of the local labour force being coloured was seen as a problem and a formal and informal quota was fixed, (3) immigrants were not commonly promoted to supervisory posts (only eleven cases of promotion to such posts were recorded by PEP in its survey of one hundred and fifty firms), (4) there was considerable resistance to the employment of coloured workers in white-collar jobs and in executive positions and (5) although all the PEP informants believed that the principle last-in-first-out should be applied to redundancies, there had been pressure at unofficial shop-floor level against the retention of coloured workers in preference to white natives.

All of this is quite consistent with the picture which we drew earlier of the role assigned to coloured workers in metropolitan society. They are accepted, but in limited areas only, and only given certain basic conditions such as a high overall level of employment. At the margins employers and white workers may seek on occasions to extend restriction and coloured workers to break it down, but the outcome is a frontier between two kinds of worker.

In fact the years between 1951 and 1969 have not produced major industrial conflicts over the employment of coloured labour. There have been small-scale local conflicts over the promotion of individual coloured workers to supervisory posts and over redundancy and there have been one or two occasions on which black workers' unofficial organization has arisen to draw the attention of both trades unions and management to their grievances. But this is quite consistent with the acceptance of a coloured labour force in a restricted role (see also Castles and Castles, 1971).

Racial attitudes may change, and it would seem that two factors may serve to bring about the change. The first is the possibility of large-scale unemployment or declining living standards amongst the native workers. The other is the appearance on the labour market of English-speaking English-educated children of coloured immigrants.

The fear that immigrant workers would become an unfair charge on the social services and would add to the difficulties of native British workers was clearly stated by a leading trade unionist, Sir William (later Lord) Carron, in his valedictory address to his union. Dealing with the economic crisis facing the Labour government and the trade unions, he discussed first the problem of

> the non-productive sections of our population who are generally found to be enjoying much higher incomes than those of us who are doomed to produce the basic commodities that make the continued existence of these people possible . . .

and then went on:

> Quite as a separate problem it would be interesting to obtain detailed statistics applying to the grand total that is consumed by educational grants, National Health expenses and subsistence payments that become immediately obtainable by the ever-growing number of individuals who were not born in the country and who in no way contributed towards setting up a fund into which they so willingly dip their fingers. As they so succinctly put it 'they know their rights'. It would be very acceptable to the rest of us if some small measure of appreciation and thanks were in visible evidence. (AEU, 1967)

Such figures as were available showed that Carron's statement was misleading. The National Institute for Social and Economic Research produced in August 1967 the account of the actual and projected social cost of immigrants as compared to the rest of the population set out in Table 5.

Table 5   *Social cost of immigrants as compared to rest of population*

| | 1961 | | 1966 | | 1981 | |
	Total popu-lation £	Immig. popu-lation £	Total popu-lation £	Immig. popu-lation £	Total popu-lation £	Immig. popu-lation £
Health and Welfare	18·5	18·4	18·6	17·4	19·0	16·8
Education and Child Welfare	12·4	13·3	12·1	13·9	15·3	22·9
National Insurance and Assistance	31·2	19·2	31·7	17·4	33·5	18·1
Total	62·1	50·9	62·4	48·7	67·8	57·9

Moreover there was some small amount of evidence on immigrant fertility. An article in the *Eugenics Review* of April 1964 (Waterhouse and Brabban) had shown that though coloured fertility is higher than English it is not as high as that amongst Irish immigrants and other surveys indicated that whereas the most popular family size amongst English families was two or three children, the most popular size amongst coloured families was three or four children. Such differences as these, which were in any case likely to decline as immigrants became more settled, did not seem to confirm the picture of an ever-rising demand for a share of social service expenditure.

By contrast with these empirical investigations there have, however, been attempts by economists to construct models based upon idealized assumptions and restrictions to estimate the effect of immigration on the British economy. An example of these is provided in an article by E. J. Mishan and L. Needleman (1966, p. 33) which develops a generalized model for assessing the cost of immigration and then applies it by taking account of what is known of the demographic and economic characteristics of Jamaicans.

Misham and Needleman's conclusion is that

> large scale inflow of immigrants into Britain over the next few years would lead to an increase in excess domestic demand and a worsening of the balance of payments situation. . . .

It should be noted, however, that, although the authors claim that they have preferred to be cautious (i.e. to underestimate the cost of immigration), they do include the assumption that immigrants will require the same amount of social capital as the native population, an assumption which means that this model does not give us an estimate of the cost of immigration in a society where immigrants have substantially less than an equal share of the available social capital.

Another economist, R. G. Opie, writing in the *New Statesman* (1968) concludes, more moderately than Mishan and Needleman, that

> It seems likely that, in the short run, immigration worsens the balance of payments and is at best neutral in its net impact on demand. In the long run it should accelerate the rise in standards of living, reduce cost pressures and strengthen the balance of payments.

What we are concerned with in dealing with these political and academic assessments of the effects of immigration, however, is not simply their degree of truth or falsehood, but their social effect. That is to say, we want to know what estimate the man in the street makes of the effect on his own economic situation of the participation of coloured immigrants in the economy and what kinds of action this leads him to. Secondly we need to know the effect on political decision makers of what they suppose public opinion on this matter to be.

From what was said earlier about the actual employment of coloured workers as replacement labour we may conclude that though the actual social frontier within which such labour is acceptable may shift, there are areas of employment in which British workers do not actually resist, even if they do not actively welcome coloured workers. The problem, however, is to dis-

cover what the popular view is of the overall effect of the presence
of coloured workers on the economy. This question is difficult to
dissociate from the question of attitudes to housing competition
and to urban deterioration which will be discussed shortly. There
is evidence, however, that the immediate response of those who
had to work and live with coloured workers was not one of
unrelieved hostility. What seemed to be the case was that the
relationship between white and coloured workers when it
occurred was a new one. Attitudes within this relationship were
ambivalent and official definitions were sought. The effect of the
prolonged debate about the rights and wrongs of immigration
was to provide definitions which defined the presence of coloured
labour in general as a threat.

The period between 1962 and 1968 saw a gradual emergence of
the immigration question as a central issue in British politics.
While public attitudes in the 1950s had been based upon the
notion of equality of British citizenship, in the early sixties
organizations demanding immigration control were set up, and,
by 1963, at least one local Conservative association has made
opposition to coloured immigration the central plank of its platform. In the 1964 General Election, the candidate of this
association in Smethwick substantially defeated a Labour
Minister, despite a massive overall swing to Labour. After 1964
the issue was kept continually alive by certain sections of the press
and in 1967 the National Front formulated as its immediate aim:

> to preserve our British native stock in the United Kingdom,
> to prevent increased strife, such as seen in the United States
> and to eradicate race hatred by terminating non-white
> immigration with human and orderly repatriation of non-
> white immigrants. (*The Times*, 24 April 1968)

In April 1968 a programme very much like this was advocated by
the Conservative front-bench politician, Mr Enoch Powell. Mr
Powell argued that it was the duty of politicians to reflect the
feeling of their constituents on issues like this and proceeded to
do so by retailing stories which he claimed came from sources
which he had verified, about the misbehaviour of coloured immigrants, of their overwhelming presence in schools and of the
increasing hostility of the white population to them. Summing up
the situation as he saw it, Mr Powell said that Englishmen

found their wives unable to obtain hospital beds in childbirth, found their children unable to obtain school places, their homes and neighbourhoods changed beyond recognition, their plans and prospects for the future defeated. At work they found that employers hesitated to apply the same standards of discipline and competence required of the native born worker. (*The Times*, 22 April 1968)

Mr Powell's speech also contained what his critics claimed were highly emotive words like 'gunpowder' and 'rivers of blood' and, when there were marches spontaneously organized by dockers and others in his support, argument broke out about whether or not a speech such as this was racist in character. Whether it was or not, however, the very least that could be said was that it offered the public a new definition of their relationship with colonial coloured workers. Most of these immigrants, Mr Powell stated in in a later speech, could not be assimilated into the British way of life; not to have stopped the immigration at the earliest possible point was a tragic mistake; and, though he called for equal treatment for those with a legal right to be in Britain, he argued that there should now be a complete cessation in inflow.

Whether, in the long run, Mr Powell's definition of the situation will become that of all political decision-makers or of the man in the street remains to be seen. If it does, however, the coloured man's position will be that of a man, who, though he is said to be entitled to the nominal rights of citizenship, is seen as a man who is only in the society at all as a result of a major policy error. Thus coloured workers and citizens would be marked as a distinct group in the society, a definition which is entirely compatible with what we said earlier about the possibility of fitting the coloured colonial into the role of the new poor and under-privileged of an advanced society.

Before we turn to the housing question and the urban scene within which the basic conflict between coloured and white workers and citizens is played out, we look finally at the definitions of their situation as workers which were adopted by coloured immigrants.

Coloured workers' response to discrimination

The PEP evidence makes it clear that coloured workers did not completely accept their positions as inferior 'replacement' workers in unwanted jobs. None the less this did not lead immediately to the emergence of a politically militant movement of coloured people fighting for their rights. Clearly the first generation immigrants were inclined, however, reluctantly, to accept their position. They were even more inclined to do so if they did not regard themselves as permanent, but expected to return home.

This situation, however, is subject to change. Such change was reflected first in the attitudes of those claiming to be immigrant leaders. Despite the accommodating attitudes taken by most West Indians, Indian and Pakistani leaders before 1964, there were already signs of appeals being made to the rank and file immigrant population in terms of slogans and ideas drawn from the United States, from the Third World and from China. Thus in 1964 Michael de Freitas formed the Racial Adjustment Association, called himself Michael X and implicitly used the slogan 'Black Power' in his appeal to his fellow West Indians. At the same time Maoist elements struggled for ascendancy in the Indian Workers' Association and in Pakistani organizations. These militant elements were probably not representative of the rank and file in 1964 and, indeed, immigrant leaders and immigrant organizations as such are at best only indications rather than exact expressions of the feelings of the man in the street. None the less, it was clear that, as time went on and white hostility received public expression, so militant definitions gained wider acceptance in the coloured community.

In fact there was in 1967 and 1968 a four-fold conflict between different definitions of the situation. The government sought through its advisory National Committee for Commonwealth Immigrants incorporating selected immigrants, along with respected leaders of extra-party-political opinion, to provide its definitions. Radical white anti-racialists sought through the Campaign Against Racial Discrimination to provide theirs. The various Black Power and Maoist groups grew in importance. And the unpolitical immigrants who probably represented the majority coped with situations as they came along. An important stage in the development of this conflict occurred when Black Power and other groups captured control of CARD. The White Radicals then turned their attention to the extension of race relations legislation to cover employment and housing and were partially successful. But the National Committee for Commonwealth Immigration was replaced by the Community Relations Commission, which seemed in 1969 to be losing significant immigrant support. In effect what was happening was a polarization between white and black views of the immigrant situation.

The growth of white support for the views of Mr Enoch Powell had an even sharper polarizing effect. The existence of such views and the support for them seemed to many immigrants, and much more to their British-born children, to make moderate and integrationist definitions irrelevant. Michael X, imprisoned for racial incitement, as well as other Black Power leaders began to attract more attention and, after his deportation from England, the name of Stokeley Carmichael began to assume increasing importance.

There is little firm evidence as yet of the experience of the young British-born and British-educated children of coloured immigrants seeking employment. What is certain, however, is that they will not accept the restricted employment frontiers which their parents were willing to do. Hence, if they do encounter the same amount of discrimination as their fathers, their frustration and presumably their militancy will increase. Thus one may have an ambivalent and contradictory reaction from these young black men and women. On the one hand they will show a strong drive towards equality and integration. On the other they will be increasingly militant and anti-white as a result of their experience of discrimination.

10

The housing of the coloured worker

All that has been said so far about the situation of the coloured immigrant relates to his position within the production system, that is, as a worker. It completely fails to touch on the most important fact of all, namely that the immigrant identifies, and is identified, much less with the place in which he works, than with the place where he lives. Thus the conflict which is perceived by the whites is a conflict with people who, in Mr Powell's words, have changed 'homes and neighbourhood beyond recognition'. And the conflict, as the blacks see it, is a conflict between themselves, as inhabitants of some kind of quasi-ghetto, and those who inhabit other parts of the city.

Peach (1968, pp. 80–2) has shown that immigrants tended to settle predominantly in towns of 200,000 population, and amongst these, in towns with decreasing population. They were much less frequently found in small and medium-sized towns which were growing. This would suggest that, far from its being the case that coloured immigrants were overstraining housing resources at the worst possible point, they were in fact 'replacement residents' just as they were replacement workers. The PEP survey has once again documented the degree of discrimination which exists in the sphere of housing and this has been supplemented by Elizabeth Burney (1968) and by Rex and Moore (1967). To start with, we may note the experience reported by immigrants of discrimination against them in the sphere of housing. This is shown for private letting in Table 6 (PEP, 1968, p. 73b) which parallels that relating to employment.

The striking thing about this table is the increase as compared with the equivalent employment tables in the 'no experience' group. This is particularly evident amongst Indian and Pakistani immigrants. The problem is to decide how far these figures are the consequence of voluntary segregation, and how far due to the fact that when discrimination is taken for granted contact with it is avoided. We shall be better able to answer this when we have discussed the dynamics of house ownership below.

Table 6   *Coloured workers' experience of discrimination in privately rented houses*

	West Indian	Pakistani	Indian	Cypriot	Total
Personal experience of discrimination claimed and evidence provided	39	15	19	8	26
No exposure through having applied only to places where known to be acceptable	40	72	71	25	53
Belief in existence of discrimination through knowledge of experience of others—avoided discrimination personally through personal or racial characteristics of luck	5	1	3	16	5
Belief in existence among others—no reason given for personal avoidance	12	4	3	25	9
Others	4	8	4	26	7
	100	100	100	100	100

Test-applications made to, and interviews of, those in a position to discriminate, confirm that the extent of potential discrimination was far wider than the experienced discrimination shown in the table. This was also true in relation to local government housing (council housing) for rent and in relation to private purchase. The most important gatekeepers here are estate agents, building societies who provide mortgages and the housing departments of city councils.

I have suggested elsewhere (1967; 1968a) that the problem of housing discrimination is best understood in terms of a model of the city, based partly on the notion of housing classes and partly on the concept of the immigrant colony. This analysis is followed here in order to illustrate what is involved in the emergence of what is somewhat loosely called the immigrant ghetto.

The city can be looked upon as a social organization structured in terms of differential rights in relation to the use of domestic and community buildings. The most desired position within this system is that of outright ownership by the head of a family of a whole house for the sole use of his family. This is, however, an ideal only rarely attained, and the usual substitute for it is a mortgaged house, in which the mortgage has all the benefits which normally accrue from ownership, but does not actually possess the title deeds. So long as this is the normal housing situation in an urban population, or at least the situation desired, the principal gatekeepers, who will decide to admit or not admit particular families to this status, will be the estate agents and the representatives of building societies. According to the PEP survey, however, only 47 per cent of the population of England and Wales were classified as house-owners. The remaining 53 per cent were in rented accommodation. This could mean that the 53 per cent were aiming at and had not yet attained the desired state of home ownership, but the fact that 26 per cent of the population were in council houses strongly suggests that council housing was an alternative destiny and alternative ideal in England and Wales. In so far as this is the case there is an alternative system for absorption into urban society, and an alternative set of gatekeepers.

The fact that only 1 per cent of the immigrant population, as compared with 26 per cent of the population at large, were in council houses, according to the PEP estimate, shows that one common housing destiny available to the British population was not available to, or was not sought by, immigrants. It will be necessary to return to this question when we have seen what happens to those who have not yet passed through the gates which lead to home-ownership or to a council tenancy. Private renting of whole houses is clearly one alternative, but this is a diminishing alternative in England where slum-clearance is continually decreasing the existing stock of houses available for rent, and rent control prevents the emergence of the kind of demand which would produce a new supply. The real problem then is to see what other forms of ownership and tenancy are available in the city. The two ways in which finance can be obtained more readily than by gaining approval from the building society 'gatekeepers' are by obtaining a shorter term loan or by being prepared to pay more interest. Many immigrants have found this the simplest way of obtaining housing without delay, and, although the business has a reputation of being unethical, various kinds of financial agency have been created to meet the need.

The immigrant who purchases a house under these conditions often makes up for what he lacks in terms of advantageous borrowing terms by his ability to rely upon friends and kinsmen. In some cases, therefore, what emerges is simply a form of group-purchase of not-much-desired small houses, in which a group of immigrants live together in overcrowded conditions. Often, however, the cost of the houses in relation to the income of the immigrants is such that they cannot meet their repayment obligations without resort to taking tenants on commercial terms.

There would seem to be two approaches to landlordism on the part of immigrant landlords. One is to distinguish sharply between those to whom one has obligations which preclude treating them purely in terms of market consideration, and those to whom one has no obligations at all and whom one is entitled to charge the rate which the market will bear. The other is simply to look on all other men as in a single category so that whether or not they are kinsmen or fellow-countrymen they are charged a 'fair' market rent.

The first type of immigrant landlord is represented by the Pakistanis whom Rex and Moore described in Birmingham, England, who, on the one hand, charged their Pakistani tenants only nominal or charitable rents, and, on the other, charged very high rents indeed for rooms let to other immigrants or individuals, who had not passed, or did not wish to pass, a gatekeeper's test.[1] The second was more common amongst the Protestant West Indians for whom individual family life and commercial relations between families seemed to be more normal. Whichever of these types of landlord we are dealing with, however, the outcome is the emergence of the phenomenon of the multi-occupied lodging house. Park and Burgess first drew attention to this phenomenon in Chicago in 1922. In Birmingham the areas concerned were called 'twilight zones'. It is the perception of these areas as a problem which produces a new and escalating pattern of racist argument and racialist practice in the white community.

[1] For contrary evidence see 'Race, Community and No Conflict', J. Davis and J. Jackson, *New Society*, no. 406, 9 July 1970.

It should be understood that the relief of this situation could be in part available through a different policy on the part of the society's gatekeepers. Even if the stock of whole houses for purchase and rent did not increase, a policy of 'no racial discrimination' at their gates would mean that those left behind would include many families who were better equipped to cope with their urban environment, e.g. native white couples who might share housing with their relations for a longer period. In this case there would be no possibility of a multi-occupied ghetto emerging. But, in any case, what happens is that policy decisions will have to be taken in circumstances where there is a continually expanding stock of houses available.

In the American situation low-cost publicly provided housing does not give much relief, and the fear is that the low-cost projects will simply become new ghettoes. So far as Great Britain is concerned, however, the popularity of council housing amongst working-class people raises the question as to whether the break up of incipient ghetto formations would not best be achieved by the action of local government. In fact Rex and Moore identify the following points at which *de facto* discrimination prevents immigrants from benefiting from local authority schemes: (*a*) the allocation systems for local authority housing discriminate against all newcomers, particularly in terms of a waiting period; (*b*) those immigrants who none the less qualify for consideration as potential council tenants may be given inferior accommodation (e.g. slums awaiting demolition), on grounds of allegedly inadequate housekeeping stands; (*c*) redevelopment schemes sponsored by local councils, and implying a right to rehousing, usually skirt the areas of immigrant settlement.

The immigrants, it should now be noted, are not the only occupants of the lodging-house areas. Any group within this local population who fail to pass the housing gates will be grateful to find that there are some landlords willing to offer them a roof over their heads, albeit at an exorbitant price. These groups will include deviants and down-and-outs of all sorts who have been selected out within the urban system because of their deviant characteristics. Inevitably, therefore, the relative segregation of the immigrant from normal urban society means that he is segregated to live with and to be identified with the city's problem people.

On the other hand the twilight zone also becomes a centre of immigrant social life and cultures. Here shops, public houses, churches, mosques and temples, social and sports clubs come into being through which the immigrant finds the necessary facilities for his social life and the security of friends whom he can trust. Thus, although his presence there is in large part due to discrimination, he none the less enjoys many advantages as a result of living in his relatively encapsulated colony, and to some degree his segregation will be self-chosen. Naturally, the greater the cultural differences between an immigrant group and the host society, the more the individuals concerned will choose segregation. Thus, for example, the grocer's shop is seen as having a crucial cultural and social role for the Indian immigrant in England. But it would seem to be the case that complete immigrant families, Protestant Christian families and families which have been settled for a number of years are less dependent upon the colony and eager to move to what, from the point of view of the urban value system, is more desirable accommodation (Desai, 1962).

What commonly existed in England in the nineteen-sixties was not strictly speaking a ghetto, certainly if the term ghetto is to be taken as implying anything approaching a 100 per cent concentration of a particular group. But it did involve the segregation of the majority of immigrant households in the equivalent of poor and underprivileged roles parallel to those of the replacement workers to whom we referred earlier. This has led on the one hand to white reactions in the form of policies designed to control and to punish the immigrants and to the emergence of racist and near-racist themes in politics, and on the other, to defensive and aggressive reactions by the coloured population.

The twilight zones as a political issue

The central theme of the debate about immigration and race relations in Great Britain has been the question of urban derioration. As we have already seen, it was this as much as or more than any question relating to employment which lay at the heart of the case made for immigration control. But apart from long-term policies of the kind, more immediate solutions have been offered.

These arise principally in connection with the work of public health and housing departments.

One factor which must be continually recognized here is the lack of fit between traditional housing policy and the problems which arise specifically in the lodging-house zone. A great deal of the legislation which has been passed in the twentieth century is designed to achieve the replacement of slum housing. But 'slum' is a technical term, which refers to houses designated as slums by local authorities, and these local authorities have used primarily physical criteria in classifying houses as slums. The recognition that living conditions might actually be worse in overcrowded houses which were still structurally sound dawned upon governments only slowly, and perhaps more slowly because the party of social reform drew its support from slum rather than lodging-house populations.

We find in England, therefore, that the powers which were given to local authorities to regulate multiple occupation of houses were quite inadequate in the 1960s. The Public Health Departments could serve notice on a landlord that his house was badly managed, overcrowded, or lacking in amenity and could prosecute those who failed to comply. Under the Act of 1964, moreover, the authorities could actually take over the management of the house themselves for a period. But there was no power to register the lodging-houses, so that the Public Health Departments had no knowledge of where the houses were, and, much more important, prosecution of offending landlords could achieve little if there was no real alternative to the service which they provided.

Unfortunately, individual local government departments do not concern themselves with matters of general policy, and it was the Public Health Departments concerned with the performance of a specialized technical function which were the pace-makers of legislative change. Hence the change which came was simply that, first Birmingham alone, and then other cities, were given the right to require registration of lodging houses and in certain defined circumstances to refuse applications to register.

The effect of the passing of legislation of this kind, in the absence of an adequate policy for making alternative types of houses available, was simply that local authorities concerned to stop the social evil of multiple-occupation from spreading would allow it to exist, but in certain areas only. The consequence of this policy could be the effective segregation of the decent and respectable areas of the city on the one hand and the twilight zones on the other. Such a division already existed in the early sixties in the main centres of immigrant settlements. The legislation merely formalized it. Thus, on one side of a main road out of the city centre, one would find quiet, smart, well-administered areas of private and council-owned houses and flats. On the other one would find the lodging-houses *and all their attendant problems.*

The phase 'all their attendant problems' refers to a whole range of problems with which the police are bound to be concerned. The question of race apart, housing conditions and the family situation of the lodging-house population mean that certain kinds of problems are bound to arise in the area. The most important concern prostitution and crimes of violence. Prostitution is bound to flourish in areas such as these both because tenancies of rooms are available at a price without questions being asked, and because, given the high degree to which normal marital relations are not possible, a clientele is readily available for the prostitute. Violence was the inevitable concomitant of the absence of family life and the fact that public houses were the principal social centres.

Those who come to the twilight zones from the respectable areas of cities are almost inevitably shocked by what they see there. The police and the social workers become used to it. In fact anyone who has to work there realizes that the standards of behaviour which are easily enforceable are quite different from those of the city at large. A question of police policy now arises. To what extent, it is asked, are prostitution and violence to be allowed? (Lambert, 1970). In 'normal' times one finds that these are areas where, despite national legislation on these matters, prostitution flourishes. Girls do solicit on the streets and there are streets of well-recognized brothels. Equally, when the public houses close, the police expect there to be a far higher degree of violence than would be regarded as tolerable in other areas. But precisely because of their tolerance the police have it in their power to increase the pressure against the lodging-house population at any time. In so far as they regard themselves as enforcing the morality of the common man, a posture commonly adopted by police, they may well be influenced by impressions of hostility to the immigrant as they arise, and the pressure may be increased.

A major area of social concern in the twilight zones in Britain is that of the neighbourhood schools. While much is written in the United States about ghetto schools and the handicaps which they impose on the children who attend them, in Britain the concern which has been expressed is that some native white children are attending schools in which a large proportion of the children are the children of coloured immigrants. But, if the problem is diagnosed differently, the most frequently proposed solution is the same, namely integration by bussing. In the British case, however, the aggrieved white parents are, in effect, not so much concerned with integration, as with thinning out. No one suggests importing a proportion of the white children from all-white schools into the coloured neighbourhood. It should also be noticed that the nature of the problem posed by the schools is usually thought of as a problem of coloured children. This seems to suggest that contact with coloured children as such is thought to be retarding, for the problem of non-English-speaking children is posed as much by Greek Cypriot as by Pakistani immigration, while it is not posed at all by the immigration of West Indians.

It would be wrong to suggest that the pattern of segregated problem areas to which coloured immigrants are confined has been completely carried through. The urban frontier, like the industrial one, is continually shifting. None the less it is possible to outline in ideal typical terms the sort of urban pattern to which present developments might lead.

In this ideal-type situation, the colonial coloured immigrant workers would be admitted to replacement employment, and having obtained that employment, would be forced by the closing of other gates to seek housing in the lodging-house area. There would be little hope of escape for any but a few of them, either through obtaining a mortgage, or through rehousing by way of the council's list or through the implementation of a development scheme. Inevitably they would be associated with bad housing and urban deterioration, with vice and violence and with deficient and overcrowded schools. Prosecution of immigrant landlords, emphasis upon the police problem, and school buses thinning out the coloured population, would all serve dramatically to affirm that they were the cause of these problems. The effect of this affirmation would be to establish that the coloured worker living in the twilight zones was, in some sense, outside the society. The quasi-ghetto of the twilight zone is, in fact, the institutionalized means whereby colonial workers become attached to without being integrated into metropolitan society.

The existence of such a social attachment, moreover, might come to have another significance. Its population could become the built-in scapegoat of the metropolitan society. If it did, one would expect that nearly all social evils would be attributed to the immigrants 'who have destroyed our towns or changed them beyond recognition', or, at least, that the issue would loom disproportionately larger in urban and in national politics.

This is an ideal type and the British case has not yet come to fulfil such an ideal type completely. None the less it does indicate a possible direction in which British urban society might move. Tending in the other direction, however, are legal and administrative measures taken by national and central government to promote integration and reduce discrimination. Under this heading may be included the machinery set up to implement the Race Relations Act which aims at preventing discrimination in housing, employment and other spheres, and the Community Relations Commission which employs liaison officers at local level to help bring about the integration of immigrants. So far, that is in 1969, it is too early to make a complete assessment of the work of these agencies (see Rex, 1968b).[1] Even those charged

---

[1] Since then, however, the ineffectiveness of the Race Relations Board has become even more apparent. The main developments which have occurred with regard to *de facto* discrimination by local authorities in the housing of coloured immigrants are the publication of the Cullingworth Report, 'Council Housing, Purposes, Procedures and Priorities', by the Ministry of Housing and Local Government in 1969; and a House of Commons Select Committee report on 17 September 1971. Both call for the elimination of obstacles to coloured immigrants being dispersed from central city areas if they wished to be dispersed. Both recognize that the arbitrary waiting periods to which coloured immigrants are subject in the allocation of council houses by local authorities are undesirable, but no attempt has ever been made to set up a national system of housing allocation to which local authorities must conform.

with directing them would not claim, however, that they can have more than an educative effect, and this has to be set against the statement of the case against coloured immigration and against integrating those immigrants who are already in the country. What cannot yet be seen is the emergence at city level or ward level of social processes which will facilitate the dispersal of coloured people from the lodging-house areas.

The result of this is that attempts are made to solve the problem without offending native born councillors or their constituents, and this means that the main burden of attack eventually falls on the immigrant landlord who is the easiest person to blame because he has no channels through which he can answer back. Unfortunately some sociologists are now beginning to argue that segregation is something chosen by immigrants, a half-truth which is used as a whole justification by local authorities for their discriminatory policies. Despite all these evasions, however, the prospect of a London whose whole immigrant inner ring became one huge twilight zone, had become so frightening to planners, for technical planning reasons, if for no others, that there seemed to be some slight possibility that a policy of dispersal might be pursued.

11

Britain's coloured immigrants and the wider context

It may now be asked what relationship this British experience has to the experiences of other countries, and especially to America where the term 'urban crises' has gained most currency. Is there some pattern common to the development of all cities with regard to black-white relations or is the experience of each country historically distinct? We begin our answer by pointing to the contrast between British and American conditions.

The most obvious difference is that, whereas in Britain the initiative is with the representatives of white society, and what is being debated is how they will act towards coloured immigrants, in America the problem is that of the negro revolt against conditions which were formerly accepted. Why should this be so?

The first point to raise is that the coloured population of Great Britain is made up largely of first generation immigrants and that they number less than one in sixty of the total population. Quite obviously new immigrants will bear much in order to gain acceptance in the society to which they migrate and, if their overall numbers are small, they have little prospect of exercising real political influence. The negro citizens of the United States, on the other hand, number one in ten of the local population, are capable of exercising the same kind of political influence as any other minority group, particularly because of civil rights legislation, and see themselves, and are seen as being, entitled to equal rights.

So far as white racism is concerned, the two countries have a similar problem. America has a moral legacy deriving from slavery, but she is also a country in which a civil was war fought, and in which the slave-owning states were defeated. There is still a battle amongst the whites between those who are committed to a policy of racial integration and those who follow the policies of leaders such as Governor Wallace. But the form of the battle has to some extent shifted. The main issue which the segrationists have to fight on is 'law and order' because of the negro revolt. They are also forced to fight defensively against the negro obtaining new rights, rather than aggressively to deprive him of those which he has. In Britain the conflict is between those who take the notion of equality between Commonwealth citizens seriously, and those who in practice distinguish in their own minds between the real British and those, principally coloured, members of the Commonwealth who come from occupying colonial roles to try to enter the metropolitan society. Within Britain the starting assumption was that the coloured British citizen had equal rights. But in fact he was accorded less than equal rights and, when he did not resist, became the target of racist hostility. It might be argued that the direction of change was different and opposite. In America the movement was either towards equality or towards racial conflict, with the negroes stronger than they had ever been before. In Britain the movement was from a starting point of formal equality towards increasing discrimination and the justification of discrimination in terms of increasingly public avowals of racist theory.

But none of the factors mentioned so far explain the relative militancy of the American urban negro and the relative quiescence of the coloured immigrant in Britain. To understand this, two other factors have to be considered. One is the question of the level of employment, the other that of relations with the police. Whereas, even when allowing for a greater incidence of unemployment amongst coloured workers than amongst white, the level of employment to be found amongst coloured immigrants in Britain was high, the American negro quarter housed large numbers of under-educated teenagers who had never worked and had little chance of working. They were frequently involved in crime and appeared to have nothing to lose by fighting back against the police.

The question of relations with the police, however, is absolutely crucial. The report of the National Advisory Commission of Civil Disorders in 1967 showed that police practices were the most common source of grievance amongst negroes in riot areas and action by the police was nearly always a factor in precipitating a riot. By contrast in the British situation, although coloured immigrants did complain about unjust treatment, discrimination with regard to employment and housing would almost certainly rank much more highly as a reason for grievance.

It must be pointed out, in drawing this contrast, that three factors in the British situation are moving in the direction of the American pattern. The children of immigrants will not see themselves as marginal members of the society, but will be in a position far more like that of the American negro. As automation and technological unemployment increase, coloured children from slum schools might find themselves ill equipped in the struggle for jobs, and there may well be a problem of negro unemployment. And finally it is possible that pressed as they are by racist propaganda the police may decide to exercise a tougher policy in the immigrant areas.

What would happen in these circumstances would be detectable in that group of associations and institutions which we referred to collectively earlier in this essay as 'the colony'. The churches, clubs, pubs and shops which help the new immigrant to sustain a social life of his own are a valuable institution from the point of view of integration. By protecting him from the buffeting of a hostile urban environment soon after his immigration, they provide him with a spring-board from which he can enter fully into the metropolitan society as a citizen and worker. The same organizations, however, could become the means whereby the coloured man detaches himself permanently from the society in which he finds himself and retreats into an insulated world which he can call his own. Further they could become the organs and the agencies of racial revolution.

There can be no doubt that there has been some movement of this kind in the immigrant colony. Whether it is more than one might expect as a result of the increasing importance of coloured men born in Britain, however, is difficult to say. On the other hand, it may be in part the product of imitation of an identification with the American situation. If this is so, the change would still be an important one. From the objective point of view of a sociological observer, however, one would not be entitled to conclude from what has been said that unless there was a negro revolt or a revolt of coloured immigrants, there was no urban crisis or problem. The crisis or problem might lie in movement in the opposite direction.

There is indeed some possibility that this will occur in

Britain. On the one hand there may be a continuous process of scapegoating, with present policy proposals for dealing with Britain's coloured population constituting only a first stage. Further stages would be represented by possible repatriation or forcible segregation. It does not seem wholly inconceivable that, at some time in the future, the proposal might be put that, since immigrants are not full members of the society, they should live in special areas or in camps of some kind.

Such developments would constitute an urban crisis just as much as does the negro revolt in the United States. The real distinction is a three-fold one: (1) one could imagine situations in which an urban society did embody institutions directed to promoting inter-racial equality and integration; (2) there is the situation in the United States in which negro militants, not content with existing programmes for achieving equality, themselves advocate black separatism; and (3) there is the type of situation in which segregation of the black population of the cities is complete, and they have been effectively deprived of the right of political protest. (This is perhaps most completely realized in the Union of South Africa.)

Conclusion

What we have been concerned with in this section is the incorporation into urban metropolitan societies of coloured workers who came themselves, or whose ancestors came, from colonial conditions. We have examined the problem primarily with British experience in mind, and, since that experience is far from complete, our results must be inconclusive. What we have found, however, is that there is considerable discrimination in employment and housing and a large measure of segregation in the cities. One possible point at which the white population might seek to stabilize this situation is one in which a limited number of coloured workers become attached to British society, but are not thought of as belonging fully to it: they would then become a kind of deprived estate within urban society. But this situation would not in fact be a stable one. Either it could lead to a revolt on the part of the deprived estate, in all likelihood uniting behind ideologies originating in the Third World, or it could lead to continuing and cumulative action against this group leading, perhaps, to its elimination from the society. Either line of development would lead to a feeling of urban crisis for many generations to come. The measures which have been taken so far to provide alternative pattern based on integration, however, do not appear to have arrested development in one or other of these directions.

12 The social segregation of the immigrant in British cities

Very few people in England have any idea of the kind of problem of race relations which faces them as a consequence of West Indian and Asiatic migration since 1950. In all likelihood the following propositions would be widely believed to be true.

The West Indians discovered the possibility of migration to Britain in 1950. Those who came enjoyed a much higher standard of life here than they could have hoped to do at home. They were inevitably followed by thousands of their fellow-countrymen and by a new wave of migrants from India and Pakistan. This represented a double threat to Britain. On the one hand there seemed to be a bottomless pit of potential immigrants who, if they all came, must have inevitably lowered the British standard of life. On the other hand, even those who were already here constituted a new and totally unexpected demand which would overtax and destroy Britain's welfare state. Immigration control was therefore necessary, but the British, being a liberal-minded people, recognized that they had an obligation to those who were already here. These would have equal opportunities and would become fully integrated into British society. When it became apparent that discrimination did none the less exist, the government immediately applied itself to considering how the existing Race Relations Act could be amended to give the coloured man a chance of fair employment and housing opportunities. Action such as this would prevent anything parallel to the rioting and arson in American cities in the mid-sixties.

In fact, this picture is almost totally untrue. There was never a 'bottomless' pit of migrants ready to set off for Britain. Those who came did not constitute a threat to the social services. The repulsive conditions under which immigrants live were, at least in part, the product of discrimination. Proposals for legislation against this discrimination were of a token nature only, and went along with other policies, the effect of which would undoubtedly be to segregate, isolate and punish the existing immigrant population. The effect of this has been to create an atmosphere of despair amongst the immigrants within which the doctrines of black power find ready support.

In order to understand this, it is necessary first to look at the situation which actually faces a West Indian worker with a family as he seeks work and housing in a British city. When this has been fully grasped the true nature of the social system of the twilight zones becomes apparent, as does the meaning of the policies applied by local and central government for dealing with them.

Let us consider the problems which would have faced a West Indian coming, say, to a Midlands city in the late fifties. He might stay for his first few weeks with friends whom he had known in Jamaica or St Kitts, and during this time would find himself a job in a factory and a small furnished room with cooking facilities. Once he had done this he would consider bringing his family over, but to do this he would have to find more adequate accommodation.

His first inclination might be to obtain a home of his own, and to this end he would go the round of the estate agents and building societies. If he was not careful, he might find that the estate agents who were most helpful were likely to charge special fees to coloured men and he would be aware of the cases of agents who had been gaoled for fraudulently converting their coloured clients' deposits. But the problem was to find an agent who was both honest and helpful. In many of the higher-class offices he would simply be told that, however much the firm regretted it, they simply could not find decent property which could be sold to a coloured client.

The building societies would also present problems. In some offices he would be told that mortgages were only available to people born in Britain, and always his financial circumstances would be subject to a far more rigorous scrutiny than in the case of a white client. He would, in the late fifties, have been able to apply for a council mortgage (although this was one of the first services to be cut when there was an economic crisis), but in the end he might well be forced to face the stark truth that house purchase was beyond his means as a technically unskilled factory worker. He would, therefore, be forced to follow the British working-class pattern and look for a house to rent.

The search for rented accommodation would lead him to the council. If he had been white, there would have been some small chance of obtaining a privately owned 'cottage' to rent, although there were fewer and fewer such cottages even for white people. But being coloured, he would recognize that the quest for privately owned accommodation was not worth the effort. He would try, therefore, to put his name on the council list. He would not, in doing so, have been seeking any special privilege. He would recognize that there was a severe housing shortage and that he would have to wait his turn. What he would not think fair, however, was that he could not even be considered for five years, and that when he was, he would still get less points for residence than those born locally. The best that he could do, therefore, was to leave his name with the housing department and ask them to put it on the main list five years later. Meanwhile, it would be clear that his main chance of getting any place at all for his family was in a multi-occupied lodging-house, owned by another immigrant or perhaps by a company doing the same kind of business as Rachmann, although perhaps on a smaller scale.

The existence of immigrant landlords depended on a kind of financial operation in which our West Indian was unwilling or unable to engage. If you could lay your hands on about £1,000 (probably twice that in London) the bank would give you, not a mortgage, but a five-year loan of about the same amount, and this would enable you to buy a large, old, terraced house with six or more bedrooms. Many Asiatic immigrants found the deposit by pooling their resources and undertook the heavy repayment obligations implied by a five-year loan on the confident assumption that they would be able to meet them out of the rents.

This was not the kind of enterprise in which the West Indian with a family was eager to engage, although some of the more economically ambitious did seize the opportunities presented either by landlordism or by rent-collecting for a company. Very often the landlord in the Midlands was a single man and very often he was an Asiatic. His tenants probably didn't like him and had as little to do with him as possible. But they saw little point in complaining about him, when he alone had enabled them to have any kind of roof over their heads at all.

The West Indian tenant now finds himself living in the 'twilight zone' of the city, a life with a style and a stink of its own. It is not the life of the slums. Slums have a place in the thinking of the welfare state. Twilight zones do not. And the squalor of the households which are established in the lodging-houses makes the life of a family in a small, red-brick slum-cottage look like a well-ordered paradise.

The basic institution of the twilight zone is the house in multiple occupation or the house 'let in lodgings'. What exactly constitutes such a house is in part a matter of customary definition. No local authority wishes to penalize the 'little widow' who lets a flat to students. Yet her house may well be included in the formal definition. So it is up to the Public Health Department to look for those houses which are likely to be ill-managed, over-crowded or lacking in amenity and to see that their landlords are kept under proper control. The landlord who presents the most serious problems is precisely the kind of landlord we have described above—the man who is compelled by his situation to grind as much rent out of his rooms as possible. It is he who is most likely to allow his house to deteriorate and it is against him that tenants seem most to need protection. We shall return to the remedial and preventive measures which are used below. Meanwhile, we should try to understand who exactly the inhabitants of his house are likely to be.

The Rachmann scandal on the one hand, and liberal fears of racial segregation on the other, have blinded many people to the fact that the typical lodging-house has an immigrant landlord and tenants drawn from a variety of races. That this should be so is inevitable, given the economics as well as the logic of the land-lords' situation. An Asiatic landlord, particularly one who comes from a rural background, will distinguish sharply between two types of tenant. On the one hand there are those to whom he feels some sense of obligation, because they are kin or fellow-villagers or because they have helped him with the deposit. For these, the rent must be as low as possible and, indeed, often is so low that it might be better to speak of guests than tenants. On the other hand, however, there are those whom the landlord has in simply because he feels no obligation to them. They will be people in one or other kind of difficulty, prepared to pay what the landlord asks. The relationship between landlord and tenant here must be based solely on the 'callous cash nexus' and, almost by definition, it will be between people of different races.

The services of the welfare state are, for the most part, based upon some test of worthiness, and the poor man who has to seek these services in a private market is usually a man who is deemed in some way to be unworthy. In any case, he wants privacy and freedom from official scrutiny and for this he is prepared to pay. Thus, when our landlord goes into business he will be providing a service which is in demand not only amongst the immigrants but amongst discharged prisoners and mental patients, unmarried couples, separated spouses, unmarried mothers, prostitutes and deviants of all sorts. The fact that there are so many for whom the housing system fails to provide is a guarantee that whatever kind of thieves' kitchen the lodging-house area becomes, it will not become a ghetto.

Within the lodging-house very little love is lost between fellow-tenants or between tenants and landlord. There is no point in the tenants taking the landlord to the rent tribunal, of course, and every reason why they should help him to lie to the Public Health Inspectors about the overcrowding. This is bound to be the case when there is no alternative accommodation of any kind available. But this does not mean that those who live together have anything in common. Each door off the corridor becomes the door of a separate home and the passages, doorways and gardens become public thoroughfares for whom no one in particular is responsible.

Social intercourse beyond the family takes place on a single-race basis in the streets and cafés and in the network of interlocking associations which make up the immigrant colonies. The high street, which reproduces in part that of Dublin, in part that of Karachi, in part that of Kingston, Jamaica, provides a separate home from home for everyone. The area begins to develop along with its reputation for squalor, a certain cosmopolitan glamour. There are, however, powerful reasons why the lodging-house zone will also become known as an area of vice and crime. The whole situation is one in which crimes of violence and sex offences are inevitable. The day-to-day encounters of tenants sharing a cooking-stove and the struggle for control of social territory between racial groups in the high street are certain to provoke situations of violence. And since prostitutes need precisely the sort of service which lodging-house landlords are able to provide and will pay well for it, the only cause for surprise is that more houses have not become specialized as brothels. Hence the term 'twilight zone' comes to refer not merely to the deterioration of buildings, to the squalor, or to the foreignness of the inhabitants. It refers to the moral twilight of streets of 'vice and shame'.

To complete the picture we have only to notice that children go to school here. Some will be Irish and they will be siphoned off into the Catholic schools. The remainder, amongst whom the coloured children are a large proportion, will go to the state schools. Some children then will be backward because they come from broken homes, some, black and white alike, will speak no English, some will be retarded through having come from different educational systems. The buildings are old and the teachers demoralized. These schools are known by all in the city to be disgraceful and all too easily a connection is established with the fact that more than thirty per cent of the children are black.

For this hell's brew of problems the welfare state has little in the way of answers, for this is not the set of problems with which the welfare state is designed to deal. What has emerged, therefore, is a set of punishments and restraints to be used against the inhabitants of the twilight zone and, when these have failed to remove the problem, plans for segregation. Unfortunately, those who are responsible for the shaping and administration of these policies see themselves as helping to solve the race relations problem. The contention of this essay is that they have become the main means through which the problem is exacerbated.

The natural target for the city's hostility as it becomes aware of the problem of the twilight zone is the lodging-house landlord. Socialists and Tories seem to agree that this should be. For the socialist he is the ultimate expression of the evils of private enterprise. For the Tory he brings private enterprise into disrepute. His tenants must, therefore, be protected and he must be forced to manage his property properly.

There is little point here in recounting the actual measures which are used against the landlord. What matters is that he appears before the courts and in the public eye as a criminal offender. The chairman of the rent tribunal and the magistrates in the landlords' courts win praise from the press for their fearless denunciation of the evil the landlords have done, and everyone agrees when the chairman of the Bench is reported as saying that it is particularly disgraceful that this Pakistani landlord should be exploiting his own kind (that is to say, the coloured population). But, even if the effect of their punishments is to force particular landlords out of business, the problem remains. There is still a demand for the sort of service the imprisoned landlord provided and a new man quickly takes his place. The officials of the local authority at least know this and, indeed, they rely upon new landlords coming forward. Hence, the effect of the punishment ritual is simply to find a scapegoat for what is accepted as a necessarily evil part of the total housing system.

This same primitive response is seen in the proposal which local authorities and central government have been discussing for dealing with the schools in the twilight zone. As we have seen, these schools have more than their share of a whole number of problems, and problem children are to be found amongst black and white alike. What is proposed as a solution to these problems, however, is that a proportion of black children, whether they have problems or not, should be dispersed to other schools by bus. It is not hard to imagine that as the buses begin to run they will be greeted with cries of 'Here comes the nigger bus'. The buses will make it clear who exactly the society holds to blame for conditions in its Plowden schools.

The proposal for school dispersal is not, of course, supported solely by racialists. Indeed, it is generally thought to be a liberal proposal. It seems *prima facie* a good thing to give some coloured children a chance of better schooling, and educational apartheid to the liberal is absolutely anathema. But no one in fact knows the likely effect on children of being publicly moved by bus to another school because they have been declared to constitute a problem. The liberals talk of an idealized scheme. In reality what is likely to occur is a half-cock scheme, providing an ideal focus for the exacerbation of racial feeling.

The other obvious way of dealing with the twilight zones, of course, is to knock them down and rehouse their population. But this is not happening. The slums which are being cleared do not include the lodging-houses. They are small, red-brick cottages built about a hundred years ago and usually housing single working-class families. The lodging-houses are younger, bigger and structurally more sound. Slum clearance does not affect them and hence it is entirely misleading to suppose that accelerated slum clearance could ever do anything to ease the situation of lodging-house tenants. If anything, it makes matters worse by ensuring that people in better housing conditions are housed before them.

Again, redevelopment has hardly affected the twilight zones. A strategy of redevelopment requires that it should begin where there can be the highest gain in persons per unit of space, and this has often become frozen into a dogma that areas of high density should be left out of redevelopment schemes. Hence, even where there is no overt intention to exclude immigrants from the benefit of these schemes, they are excluded *de facto*.

Given that the problems of the twilight zones themselves are not being and cannot be tackled, the local authorities have become concerned to stop them from spreading. Birmingham has been the pioneer in this matter and obtained the passage of a special Act of Parliament for this purpose. Since this Act was recommended for general adoption in the White Paper on Commonwealth Immigration, it is of some importance and deserves study by all those concerned with either segregation or integration. Quite rightly and necessarily, the Act gives the local authority power to compile a register of lodging-houses. This is necessary if the council is going to retain control of the public health situation in the city. What is not necessary is a clause which gives the local authority the right to refuse registration, if the amenity of a neighbourhood would be injured by allowing multiple-occupation there. Of course, such legislation could in theory be used to thin out existing lodging-houses. But, as we have seen, the pressure of demand for rooms makes this unlikely, and, if this is so, the sole effect of the legislation will be to segregate the twilight zones from contact with normal society.

When it is recognized that the whole way of life of the lodging-house areas is different from that of other parts of the city, that a level of violence and sexual deviance exists and is permitted there which is not allowed elsewhere, legislation like that which now operates in Birmingham can only mean the social and moral division of our cities into two parts. Coloured immigrants will be very largely confined to one of these, the problem part, and the landlords' courts and the school buses will make it clear to all who is held responsible for the problems.

The acceptance of this *de facto* plan for the segregation of these problem areas and people from the clean sectors of the welfare state was laid down in the White Paper on Commonwealth Immigration and ironically in those sections which dealt with integration. The need for central government to intervene to ensure that immigrants had equality of housing opportunity was passed over. Indeed, the White Paper warned against the danger of discriminating in favour of immigrants. It was then proposed that the Birmingham Corporation Act should be extended to other areas.

Since the publication of the White Paper, such government action as there has been affecting immigrant housing has been designed to protect them against their landlords, without suggesting any alternative source of accommodation. Moreover, housebuilding for those who qualify for rehousing under present discriminatory systems has been stepped up on the grounds that the areas concerned were areas of high immigrant density. Thus the native-born Brummy has been given an even better chance of housing because there are immigrants in Birmingham. The immigrant himself is excluded by the five-year rule.

None of these facts is altered by the proposed amendment of the Race Relations Act, by its extension to cover employment and housing. It is in the nature of legislation against discrimination that it can only affect overt discrimination and no local authority overtly refuses accommodation on grounds of colour. Thus, while some small landlord may be affected, the local authority system will continue much as before. After two years of work by the National Committee for Commonwealth Immigrants, which had strongly urged central government intervention, the Minister of Housing had not yet in November 1967 (two years after the White Paper) taken the elementary step of politely asking local authorities to stop discriminating.

There does not appear to be any strong force standing in the way of the present drift towards racial segregation and, useful in its small way though the reform of the Race Relations Act is, the danger is that politicians will now be misled into thinking that matters are in hand. In these circumstances, it becomes important that immigrants should speak for themselves. For far too long the Government, in so far as it has taken advice at all—sometimes in 1965 it deliberately avoided contact with advice—has taken it from its own appointed experts, most of whom have been white, and immigrants, finding themselves without any channels of communication with those who make policy, have begun to see their only hope in a Luddite policy of 'burn-baby-burn'.

What really makes it likely that racial violence will occur in our cities is not the preaching of the apostles of Black Power. It is the complacency of those who have to make the crucial decisions affecting integration. Here and there they make a small gesture like reforming the Race Relations Act and they keep their liberal advisers furiously at work, but these are token gestures only. The steady drift of political advantage is towards identification with racialism and racial segregation and, in the long run, this may well prove decisive in determining Britain's inability to do anything else than get firmly on the White Supremacy side in the racial war which is gradually shaping up in the world. But our future was not yet completely determined. In 1969 a small amount of idealism and courage in the Government, particularly at the Ministry of Housing, could have done a great deal to reverse the trend. By 1970 it was probably too late.

Theory and research on colonial migration

Part III

New minorities in Scandinavia

Some comments on current research perspectives

This chapter was promoted by an interchange which took place between the writer and a group of graduate students of the University of Lund after a conference on minorities in Scandinavia held near Korsor in Denmark during April 1970. The writer and his students both felt that the approach of the Korsor conference was inadequate in two respects. On the one hand it sought to include all minority problems (e.g. those of the Lapps, the gypsies, the Jews, the Finns in Sweden and the Swedes in Finland, Yugoslavs, Greeks and Turks in Denmark and Sweden as well as the problems presented by the exploitation of colonial labour in Greenland and in the Norwegian merchant navy) within a single frame of reference. On the other it adopted a welfare-based approach assuming that at a governmental level there was no motivation other than that of ensuring justice for immigrant groups and, in some sense of the term, their integration into the several Scandinavian societies. What the Lund seminar tried to do was to focus attention upon one specific type of minority situation, namely that of the Southern European minorities in Sweden and to adopt a more realistic approach in estimating the likely motivation of participants.

Central to the perspective of the seminar was a critical approach to the question of the relation between the advanced industrial nations and those which are industrially more backward. Contrary to the commonly held view that the advanced countries are concerned to help the backward countries to achieve an economic takeoff, it was suggested that, as a hypothesis worth exploring, many of the so-called underdeveloped countries had in fact been systematically de-developed by the advanced ones and that, over time, whether by deliberate decision or not, the advanced countries were likely to have a vested interest in keeping other nations dependent. Such a situation reaches its extreme form in the kind of relation existing between the Republic of South Africa and its neighbours Botswana and Lesotho. Clearly it does not yet exist in anything like as severe a form in the relations between Germany and other north-west European countries and those of south-eastern Europe. None the less there is a tendency in this direction to be detected. And the existence of such a tendency affects the kind of situation which is projected into the cities of the advanced countries as immigrants arrive.

What is suggested here need not take the strong form of suggesting that the advanced countries and the capitalist entrepreneurs in those countries are simply looking for and finding an industrial reserve army which can be used to undermine the conditions of native born workers. Such a factor may affect immigration policy, but it is likely to be modified both by the interventions of a government oriented to some measure of economic planning, including the planning of a labour force in an expanding economy, and by the fact that the initiative in migration might well have been taken by the immigrants themselves. What is likely to be the case is that at the actual point of decision-making at national and local level the decisions reached will be affected by a number of cross-pressures, so that a first question in all minority research should be that of discovering what these pressures are. Too often minority research operates with an idealized picture of the motivation of those in authority.

The structure of the situation which the immigrants enter, however, will depend not merely upon the motivation of the decision-makers but also upon the situation, beliefs, motivations and likely behaviour, both of the native working class and of the immigrants themselves. Basically it is likely to be a situation of severe competition, but the degree of inequality of opportunity within the competitive situation will vary from one context to the next. Southern European immigrants may come either from urban or from rural and peasant backgrounds. In the former case they will already be geared to some type of urban social system as regards such matters as jobs, housing and education. In the latter case, they are likely for a while at least—perhaps for a whole generation or more—to seek to maintain links with their own society, while trying to build around themselves some sort of colony structure within which they can defend their traditional way of life.

Further, there will be a distinction between short-term and long-term migrants, between those who come from areas of subsistence and cash-crop agriculture, and between target migrants working for a limited target of capital accumulation and those who are seeking a more continuous income. It can be misleading to assume, therefore, that all immigrants desire integration. But it can be equally misleading to assume that because some do not want it, others will not suffer discrimination if the way to full integration is not open. Thus, for example, in the writer's experience in England, the fact that some Pakistani peasant migrants are willing to settle for a temporary status, segregated from the main social system, is used as a justification for discrimination against West Indians. On the other hand, where a demand develops for integration as a way to achieving improved race relations, the fact that many Asian immigrants do not want integration may be overlooked, or, if it is not overlooked, deplored. What is necessary, therefore, in any serious research on the newer immigration is a careful assessment of the background situation and motivation of different kinds of immigrant.

So far as the native working class is concerned, a careful study is necessary of the ways in which the representatives of labour influence the allocation of jobs, houses and educational opportunities. At some time all labour movements have gone on record as being opposed to discrimination on grounds of race, religion, or ethnic origin, but the extent to which such idealistic motivations operate when workers have a say in the disposal of limited resources will clearly vary. One can imagine a social democratic movement in which members had been educated with regard to the long-term policies of labour recruitment in an expanding economy and applied itself to ensuring equal rights for all workers. Far more usually, however, social democratic leaders are themselves ambivalent as to how effective planning is likely to be, and the working class, having only a short-term perspective with regard to employment problems, approach the problem of their relations with the new workers with real anxiety.

The consequence of these attitudes is that the actual situation which the immigrant faces is one of intense competition for scarce resources and a pattern of discrimination which ensures that the more privileged positions will not be available to him. No doubt this pattern of discrimination is not as severe as in those ex-imperial countries where race and colour make the immigrant clearly distinguishable and his former role in colonial society make possible a perception of him as being entitled to something less than the full rights of a worker. None the less, unless the receiving country not merely has clear policies but also succeeds in explaining them to those who might otherwise feel themselves threatened by immigrants, some pattern of discrimination is likely. It is of the essence of any research programme that such a pattern of discrimination should be exactly described.

The most obvious starting point for this analysis of discrimination is in the sphere of employment. The distribution of a new immigrant minority by industry, by skill and by level of employment has to be compared with that of the population at large. The views of employers and workers in particular industrial contexts on the employment of the minority have to be discovered, and means found of distinguishing between genuine reasons offered for excluding the minority and rationalizations of a predisposition to discriminate. The experience of immigrants in seeking employment may be studied after the event, but evidence derived from this source may usefully be supplemented by job-testing programmes in which, say, a pair consisting of one Yugoslav and one Swedish worker are sent to apply for an advertised vacancy. Apart from all such investigations of the level of employment, moreover, there is the question of the average level of unemployment in the immigrant community and the community at large in good times and bad, and the questions of what happens when an immigrant is promoted and who is discharged in the event of redundancy.

A total description of this kind would be capable of being quantitatively compared, both with a hypothetical state of complete equality of opportunity, and with the sort of situation where discrimination is severe, as it is in the case of colonial minorities in London and Paris. More important even than this, however, would be not simply the quantitative comparison, for mere figures based on routine classifications of the population can be misleading, but whether the new immigrant minority had succeeded in breaking into those areas of industrial life thought to be most typical of the native population. What is likely to be the case to some degree is that the immigrant minority is forced, at least initially, into the position of an industrial underclass, fulfilling industrial roles which are entirely unacceptable or less than completely desirable to the native workers.

Even more important than discrimination in employment, however, may be the question of discrimination in housing. There is a geat deal of evidence to suggest that, although social contact may be common between members of a minority group and native workers at the place of work, segregation and lack of contact is the rule after working hours. This takes place within an overall framework of discrimination in the allocation of the housing stock. In Birmingham, England, for example the writer suggested that there were about seven major types of housing situation and that access to the more desirable situations was controlled either by loan-making agencies, by housing associations or by local councils. Those who controlled the housing stock brought about a pattern of segregation either through overtly discriminatory rules or by rules which *de facto* prevented immigrant minorities from achieving the more desirable housing situations. The actual pattern in any country, however, will vary, and before it is possible to understand the situation of the minority it will be necessary to discover the actual variation in the types of housing and of housing tenure available, the scale of values in terms of which these houses are rated as being desirable or undesirable, and the manner of the allocation of the various sorts of housing. This will vary considerably from situation to situation, but here, as in the case of employment, a situation of equality of opportunity as between minority and majority groups would be very unlikely indeed. What has to be avoided in research is the too ready acceptance of evidence of such equality on the basis of statistical information derived from routine census categories. To quote only one example the category of 'owner-occupier' in the writer's experience has turned out to include those who own and fully occupy their own houses, as well as those who technically become owners and occupiers, although the whole of their housing operation is dependent upon their crowding their houses with tenants while living in one or two rooms themselves.

Educational discrimination is in part the consequence of

discrimination in housing, since the principle of neighbourhood schools amongst the younger age groups means that those who live together will be educated together, but it also turns upon other autonomous factors. What seems to happen is that whatever disadvantages the minority suffer, of which inability to speak the language of the country of settlement is the most important, these will be multiplied by the fact that those who share such disabilities will be concentrated in particular schools. Moreover, once this happens the already low status and standards of the immigrant schools will be exaggerated and those who belong to the majority group, but whose children remain in the deprived areas, will demand some measure of protection for their children, either by the segregation of the minority, or through their dispersal to a larger number of schools in a kind of thinning-out operation. These segregative and discriminatory processes may, moreover, be aided and abetted by certain 'liberal' misunderstandings of what is happening. On the one hand the thinning out of the immigrant children (what is called in the United States 'integration by bussing') may be represented as for the children's own good. On the other it may be pointed out that receiving instruction in their own language is a privilege which the older and established minorities are continually fighting for. Thus the most discriminatory acts take on a mask of liberalism.

What one sees in the sphere of employment, housing and education, as well as in other spheres where different minority communities compete for scarce resources, is a situation in which the minority group may take on some of the characteristics of an underclass. This is to say that whereas the native workers have found ways of ensuring that within a framework of competition overall they can defend their rights to jobs, houses and education for their children (it is this which has led to the establishment of a relative social consensus in the modern welfare states of which the Scandinavian countries provide the prime examples), the minorities are minorities not solely because of their numbers but because they have been excluded from the general welfare and trade union bargain.

It should be emphasized at this stage, however, that what we are trying to do here is not make substantive statements about the structure of, or the actual degree of, discrimination in Scandinavian society, but rather to suggest the questions which must be asked in order to discover what degree of discrimination actually exists. When this has been done, then it should be possible to trace the processes which permit minorities to move out of their underprivileged position over time. It seems possible that such movement may occur and is occurring in Scandinavian countries since there is nothing quite equivalent to the predisposition to oppose permanently the full acceptance of the minority which operates in countries whose minorities come from former colonies. None the less there are instabilities in the processes, and any political or other movement which suggests a permanently inferior status for the minority would bear investigation. It could be that in conditions of economic depression such movements would flourish.

Once it is understood that there are tendencies towards discrimination against minorities and once these have been measured, it might then be admitted and, indeed, be expected, that there would be certain countervailing tendencies within the society helping to arrest the discriminatory process. There are a number of agencies which might be expected to play a role in this respect. Clearly there is in the political ideologies of the main Scandinavian political parties much which would lead one to expect that they would produce forms of social action opposed to discrimination. So also one might expect some such action from the churches, although the fact that difference in ethnic affiliation is often correlated with difference of religious affiliation would run counter to this. Finally we might expect that the universalistic professional orientations of civil servants, local government officers and social workers would work against discrimination. In all of these cases of course, 'prejudice' and a tendency to discriminate are likely to occur, and it is most important that research studies should not idealize the motivations involved; but once this potentiality has been understood, there is considerable scope for investigating the way in which the various sorts of institutionalized behaviour mentioned place a brake upon the process of discrimination and segregation.

Apart from countervailing tendencies arising from the receiving society, however, it is most important that we should also look at the defences set up in the organizations of the minority communities themselves, but in order to do this one has to consider a little more widely the social functions of minority group associations. We do need to stress that such organizations are, *inter alia*, 'trade unions' of the minority groups, i.e. organizations which serve to defend the groups' interests where these are opposed to and opposed by those of the receiving society. But this function is allied with others which have to do with preserving the morale of the individual immigrant in what for him is a crisis in his social life, and with gradually helping him either to insulate himself from or effectively to enter the social system of the country of immigration.

When a research worker lives amongst a new minority community he very quickly becomes aware of the prolific growth of associations of one sort or another which sustain the separate life of that community. They may include ties drawing upon kin and village connections in the country of emigration, they may include religious organizations, communities and congregations, they may take the form of sports clubs, friendly societies and charitable associations or they may be based merely upon the clientele of particular shops, cafés and other commercial enterprises. But what also becomes apparent is that any of these organizations, whether it calls itself religious, political or social, is engaged in the same kind of work and fulfilling the same kind of functions. Elsewhere these have been referred to as the overcoming of social isolation, the defence of group interests, the carrying on of social or pastoral work amongst group members and the affirmation of beliefs and values.

Obviously it is true that a church will be more concerned with the affirmation and recreation of group values, that a political party will be more concerned with the defence of group interests, that there will be friendly societies which service the group in terms of personal needs, and that there will be social clubs where individuals go for company. But, with this said, it is important to notice that a football club or a church or a drinking club might all fulfil all functions and that the individual immigrant could live his life primarily or even wholly within the network of social relations provided by only one of these.

What is important and of truly sociological significance is, of course, not the manifest but the latent function of such organizations. It is not the particular type of organization which matters, but the fact that it happens to be the explicit form taken by the social relations of the immigrant colony in that society. It is this colony structure and its functions which is of greatest importance to the sociologist.

The nature of the colony and its relationship to the city as a whole are often misunderstood. It need not represent a permanent structure within which a group lives continually in a state of pluralistic accommodation to the society. Nor need it become a place of forced residence i.e. some kind of ghetto. Both of these are theoretical possibilities and the latter is a possibility which most societies would actively seek to avoid. But the far more likely possibility in a country like Sweden or Denmark dealing with immigrants of Southern European origin will be one in which the colony acts as a kind of temporary refuge for the new-comer and as a springboard from which the second generation at least can begin to make the transition to full urban participation.

Failure to understand these issues has led to an unreal argument arising out of the theories of Robert Redfield, Oscar Lewis and Louis Wirth. Clearly, according to the view taken here there is such a thing as 'Urbanism as a Way of Life'. But this does not by any means imply that there is a simple statistical correlation between size of population, density of settlement or nearness to the city centre and the intensity of social ties. What we would expect is that, when a substantial group of immigrants arrive from the same country, social ties between them will become even more intense than they were in their native country. But this intensification of in-group interaction in the colony is in fact the precursor of a gradual process of absorption, in which the newcomers and their children became lax in the fulfilment of their native cultural and religious obligations and less concerned to associate with their own kin and kind, as they move into a more individualistic and secularized society and as they come to rely for their security more upon their own property and the services provided by state and commercial bureaucracies.

The colony, however, is not usually a completely distinct ecological or geographic area of the city. The concept as it is used here is a social rather than a spatial one. The minority, in fact, is to be found living most usually jumbled up with other minorities and sub-communities as well as with the most problematic and interesting of the city's population. The research problem for the sociologist is to trace the way in which this 'jumble' becomes a system of interaction and conflict and what kind of outcome is likely to ensue.

The best known and most feared outcome is that in which populations other than those drawn from the most deprived minorities move on and leave the neighbourhood to become a ghetto. This is the frightening prospect which has been forced to the world's attention since the mid-1960s by the American negro revolt. Far more likely, however, is a situation in which a part of the city becomes a permanent intake area taking in successive waves of immigrants, in which each new group finds itself in conflict with other groups and in which such conflicts either escalate to the point of violence or racial persecution or become subject to some system of management, through the creation of local intercommunal organizations.

The sociologist *qua* sociologist does not have the task of saying what must be done in these circumstances. His task is to indicate what possibilities exist. As we have pointed out above, the confusion of value judgement and sociological research in the welfare-oriented approach too often leads to make-believe and pretence about the motives of the decision-makers and the powerful in any society. Once we have a clear picture of the actual possibilities in the situation, it becomes possible for the sociologist, declaring his value judgements openly, to point out what would have to be done, say, to create a situation in which the security-giving function of the colony could be maximized while at the same time facilitating the transition of any member of the minority who wishes it either to a position of absorption into the social system of the city or to a position in which, while receiving all normal rights, he is none the less able to maintain his cultural distinctiveness. If such a policy problem is discussed after the process of social research has been carried through rather than at its outset, the mischievous idealizations which are so frequently found in the sociology of minorities will be avoided and a more realistic perspective for social change will be attained. It should also prove possible for those who do not accept particular value judgements (for example those who do not accept that the petit-bourgeois norms of the suburb should be the goal of the incoming immigrant) to make clear their value disagreements and to suggest alternative goals and alternative means of attaining them.

What has been outlined here is no more than a series of

questions which it is hoped might facilitate minority group studies in Scandinavia. It is in no sense an account of any actual situation which prevails. What it seeks to do quite clearly, however, is to suggest a realistic perspective which takes full account of actual situations of inequality and conflict and the confused and ambiguous motivations of governmental authorities as well as of the ignorant and prejudiced man-in-the-street who too often emerges as the villain of reports on minority research. Perhaps a genuinely liberal government or governmental agency would be prepared to finance research of this kind. If it is not, however, the serious student of minority sociology would do best to do without the government money and address himself to the real problems. This is what the writer took to be the serious point being made by his Swedish students.

14 **Urban and other elements in race relations theory**

The perception that there is a problem of race relations occurs in different circumstances at different times in history. In the United States, for example, the problem in the 1930s used to be perceived as one of a dilemma between the high ideals enshrined in the constitution on the one hand and the actual practice of *de facto* disfranchisement and Jim Crow in the South and of segregation in the urban ghettoes of the North. In Britain, in the immediate post-war period, the problem was usually seen as that of the colour bar, recognized with varying degrees of moral clarity as a problem in the settler colonies in Africa, and to a small extent with regard to the housing and employment of coloured workers in Britain, or, alternatively, of the strangeness and inscrutability of the customs and ways of the inhabitants of the oriental empire. In Europe, on the other hand, the problem was a more diffuse one. The colonial powers which had black populations, e.g. France and Portugal, knew no colour bar as such, but all of the more advanced countries used immigrant labour operating under relatively unfree and restricted conditions, to supplement the native working class and to staff the societies' more menial jobs. Germany, during Hitler's rule, saw a violent extension of this form of labour, with the creation of concentration camps and the use of slave labour, the whole operation being justified in specifically racist terms.

All these perceptions have been changed dramatically by the experience of the past twenty years. The doctrine of white supremacy coupled with a partial segregation of the politically deprived racial groups, has been systematized in South Africa, creating a society and a political economy of an historically new kind and one which becomes increasingly morally isolated from the rest of the world. The American negro has become more and more politically demanding, more and more militant and has literally set the cities of the United States ablaze. And, though north-west Europe has quietly absorbed its southern immigrants the British, faced for the first time with black immigration on a considerable scale, some of the migrants having a plantation background not unlike that of the American negro, now ask themselves a terrified and anxious question, 'can the American experience be repeated here?'

World sociology has approached these problems with a mixture of moral earnestness and conservatism. That is to say it has tended to assume that there is one single problem called the race problem which can be tackled as a particular problem within the existing order and our existing models of how societies work. For orthodox conservatives the question has been 'how can this type of labour be used without creating a danger of riot and revolution?' For conservatives of the Marxist sort it has been 'how can the new stresses and strains represented by black or immigrant discontent be fitted into better understood patterns of revolution?'

One enormous oversimplification of our problems, however, has recently been exported to us by our American colleagues. This is that the problem of race relations is at bottom a problem of the cities. If, therefore, we can only get our urban problems right, the so-called race problem would not get out of hand. On this basis the Institute of Race Relations has recently embarked upon a comparative study of race relations in cities in various parts of the world, and though there may be disagreement between the researchers on whether their commitment should be to the urban revolution or to the maintenance of law and order, the urban focus remains.

It is because I was one of the first researchers in this country to relate the problems of race relations to a framework of urban sociology that I have decided to return to this question here. What I want to do, therefore, is two-fold. First, I want to insist that it is a gross oversimplification to say that the race relations problem is a problem of the cities purely and simply, but, second, I want to show how, given pre-existing economically and historically caused tensions, the industrial city provides the social mechanism whereby racial confrontations are organized and racial conflicts ensue.

The setting of contemporary racial problems within which the urban explosion takes place appears to me to be provided by two main historical processes which are going on at the present time. One is that of the widening gap between the advanced industrial countries on the one hand and the so-called underdeveloped countries on the other. The other is the usefulness in a capitalist or partly planned economy of having a clearly distinguishable labour force, which is readily dispensable and can be disposed of without too much interference and resistance by working-class organizations. Thus one finds immigration from the poorer countries to the richer, but this immigration is to 'underclass' positions, from which a minority might rise truly to enter the society, but which will for most be permanent positions. Given that this is the case, the city provides the machinery through which interchange occurs between this underclass and the native population.

The usual view of the relationships which hold between coloured immigrant workers and the so called host societies of the metropolitan countries is, of course, not like this at all. It is that there simply are countries, which are economically backward and likely to remain so for many years to come, despite our efforts to provide them with aid, and that, in the meanwhile, immigration into the metropolitan economy and society is likely to be to the advantage of all concerned. Moreover responsible trade unionists are expected to concur in the view that, far from threatening an undercutting of their living standards, immigration creates the possibility of overall economic growth and of promotion for themselves; provided only that the immigrant worker has trade union rights there is, according to this orthodox view, no reason why temporarily or permanently he should become a member of any sort of underclass.

For the purposes of my argument here, I do not even need to assert that this orthodox view is untrue in its entirety. But what I do assert is that there is a great deal of wishful thinking about it, which can best be corrected by considering an alternative extreme theory of a more cynical and pessimistic source. It is in terms of this sort of theory that many of the more articulate immigrants see their position and it is increasingly the kind of theory in which a younger generation of sociologists are beginning to make sense of race relations and immigrant problems.

The first part of this theory deals with the so-called underdeveloped countries and it owes a great deal to the development economist turned sociologist, André Gundar Frank.[1] According to this view, what these countries suffer from is not under-development, but systematic de-development which has been going on for a very long time through the operations of the representatives of the developed nations in these countries. Even so-called aid is often a means of ensuring that they remain in a condition of underdevelopment, and immigration into the metropolitan countries, while its harm may in part be abated by the flow of remittances, strikes a death-blow at their economies through the disappearance of a large part of the able-bodied labour force. To put the point at its strongest, the underdeveloped countries are not merely not catching up but are subject to social and economic processes which ensure that they will always remain underdeveloped, offering their aid to the advanced countries by allowing their economies to be distorted in the interests of others and their able-bodied workers to go and work for someone else.

Obviously if this model has truth at all, it has it most clearly in the case of purely colonial countries. In the hey-day of colonial-ism imperial armies ensured law and order while tribute was exacted. What is less commonly realized, however, is that it may be just as true today both in the ex-colonies and in poorer more dependent countries which have never been colonies at all. Thus the successor governments of the colonial regimes find that the options open to them in planning are very limited indeed. Quick returns for some of their people can be bought only at the cost of developing in those directions which suit the former colonial powers. And, on the other hand, there are countries like Turkey, Greece, Yugoslavia, Italy, Spain and Portugal which drag behind their Northern neighbours economically and which must export their labour surplus to keep the population alive. To grossly overstate the case, they tend to become to northern Europe what Botswana or Mozambique has become to South Africa.

In all cases, but especially in the case of the immigrants from former colonial countries, the role from which the worker comes is very different from that of a free wage worker in a modern industrial society. The latter may be exploited by capitalist entrepreneurs or by planners in the public sector, it is true, but

[1] A. G. Frank, *The Sociology of Underdevelopment and the Under-development of Sociology*, Copenhagen, n.d.

over a period of a hundred years or more he has worked out the means to self-defence. He has unions and he has political parties which enable him to bargain over wages and conditions at work and to win some degree of redistribution of wealth through the set of agencies which at their best we call the welfare state. The colonial worker, on the other hand, may be the descendant of a slave or an indentured labourer, but in any case will have been used both to some degree of unfreedom and to sustained unemployment. Alternatively he might like many immigrants from non-colonial backward countries, have been simply a peasant, perhaps in the hands of the money-lender but barely able to contemplate more than the most meagre subsistence. The problem of immigrant labour, therefore is the problem of incorporating men whose image at least is that of unfree men.

Western sociology has scarcely considered the implications of a society of an imperial kind, that is to say, one which includes not merely the forms of stratification division of labour and conflict which occur within the domestic metropolitan context, but also those patterns of social relations which characterize dependent colonial societies and which form a part of the total imperial social structure. Yet the problem presented by colonial immigration can scarcely be understood unless this is taken into consideration. The immigrant is not simply another human being seeking to enter into the role of worker. He bears a certain contamination arising from his former colonial role or what is believed to have been his colonial role. Rightly or wrongly, therefore, he is perceived by the native worker as a threat, a threat that the hard won rights of the free wage worker will be undermined by the presence of workers used to something less than normal standards of welfare and freedom.

I do not wish to be misunderstood in what I am saying here. I am not saying that immigrant workers in Britain or elsewhere have undercut trade union standards. Indeed, such evidence as there is points in the opposite direction. But whether he wills it or not the immigrant is likely to be perceived as a threat in so far as he is understood as having come from an unfree colonial context.

What I now want to suggest, however, is that there are advantages to the entrepreneurs or planners of a metropolitan society in having, alongside of the normal unionized and protected free labour force, another more disposable force which has nothing like the same rights and is liable to some degree of harassment. The system reaches its extreme form in South Africa's towns, in the institutions of the compound and the location, but legal and illegal immigrants living in employers' hutted camps, in bidonvilles or in multi-occupied lodging houses subject to public health control, are all subject to some such degree of harassment. The ever-present threat of deportation for the controlled immigrant is something which is already well known in Europe and which is simply a new twist in the British story.

But it should not be thought that the use of harassed immigrant labour is simply something which accords with employers' interests and conflicts with those of other workers. Far from this being the case, there are circumstances in which the existence of an immigrant labour force must appear at least to those in responsible planning positions and in the trade union movement as thoroughly desirable. The uneven rate of technological advance means that there are jobs still in existence from an earlier indus-trial age as well as some jobs brought in by a new technology which are simply not acceptable to native workers. Yet they must be done none the less and it is a matter of convenience that they should be done by the immigrant labour force mentioned above.

Ideally, of course, the system when taken to its logical con-clusions would also demand that the immigrants were disposable in times of unemployment so that the unemployed could move down into them, but this has only really been systematically applied as a policy in South Africa of the nineteen-thirties when certain unskilled jobs on the railways were closed to all but 'civilized' (i.e. white) labour. What does happen, however, is that because the immigrant is perceived as a threat both through try-ing to move up into a true free labour position in times of full employment and through occupying the least desired jobs in times of unemployment, the likelihood is that native workers will be sympathetic to demands for immigration control and to measures which have the effect of harassing the immigrant and making him unfree. The notion of immigrant labour subject to police control was proposed by the Conservative government in its Commonwealth Immigration Act of 1971.

Thus what we have said so far is that in the relationship

between native and immigrant workers where the latter come from a colonial, neo-colonial or quasi-colonial society, the immigrant starts out identified as having come from an inferior social position and he tends to be pushed into and segregated within inferior occupational roles in the metropolitan economy. Thus we have what I have called an underclass. In some cases, of course, the actual personnel of that underclass will change as immigrant workers or their descendants push their way upwards within the class structure. But characteristically, where the immigrants are easily recognizable by physical or cultural signs there may be some tendency for them to stay permanently in the underclass. This is, of course, most true of black workers in the United States, in Britain and in British territories abroad.

Conflict between immigrant and native workers is, of course, likely in industrial contexts and such conflict has occurred in characteristic form in most European countries. What appears to have happened is that in any dispute in which the interests of a separate immigrant group have been threatened they have had little if any support from the trade unions of the host society and have in the last analysis simply had to accept defeat. On the other hand where there have been major clashes on an industry-wide or national and class basis there is very little evidence of immigrant workers allowing themselves to be used as blacklegs (Castles and Castles, 1971). These facts stand out only more sharply against a background in which there appears to be day-to-day collaboration at the workbench and in which national trade union organizations frequently affirm their opposition to all forms of racial discrimination.

Yet even with this said, one has to notice that the underclass status of the immigrant in relation to the welfare and trade union bargain which assures basic stability in the advanced countries is not expressed only or primarily in industrial terms. When one looks at the way in which the immigrant or race issue has emerged in politics in these countries, what has been discussed has usually been not in terms of the industrial rights of or the industrial threat posed by the employment of immigrant labour. What has been much to the fore has been the question of rights of immigrants to welfare benefits of all kinds, but most particularly the rights of the immigrants in relation to the housing system. This is not to say, let me repeat again, that it is the housing crisis or the urban crisis which is the prime cause of race relations problems, it is to say that the incorporation of a group which in some degree has an underclass status into a complex industrial society is itself a complex process. Class position in a modern society cannot be solely and simply defined in terms of men's relations to the means of production or simply in terms of the workplace. It refers to a whole complex of rights which, though they may be in the long run derivative from a man's industrial position, has implications in many other social spheres as well.

So far as housing is concerned a separate point must be made. This is that it has been shown frequently that, even though workers of differing racial and ethnic background may work together and collaborate at work, the same workers do not tend to mix in extra-industrial contexts. This is particularly true with regard to black immigrants in Britain, but, in any case, social mixing apart from work and, particularly, intermarriage is at least beset by obstacles. Moreover, the growth of industrial cities and the suburban migration of the affluent means that to a considerable extent the residential community unit and the industrial unit do not coincide in their membership. It is true, in the broadest possible sense, the poorly paid occupy inferior industrial roles and also live in inferior urban districts. But, within this, the actual structure of the inferior social districts and their relationship to the more desirable ones produces peculiar complications, which have a special significance for the immigrants and their native fellow residents.

The particular contribution which I have been trying to make for the past few years to the study of immigrants in advanced industrial countries is to explore the networks of relationships in which they become involved as a result of their position in the housing market and in the total urban status situation. I have tried to formulate what I have to say in terms of a theory of 'housing classes' arguing that it is the existence within the city of a system of differential access to housing and a kind of status and class order that goes with it, which does much to explain urban politics and, within the pattern of urban politics, of race relations and immigrant-host relations.

A more extended account of the theory which I first put

forward in the book which I wrote with Robert Moore on Sparkbrook in Birmingham can be found elsewhere, but a brief summary of the argument can and must be offered here to make clear what it is that I am saying. In the first place, I should like to emphasize that my theory is a historically and politically based one. That is to say, that I accept that in unplanned industrial cities of the nineteenth century, but also in those which have been fully or partially planned later or have attempted to graft planning on to a competitive base,[1] there is an underlying political conflict over the use of land and when buildings have been erected, competition for the use of old buildings for new and alternative purposes. Out of this conflict of interests and out of the possibility that an individual may improve his situation in the housing market by moving from one market position to another, the housing class system operates to structure the social, cultural and political processes of urban life.

One can be more or less sophisticated about the housing class model which one uses in urban sociology and one should be clear that the model which is appropriate at one time and place is not necessarily appropriate at another. I have increasingly felt the need for greater sophistication and refinement of my own model, since the Sparkbrook study was published, both in order to apply it to problems other than those of immigrants, and to apply it to the sorts of problems which are engendered by the movement of immigrants from the inner city areas. With this said, however, as a basic model which served to explain some of the main racial and political tensions in the cities of Britain in the 1960s I think it still has something to commend it.

The model assumes in the first place a pattern of historical development in the city in which an initial bipartite division of residential land is supplemented, first by the growth of an intermediate sector of housing for white-collar and skilled workers, and then by a three-fold migration, first of the big bourgeoisie and their friends, then by the white-collar people to mortgaged houses in the suburbs and, finally, of the established working classes to suburban council estates of rented houses. Within the scale of security of tenure and of status honour which results from the

---

[1] Dr Musil of the University of Kent has suggested that the theory of housing classes as stated is applicable in the planned economies and societies of Europe.

forms of housing so created, the positions of highest security and status are those in the outer districts, with the exception perhaps of a return inwards in large metropolitan cities by the very rich to town houses. The implication of this statement is that the simple distinction made equally by the registrar general and by radical Marxist sociologists between landlord and tenant is not the most important one in the city. To be a member of the native working class, and to have an entitlement to a council house for rent is to have a considerable social property, and one which is thought to be a far more desirable alternative than struggling to maintain ownership of some kind of an inner-city slum.

I have suggested that in most British cities urban politics are conducted basically by the owners of residential property on the one hand and the representatives of the council house tenantry or aspirant council house tenantry on the other. This does not mean that this division is more important than others. To say that would be to deny what I have said in the previous paragraph. What it does mean, however, is that the welfare deal on which modern industrial society is based permits the existence of a two-party system, which fails to make provision for the representation of the truly deprived and under-privileged. Whatever the parties are called, and whatever appeals they may make to the ideals of the property-owning democracy or of welfare and equality, they do not represent interests other than their own with any degree of effectiveness. Thus one of the crucial processes now happening in the city is the struggle of the under-privileged and unrepresented to make their voice heard through political channels or outside them.

The underprivileged to whom I refer consist of the major groupings who occupy central city areas for residential purposes after the suburban migration has begun and before these areas are themselves bulldozed and rebuilt. They include the occupants of slums, i.e. an administratively defined category of buildings usually referring to small redbrick terraced cottages of a hundred years or more in age, the tenants of flats and rooms in multiple-occupied property, and resident landlords who, if they do make a profit out of their houses, do so by occupying as little space as possible, and letting off as much as possible, so that their conditions are very much inferior to those of the normal owner-occupier.

In this greatly oversimplified picture then we may say that there are three privileged housing classes: (a) the outright owners of 'desirable' property commonly outside the inner city; (b) the occupiers of desirable and usually suburban property; (c) the tenants of publicly provided rented houses of high physical standard, and three underprivileged classes: (a) the tenants of slum property awaiting demolition; (b) the tenants of rooms and flats in multiple-occupied lodging houses; (c) the resident land-lords who actually live in some of these multiple-occupied lodging-houses with their tenants. It might well be added that there are a number of other groups who survive in the inner ring. Some of these are in better flats or lodging-houses by choice and some are the owners of ageing inner ring property. The latter of these two groups in fact might play a fairly crucial role in what are commonly called the twilight areas.

The crucial political decisions about the twilight areas are taken very largely by people who either do not live in them or, living in them, have some plan for leaving them and taking their own kind with them. The great political achievement of Labour in the town hall is to ensure that some of the inhabitants of the twilight zones can look forward to leaving. This is not the case in countries where there is no strongly organized labour and trade union movement. But great though the achievement is, it is also limited. The people whom it helps are primarily the long-established working-class families who live in slums in single-family occupation. This is largely because length of residence within the city is taken to be an important criterion in the allocation of the public stock.

What has happened in the so-called twilight areas is the opening up of a division between the orthodox slum-type houses and the multiple-occupied lodging-houses and for a variety of reasons, in the early 1960s at least, it was the orthodox slum which received most attention from formally elected politicians, and the public servants who carried out housing and public health laws designed to meet the problems of the thirties. The houses concerned were, of course, older. But a more important consideration than this was probably that the tenants, coming as they did in fairly small family units and having votes which the politicians wanted, made them fairly easy to move. To turn attention to the lodging-houses which in sheer physical terms were bigger and younger and, therefore, not yet slums, appeared to create considerable political difficulties. They were thought of as essentially good houses which could be kept in control by good public health law.

Yet it was clear by the time of the Milner Holland report on housing in London (HMSO, 1965a) that the really serious problems which London and other cities faced were not the problems of the orthodox slums of the East End, but the new multiple-occupied houses of Paddington and Notting Hill. It was here that the most squalid and insanitary living conditions were to be found, even though the houses concerned figured in no slum-clearance or redevelopment programme. It was not until the end of the sixties that public attention became focused on the older, larger houses which had not yet become slums. But even then the approach to the problem was in terms of irrelevant programmes drawn from the past. The landlord was seen as someone who had to be controlled and aided to run his house better. But little attention was really given to the question of the motivation either of landlords or tenants, who were assumed to be people who wanted to improve their property, as though they were suburban property owners, whereas a great many of them were in effect desperate men and women, who had turned to that kind of housing with all its defects for reasons other than purely economic ones.

The so-called twilight zones were areas in which there were large proportions of houses which had gone over to multiple occupation. In order to understand them we have to understand first the nature of the lodging-house itself and secondly its siting amongst and its relationships with buildings of other kinds. It is the interplay of interests both in the lodging-house and between lodging-house residents and their neighbours which is the most interesting phenomenon of all. As I understand it, it is in an area such as this that the main interplay between housing classes occurs, even though it also takes place within a wider kind of housing class conflict at the level of the city hall.

The problem of multiple occupation of privately owned houses in the inner ring comes into existence because there are many groups who are not adequately catered for in any other housing policy. If both the city council and the building societies decide that a man is unfit to have a tenancy or a mortgage then there is a demand for a different type of housing and, unless someone intervenes to stop it, an alternative source of housing supply will emerge. In England, where public health and housing legislation is relatively strict, the main alternative has been the conversion of older large terrace houses by private landlords.

On the whole the entrepreneurs in this housing field have not been large-scale capitalist absentee owners. There have been some of these, but one of the misleading consequences of the prominence given to the activities of Rachmann in London has been the assumption that the whole problem here is one of unethical capitalist enterprise of a large-scale kind. In my experience at least, another pattern seems to have emerged. This is that within some of the immigrant communities there are those who have taken the initiative in housing themselves, their friends and kinsmen, and anyone else who is willing to pay. The landlord may sometimes be an absentee, but very often there is a kind of loan-chain within a tight-knit community which makes it very difficult to say who the owner is; and in any case, one aspect of the whole business of lodging-house proprietorship which tends to be overlooked is that it contains within itself a considerable element of simple charity. Landlords establish houses to provide for kin and friends newly come to the city. If they did not so so, the newcomers would have nowhere else to go.

But precisely because owning a lodging-house involves this element of charity it also involves its opposite. That is to say that if a house-owner is going to accommodate some of those to whom he feels he has a charitable obligation at less than the going rate, he must have other tenants who will carry the cost. These other tenants are drawn, therefore, from other immigrant groups and from certain groups in the host society, essentially people with broken families or broken lives, who will fill up the houses, living in inadequate rooms, and paying exorbitant rents for them. Thus even if we look at the lodging-houses in isolation we find, not a ghetto, but an essentially multi-racial institution. This might not be the case, of course, if the whole enterprise were run by absentee capitalists. They might well seek to cash in on the fact that immigrant workers were homeless and let off large blocks of property to a single immigrant group. On the whole this is not what has happened in Britain.

The relations between landlord and tenant in a lodging-house are essentially ambivalent. So far as his kinsmen and fellow countrymen are concerned, they might be quite cordial. But, so far as relations with his other tenants go, there is often a consciousness of the harsh and exploitative terms which the landlord offers on the one hand and at the same time a certain feeling of gratitude to him as someone who provided rooms which no one else could supply. It is not easy, therefore, to imagine large numbers of such tenants seeking to solve their problems by appealing to rent tribunals.

One very important fact about the tenants of lodging-houses is that many of them are there because they are seeking anonymity. They may be deviants of all sorts, people with broken families or people with problems. But it is all too easy for their deviance and their problems to be blamed on the area or the form of house-ownership. In fact they have been drawn to the area because of the facilities which it offers for their way of life. They have not adopted that way of life because they are there. Obvious though this may seem, the fallacy of purely physical strategies of social planning and reform is that if only one does away with a certain kind of housing and environment problems will automatically disappear. So far is this from being the case that we should say that if these houses were bulldozed away they would crop up elsewhere in some new form, because they answer a real need.

But whatever the rational explanation of the lodging-house phenomenon, one thing is clear. This is that the image of the immigrant is associated by their existence with vice, squalor and the worst sorts of exploitation and landlordism. And the people who are likely to be most immediately conscious of this are their nearest neighbours, those who live in the slums and those who seek to make status ends meet in the rapidly declining number of small old houses which are privately owned. For the first of these groups the formula explaining the way things are is likely to be 'It's not fair that they have better houses than us and quite wrong that they should be able to so misuse them'. For the second it is that 'they cause property values and other social values to decline'.

To say all this is not to say that a sociologist doing a survey in one of the twilight zones is likely to find a high correlation between a man's housing situation and his racial attitudes. I doubt, myself, whether such attitude studies have any real significance at all. What matters more than attitudes is the way in which the whole socially structured world view which the inhabitants of such areas have is affected by their membership of housing classes. What I expected, and what I found, in the area which my colleague and I studied in 1963–4 was that there was a great efflorescence of associational activity going on in the area, and that the associations were, at least in part, oppositional ones, giving scope for the expression of ideas and definitions of the total situations, which were in the interest of particular groups.

On the other hand, the associational life of the community was not solely determined by the needs of the immediate conflict situation. The associations represented there were not simply confined to one place or time. Thus 'prejudice', if it was expressed, took highly complicated and veiled forms. People simply lived their lives within partial communities which provided mutual aid and which incidentally helped to shape their world views. What mattered in the last analysis was the balance which was struck between the universalistic ideas intruding into these organizations from outside and those which interpreted the received doctrine in such a way as to deal with the immediate problem of living with one's neighbour.

In some areas this ambiguity in the goals of associations and organizations meant that it was possible for them in some limited measure to work together, and one of the most interesting phenomena which we observed was the way in which small groups, usually having outside roots of some kind, were able to meet together and encounter problems with definitions distinct from those offered by the various separate associations. If, indeed, it was one's goal to promote good community relations, then this was the level on which there was most hope for, despite their special interests which they needed to defend, there were those in all groups who were conscious also of limited common interests, at least in maintaining an overall peace within which conflicts could have been resolved.

Whatever the goals of community leaders at ward level were, however, there was always the possibility that the whole developing pattern would be upset if what had previously been merely guiltily held opinions involving inter-ethnic hostility were given a degree of respectability by being incorporated into political programmes. But this is precisely what began to happen in

Britain from 1962 onwards. The first Commonwealth Immigration Act, the Smethwick campaign, the 1965 White Paper on Commonwealth Immigration and subsequent speeches by front-bench spokesmen on either side of the House all moved towards accepting those definitions of social reality which local community associations were trying to avoid. And at a city level, local government leaders looked at the twilight zones and felt justified in explaining them away as being due to the presence of immigrants. Thus the tensions of the twilight zones which might perhaps have been resolved by effective community relations work at ward level were actually exacerbated, while at the same time, far removed from the actual sites of intercommunal tension, that is to say at city hall level. Community Relations Councils were formed which concentrated on those aspects of the problems of minorities which caused least political difficulty. But the idea of community relations, even at this level, came under attack. What was being debated in Britain by the 1970s was not merely the local problem of community relations, but whether immigrants as such should be subject to new forms of deprivation and harassment. Those who had previously been concerned to establish good community relations now found themselves dealing with the problem of racism, and racism feeds as much as it does on anything on the problem presented to the city by the twilight zones.

What I am saying, therefore, is that we have created in this country an underclass, whose membership is largely drawn from the immigrant community. It has become identified particularly with certain areas of the cities, which it would be wrong to call ghettoes because they are by no means confined to single ethnic groups, but it is the immigrants in these residential areas who form the prime target of attack in racist speeches. Increasingly too, these areas become socially segregated from the rest of the city, the more so as neighbouring slum areas are cleared away.

What then may be expected in the future? What many people fear, I imagine, is that in some way the American experience will be repeated here, and that there will be black urban riots. For myself I do not think this is likely. Whatever may happen in Trafalgar Square, what matters are the grass roots problems of urban industrial areas, and, so far as these are concerned the problem is the continuing one of clearly defined areas where immigrants are very largely confined, and which will continue, so long as they exist, to provide a programme for British racists. And as things stand at the moment it is the racists rather than the advocates of Black Power who are making all the running.

The hope of the Labour government of 1965, in fact, does not seem to have been fulfilled. That hope was that if immigration was slowed down or even halted, those immigrants who were already here would gradually gain more acceptance, would be absorbed into our industrial structure, and would find their way out of the twilight zones. This overall process of assimilation, it was thought, would lead to a decline in racism as a factor in politics. Instead of this, what has happened is that the twilight zones remain much as they were, the immigrants are to be found much where they were and their visible presence in deteriorating urban areas makes them an ideal scapegoat for nearly all the society's ills. Thus each new concession to racist opinion leads to a stepping up of racist demands.

There can be only one way out. I advocate it here in the hope that it will have some influence, but I am not optimistic that it will be taken up. This is that the forms of discrimination which prevent those immigrants who wish to move outside the twilight zones from doing so should be abolished and that so far as the remainder are concerned, we should be actively investigating the ways in which the needs of tight-knit immigrant groups with regard to housing should be met. If we were to take up these questions instead of responding hysterically to the presence of black people with a cry of 'send them back home', there might be some chance that a way could be found of integrating an immigrant population which the British economy certainly has needed and may continue to need.

15

Policy-oriented research and the sociology of race relations

The theme of this paper may be simply stated. It is that professional sociologists in Britain may have made virtually no contribution to the understanding of race relations problems in Britain, or, to put the matter more correctly, to the understanding of problems which are defined in the public mind as problems of race relations. The result of this has been that the task of analysing race relations and immigration problems has fallen to those whose subject-disciplinary commitment is far from clear, and who are mainly concerned to discuss administrative problems as they appear to those in government. Such research does, of course, have a long and not entirely dishonourable record in Britain. Where no major value-judgement has been in question it has been possible for a small administrative élite (commonly with degrees in history, classics or modern greats) to produce dispassionate work which throws light on crucial policy areas. The limitation of this type of work, however, lies in its inability to bring questions of value out into the open and to subject them to scrutiny. Moreover the social perspective of this élite is so much shared with those in higher echelons of government that it is quite impossible for its members to record the actions of government as open to enquiry and analysis on the same basis as the actions of ordinary people.

What I propose to do here is to consider the central organized study of race relations of the past twenty-five years, E. J. B. Rose *et al.*, *Colour and Citizenship* (1969) and the implications of its publication and reception for sociologists. Quite widely this book is regarded as a sociological study, despite disavowals of this by its authors, and many sociologists have found it difficult to define their own position in the argument which has followed. The crux of any serious discussion of the work by sociologists must, therefore, lie in an attempt to disentangle ideological, empirical and theoretical strands in the argument. Those more widely interested in questions of the social responsibility of the scientist may find this process of disentangling particularly important.

I think I can best explain my own approach to *Colour and Citizenship* by disagreeing sharply with a review of the book by Dipak Nandy (*New Statesman*, 11 July 1969), whose organization, the Runnymede Trust, is itself commended within the book. What Nandy suggests is that *Colour and Citizenship* is an English equivalent to Gunnar Myrdal's *An American Dilemma* (1944). Indeed he goes further and suggests that, while being comparable to Myrdal's work in aim and scope, the Rose-Deakin (1969) survey is even greater in its achievement.

Now I am not concerned here to award prizes and there may indeed be some respects in which *Colour and Citizenship* surpasses *An American Dilemma*. Specifically I am quite prepared to recognize the great value of *Colour and Citizenship* in bringing together in a summary way some of the problems which immigration has thrown up in the various social services. What I want to raise here, however, is a point which Nandy ignores or, perhaps, fails totally to understand. This is that, in sociological literature, Myrdal's work stands out as one in which the question of the three-fold relationship between value standpoints, theoretical hypotheses and empirical observation is made thoroughly explicit. In *Colour and Citizenship* on the other hand these three remain totally confused.

What Myrdal did, it will be remembered, was to say that he would take as his value standpoint, in judging the adequacy of American institutions, that state of rights and relations between men which could be deduced from the American Constitution as interpreted. Quite explicitly, however, he showed that the actual state of Amercian social institutions was at odds with the ideal. While one might criticize him, therefore, for using a too-diffuse value standard one could not accuse him of confusing the ideal with the reality or of idealizing the reality.

Colour and Citizenship is extremely confusing in its discussion of these issues. Myrdal is misinterpreted as saying merely that there was, as a matter of empirical fact, a contradiction between American ideals and American practice and that the American nation therefore suffered from a moral dilemma. It is then easy to argue from this that current British ambivalence about according citizenship to immigrants may be diagnosed as resting upon a moral conflict between what is described as 'the British ideal of fair play and equality before the law' (p. 4) and actually observed social and political practice. What is missing here is any real distinction between the standard of value-judgement of the researcher and the alleged moral ideals of those whom he observes. No evidence is either provided or thought to be necessary regarding the alleged British sense of fair play. The function of the notion in the argument appears to be simply to suggest that there are certain agreed moral and political ideals and that a critical confrontation of a declared value standpoint on the part of the researcher and the values operative in government is, therefore, not necessary.

There is, however, more to it than this. One might still, despite what I have said above, argue that, unclear though the notion of the British ideal of fair play is, it is none the less a possible basis for some kind of sociological comparison between social ideals and social reality. Any hope that this is the case, however, disappears with the enunciation of the doctrine of 'the passing of the liberal hour'. The liberal hour, according to Deakin (1970,) 'is the moment when men of all shades of opinion, from radical to conservative, accept the necessity of a movement in policy on a social problem issue in the liberal direction.' But 'for race relations in Britain the liberal hour has already passed'. Therefore,

> the implication of this book is that appeals to idealism are no longer in order. Any proposals for the amelioration of relationships between minorities and majority—and this book is intended principally as a constructive contribution towards policy making in this field—must be justified in purely practical terms. That is to say they must be seen to have an application to the real problems of the adjustment process and relate to the short run as well as the long term, the back-streets as well as Whitehall. (p. 21)

Now if this injunction were taken seriously, it would lead to an analysis of the aims of government and of people in the back-streets, and 'recommendations' would only be made if they were in accordance with these interests. What then if sociological research suggested that slavery or the establishment of concentration camps was in the best interests of both? One supposes that such a conclusion would be suppressed. Thus only those recommendations would be made which were both in the interests of the back-streets and Whitehall and in accordance with 'British traditions of fair play'. The temptation, however, is to pretend that the two coincide, that recommendations can be made as regards policy which disregard the empirical evidence of goverment action in a contrary direction and that, the movement of opinion in support of Powell notwithstanding, the British people can be shown to be basically 'tolerant-inclined'.

The latter chapters of the Rose-Deakin survey provided by Dr Mark Abrams (pp. 551–603) have, I think, now been widely recognized as an example of how preconceptions of the use of crude survey techniques can combine to produce whatever conclusions one wishes. The former implication is less widely recognized.

What strikes one as one reads many of the more 'liberal' recommendations is the unwillingness to consider their political practicability. Thus one might ask whether there is much to be gained from recommending in general terms against discrimination in the allocation of council housing, without noticing that, despite clear evidence of discrimination produced by the PEP survey and other studies, since the housing of coloured people became an election issue in 1964, no steps were taken to do anything about it until the subject was included amongst many others in the terms of reference of the Cullingworth Committee in 1968 (HMSO, 1969). This Committee recommended the abolition of the waiting period which many immigrants were forced to undergo before going on local authority waiting lists and gradual reduction of special periods of residence for those on the housing list. Even these modest recommendations, however, have been ignored by successive governments and it would appear that the attempt by the Race Relations Board to secure the alteration of one housing authority's residential qualification period has produced only the most derisory token alteration. My object in pointing these things out here is not to raise the political issues involved but simply to argue that a comprehensive sociological study of the question would necessarily involve considering the political forces which permit or prevent the implementation of recommended policies.

The point to be emphasized is that it should be the hallmark of a sociological study that the behaviour as well as the ideals and policies of government are a matter for empirical study. A sociological study would not confuse statements of good intentions for predictors of behaviour as the Rose-Deakin survey is inclined to do. The survey, however, is bound to do this since it is in terms of a political strategy of trying to persuade ministers and civil servants to pursue new goals without any kind of critical view of what they have done hitherto.

This over-optimistic assessment of government policy is, of course, at odds with the claim to political realism expressed in the doctrine of the passing of the liberal hour. Indeed by the end of the book this doctrine has been replaced by another which one might call, with due respect to the founder of our subject, Deakin's Law of the Three Stages. According to this, British policy towards immigrants has gone through three stages of laissez-faire, of panic and emergency legislation, and, finally, of coming to grips with the problem. Referring to the third stage Deakin says (1970, p. 143) 'by a process of trial and error repudiating and then adopting their critics' proposals, the government had finally reached a position where the weapons for a dramatic assault on the problems associated with immigration had been forged in the Urban Programme and effective anti-discrimination legislation'. True, Deakin follows this by noting that these instruments were forged at a time when liberal morale was at its lowest ebb. But he does not consider the possibility that these policies themselves might be inadequate, both in their conception and implementation, so far as overcoming discrimination is concerned, and that the real effect of their existence may simply be to overcome a gap which exists between ideals and practice. Once again it should be noted that Myrdal understood this point. In another of his great appendices he pointed out how belief systems including statements of moral ideals might simply serve to rationalize the departure of practice from theory. Of course, Deakin might plead that unlike Myrdal he was not making a sociological analysis, but, if this is true, the comparison of *Colour and Citizenship* with *An American Dilemma* is misleading.

I would not myself wish, on the basis of internal evidence, to suggest that Rose and Deakin's vacillation between realism and idealism rests upon anything as simple as an attempt to devise solutions in the interest of the capitalist economy.[1] This seems to be the implication of a recent paper by Robin Jenkins (1970) and an earlier neo-Marxist analysis given by Corrigan and McGreal to the British Sociological Association's study group (1969). What I do think to be the case is that the question of the function of expressions of good intentions by the government is a matter for empirical study and theoretical analysis of a sociological kind.

So far sociology has not measured up to the challenge presented by the Rose-Deakin survey. What it has produced are (a) piecemeal analyses of particular problems within the terms set by the Rose and Deakin study, (b) the assimilation of race relations studies under other headings of sociological research, (c) retreats into dogmatic Marxist counter-assertion and (d) more conservative ideological responses concerned with the question of the integration of coloured people into British society. Before we turn to these responses, however, it is worth considering in its own right an important contribution to the debate about race relations made by the leading British sociologist in this field up until 1960, namely Michael Banton (1969).

Banton's pre-eminence in the field of race relations in Britain is undisputed. He has produced a number of major books of an empirical and theoretical kind, dealing with both metropolitan and colonial situations and he has been writing about the topic longer than any other British sociologist. His contribution to the Annual Conference of the British Sociological Association was, therefore, one which was awaited with great interest, the more so because he chose to address himself to the question of 'racism' shortly after the two speeches of Mr Enoch Powell had made their dramatic political impact.

Banton distinguishes first between racism and racialism by confining the first term to 'doctrine' and the second to the practice of 'doctrine'. His problem then is to explain the existence of racial doctrine and he lists three possible form of explanation:

1. the Marxist approach [which] attempts to explain the mistake by showing the function it serves in capitalist society.

[1] Subsequent developments in the Institute of Race Relations have led me to the view that Jenkins was nearer to the truth in this matter than I allowed.

2. the inductivist explanation [which] is that the error was caused by bias on the investigator's part.
3. the historical approach [which] explains the mistake by relating it to the intellectual context of the period.

The surprising thing about this classification of types of explanation of racism is that it is neither logical in its basis nor exhaustive. Clearly the three categories of explanation overlap, but, much more important, they leave out any kind of explanation which refers to the function of racist belief other than a narrowly defined Marxist one.

Such theoretical confusion might perhaps be excused on the grounds that it clears the way for Banton to develop in an interesting way his own review of the historical context of racism. What it leads to, however, is a discussion of contemporary doctrines which have been thought to be racist and the conclusion reached is that those who now seek to deny equality to immigrants do so on other than biological grounds and are, therefore, not to be classified as racists.

Banton does consider that some commentators have defined the term 'racism' in terms of its function but dissociates himself from this approach. Thus there is no basis left for considering whether doctrines advanced by Enoch Powell and Peter Griffiths, two politicians whom he specifically mentions, might not have the same function as racist doctrines based on biological theory. All that can be said about them is that what they say is not racist.

Since writing that piece, Banton has been made director of the Social Science Research Council's Race Relations Research Unit. It would be unfair to him to take his analysis of the problem of racist doctrine as representative of his views on the sociology of race relations,[1] but it is perhaps worth noting that the SSRC Unit was set up precisely in order that there should be a centre where theoretically oriented research removed from immediate policy considerations could be pursued. The theoretical approach of the centre will, therefore, be extremely important. It would surely be most unfortunate if the centre simply described all sociological explanation as Marxist and, therefore, dismissed it as readily as Banton dismisses Oliver

[1] Banton's book *Race Relations* (1968) does give some indication of a general theoretical perspective but this gives way to *ad hoc* theories as he deals with the problems of different regions.

Cromwell Cox. Clearly there is a problem of a theoretical vacuum in British sociology and this problem will affect the operation of the Bristol centre. It is little wonder, therefore, that A. H. Halsey and others have sought to offer advice on this matter (Halsey, 1970). I shall return towards the end of this paper to the question of the theoretical and political bias of that advice.

Most of the research which is going on at the moment, as can be seen from bibliographies of work in progress, is that which is pursued within the context of 'the race relations industry'. Community relations councils are aware of what are defined as problems at a local level and encourage research on these. Usually, however, their researchers are neither trained sociologists nor capable of understanding the degree to which the problems which they discuss are posed in such a way that they are profoundly value-laden. None the less, the sheer volume of this work is such that it results in the development of its own kind of expertise—either one based upon good or bad market research or one based on familiarity with issues on social policy. Unfortunately these kind of expertise come to be accepted as being in themselves sociological. The need for a serious objective sociology of the structure and dynamics of race relations situations in our society is then totally overlooked.

The race relations groups of the British Sociological Association did not alter the pattern very much, for although it did discuss the theory of pluralism at its first meeting (a potentially fruitful point on entry into an argument about the sociology of colonialism and race relations), the bulk of its original work was concerned with topics arising out of *Colour and Citizenship*. Thus it heard a report on the monitoring of racial attitudes, a critique of Mark Abrams's survey of attitudes and discussions of housing and educational policy to questions of sociological theory. None of them raised any questions about the structure of the society within which people had attitudes, facts occurred or policies were pursued. In most cases the effect of this was harmless, but in the case of the paper on education the limitations of the discussion could only be described as mischievous. The author of this paper, a lecturer in Social Administration at the London School of Economics, set out to discuss what she called the 'pros and cons' of the policy of dispersing coloured children, and went out of her way to call on her audience not to be prejudiced about looking at the pros as well as the cons of this policy (Blackstone, 1969). What remained absolutely unclear, however, was the set of standards in terms of which factors were judged pro and con, and, even more important, what the larger context was within which the issue was to be judged. Clearly if a decision to disperse is taken as the result of a racialist demand for 'thinning out', it is a quite different decision from one taken by educational administrators as a part of a strategy to overcome social deprivation.

More subtle, however, than the temptation to avoid studying race relations questions by absorbing them into social policy discussions is that of absorbing them into the general sociology of social stratification. This is, of course, more than merely a subtle temptation. There *are* hypotheses worth exploring regarding the relationship between minority groups of various kinds and the stratification system, but this by no means justifies an attempt to bully the facts of race relations situations into traditional categories for the study of social stratification, nor does it justify the assimilation of the problems of coloured minorities to those of a wider category referred to as the New Poor. I must confess that my own work with Robert Moore could have been misunderstood as pointing in this direction. What we did, however, was to suggest that, given a wider background of problems of colonialism and immigration, the exacerbation of racial conflict could be understood in terms of the sociology of the city. We would never have committed ourselves to the proposition advanced by John Lambert recently in a discussion of Handsworth that 'the deprivation of the area inflicts suffering and anxiety *indiscriminately*. White and black families *alike* have to respond to overcrowded housing, poor amenities and what seem to be uncaring authorities.' (My italics; Lambert, 1970.)

We cannot, of course, say simply that this statement is untrue. But, given the known facts about discrimination against coloured people in the housing market, it would be surprising indeed if the 'deprivation of the area [inflicted] suffering and anxiety indiscriminately'. And certainly no contrary evidence is provided by this study of Handsworth. One cannot help wondering whether statements such as this are written because they help to bolster 'liberal' beliefs that the extent of racial conflict is exaggerated, rather than because they reflect the actually observed situation.

The failure of sociologists of race relations either to look carefully at the facts or to develop an adequate frame of reference had led some left-wing critics into arguing that it is the absence of a specifically Marxist perspective which makes it impossible for them to do so. Thus Robin Jenkins, for example, in dismissing Deakin's approach to the existence of a sub-proletariat responds by quoting Baran and Sweezy: 'when it comes to housing, education and private employment, all the deeply rooted economic and socio-psychological forces analysed above come into play. It was capitalism, with its enthronement of greed and privilege, which created the race problem, the ugly thing it is today. It is the very same system which resists and thwarts every effort at a solution.' (Jenkins, 1970.)

Thus it would seem that the root of the failure of Rose and Deakin to understand the problem with which they are dealing is simply that they do not approach it in terms of a simplistic Marxist model of capitalist society. For the genteel self-praise of the Home Office analysis we have substituted the holy writ of Baran and Sweezy.

My response to this is not to deny Jenkins's view about the unlikeliness of gradual change and reform in the pattern of British race relations. In fact, my own analysis is far more pessimistic than his. What I am claiming is that a real understanding of what is likely to happen depends on our making a fundamental structural and dynamic analysis of British imperial society, including both free labour in the metropolis and what Jenkins himself has called elsewhere 'fettered labour' in the colonies. I do not believe this analysis can be adequately contained within the categories of traditional Marxism. We have to make our own analysis of our own circumstances starting with the political economy of contemporary imperial and neo-colonial society. This, after all, is no less than what Marx himself would have done. This reaching out for a genuine sociology of imperialism, colonialism and race relations can be inhibited by dogma of any kind. Most of all it is likely to be inhibited by the use of obscure and half-understood terminology. Thus I do not believe that it helps us at all in the understanding of these questions to phrase them in terms of the neo-Marxist vocabulary of Louis Althusser

(1970) as many of the younger generation of sociologists are inclined to do. I sympathize at their frustration with the inadequacy of the sociology of race relations that they have been taught, but I would ask in all seriousness whether it helps our understanding of what is going on in Jamaica, South Africa, Bradford or Southall to use terms like 'social formation', 'conjuncture', 'practice' and 'contradiction'. These are forms of speech which have become necessary in a particular tradition of Hegelian and Marxist argument and which may perhaps be useful in analysing the revolution in Russia or the acceptance of the absence of revolution in France by the French Communist Party. It is certainly no indication of whether or not a sociologist is genuinely seeking to understand the patterns of class formation and other social structures in a society that he should use or not use these terms.

What I wish to see, and to see developed urgently, is a framework for the analysis of all race relations problems which is both realistic and undogmatic. I believe that we need to develop typologies of colonial social relations of production and wider colonial societies. We need to understand the varieties of neo-colonialism and we need to understand the process whereby men and women from colonial and neo-colonial societies seek to enter and are excluded from the established social order—whatever that may be—of the advanced capitalist societies. Such an understanding will not do much to help those who are simply concerned to maintain the stability of British society at any cost, nor will it help those who wish to score points for this or that political-intellectual set. What it will do is to give us a realistic basis for assessing what is likely to happen so that, given explicit political commitments, we may better understand what has to be done to alter our future history. There is very little evidence indeed of this kind of sociology being pursued in Britain. My own recent book (Rex, 1970) is a very small first attempt to get a discussion of these larger issues going.

Unfortunately, in the meanwhile, A. H. Halsey of Nuffield College, Oxford, has intervened in the debate to suggest that what the study of race relations needs is a theoretical framework of a quite different kind (*op. cit*). I see this framework as being conservative and value-laden as well as being entirely insular. It seems worthwhile to conclude this chapter by looking at Halsey's argument in some detail in order to understand the main directions in which leading sociologists, now intervening in the study of race relations for the first time, are likely to push race relations research.

Halsey's piece was entitled 'Race relations: the lines to think on' and was specifically offered as an attempt to provide a theoretical framework for the Bristol Research Unit. Halsey writes as follows:

> Looking back at the history of theory one is struck by its pragmatic quality. Thus the stranger hypothesis was a theoretical refinement by Banton and others of a simplistic policy of assimilation.

But now:

> Both theorists and policy makers . . . are forced to recognize that the assimilation theory has gone with the end of the immigration or newcomer period.

In the new circumstances:

> The changing scene points to the need to develop a complex theory of integration.
>
> The basic outline of such a theory and, therefore, the framework of a research programme for the Bristol Unit, is I think, at hand. It was formulated briefly by John Goldthorpe in a presidential address on 'Social Inequality and Social Integration in Modern Britain' to the Sociology Section of the British Association [1969]. . . . [Goldthorpe] took his illustrations mainly from the social relations of work and, oddly enough, made no mention of race relations to which the generality of this theme dramatically applies and which also serves to emphasize the derived character of a theory of race relations, derived that is from general theories of the social science disciplines.

What then is the more general theory to which Halsey refers? It is, of course, a theory about social integration. What is surprising, however, is that it shares certain of the ideological assumptions of the Rose-Deakin survey. Thus Halsey continues:

> As Goldthorpe points out, the effectiveness of the deliberate pursuit of equality through governmental action in the

twentieth century has been severely limited in respect of the relative chances of the working class. Insofar as the integration of Africans and Asians is thought of as a recapitulation of the gradual admission of the working class to full citizenship, the task calls for much more politically forceful action than is embodied in the Race Relations Act of 1968 or the mild gestures towards positive discrimination which have followed the Plowden Report on primary education.

No evidence is adduced of the deliberate pursuit of equality through government action. Indeed it would be difficult to adduce evidence for so studiedly ambiguous a notion, but it is also assumed that there is some sense in which it is conceivable that equality might be sought through governmental action for coloured immigrants. As a matter of fact the only serious meaning that can be given to the notion of the 'deliberate pursuit of equality through government action' so far as the British working class is concerned, is that the working classes have themselves sought to gain and use political power on their behalf; but this is clearly not what is intended by Halsey in the case of coloured immigrants. In their case the basic question is 'will they revolt?' and even if they are unlikely to, there is a danger that they might none the less be unintegrated.

Halsey refers to Goldthorpe's analysis of the 'paradox of the existence of gross inequality with a high degree of political consensus'. Goldthorpe's own analysis of this paradox is said by Halsey to be 'culturalist' rather than psychological. Halsey describes it as follows:

> The British political culture is in practice characterized by a balance that holds even across lines of class and party, between participant activist attitudes on the one hand and acquiescent, passive attitudes on the other, between emotional commitment to political principle and cool pragmatism, between consensus on matters of procedure and conflict over particular issues.

Socialization into this culture, Halsey adds, 'makes for apolitical and unfantical citizens'.

(It should be noted that there is a distinction between what

Goldthorpe actually said and Halsey's gloss on it. Goldthorpe should not be held responsible for the general approach to race relations which Halsey has developed, even less for the implications which follow.)

Having stated this by no means uncontroversial view of the nature of British society, Halsey then asks with scant regard for recent developments in the etiquette of reference to minority groups: 'Will the coloureds tear this fabric apart?'

It is hard to believe that an approach of this kind can be seriously intended as the basis for objective sociological race relations research, yet Halsey's role in British sociology is so significant that it cannot be ignored. It must, therefore, be pointed out that what is offered here as a theory is conservative, value-laden and extremely insular.

Quite clearly what Halsey is asking us is simply that the Bristol Unit should adopt on a more abstract level the same policy-oriented approach as the Rose-Deakin survey. He is not asking for a systematic analysis of the possibilities inherent in race relations situations. What he is asking for is simply systematic investigation of how Britain's existing political culture might best be preserved. Coloured people are seen principally as a threat to this political culture. Even if one accepted this limitation of our range of interests, however, one cannot but notice how limited are the range of ideas on which Halsey draws. Surely there are other writers in Britain apart from Runciman and Goldthorpe who have commented significantly on the inequality and class divisions which exist amongst British people. But, in so far as we are talking about the integration of West Indian and Pakistani immigrants, what they have to say is even more clearly limited in its scope. It is surely extraordinary that any sociologist writing about potential social conflict and pluralism in English society should ignore that whole literature which includes writers such as Furnivall, Lloyd Warner, M. G. Smith, Leo Kuper, Talcott Parsons and Melville Tumin, apart from a whole range of writers in the Marxist tradition as well as the new schools of comparative history which have arisen in connection with North and Latin American Studies. To ignore this literature is surely to end up with a very impoverished theory indeed.

Thus my conclusion is that in the wake of the Deakin and Rose report, which I would only wish to criticize in so far as it claims to be more than a well-informed ideological discussion of policy, sociologists have had all too little to say. Banton presides over the SSRC Unit at Bristol 'which will concentrate on fundamental research aiming to help explain such questions as the origin of prejudice, the pattern of discrimination and family structure in immigrant communities'. It must be hoped that he and his colleagues will develop an adequate theoretical approach. Unfortunately there is no kind of tradition of argument out of which such a theoretical approach could grow in Britain. The advice offered by Halsey would, in fact, direct the research in a quite disastrous direction. In fact it is hard to see how anyone at this particular point in history could even think of formulating as the main aim of race relations research 'how the coloureds can be prevented from tearing the fabric of our political culture apart'.

The Halsey approach to race relations like that of Banton's address to the BSA and Lambert's paper for the Runnymede Trust seems to me to be based partly on wishful thinking, partly upon a more or less deliberate attempt to rule out those definitions of our contemporary situation and likely future which raise the possibility of the disintegration of the social fabric, or the exacerbation of conflict. Of course, if these definitions of social reality happen to be nearer the truth than their own, it would only be a short step to go on to argue that the coloureds must be prevented from revolt. Thus what starts out as a theoretical perspective finishes up as a political programme. It is hardly surprising, therefore, that an ideology of this kind has led to a counter-ideology of revolt. Thus I find that there are some young sociologists who are asking 'how can social fabric be torn apart?' and some who see their function as supporting what they call 'The Black Cause'.

In this situation I want to emphasize the importance of achieving a definition of sociological objectivity and of not subordinating our discipline to propaganda of any kind. I am well aware of the difficulties in the way of attaining objectivity, having been brought up on Mannheim's *Ideology and Utopia*. None the less I believe that it is possible for us to explore systematically patterns of social relationships, of integration and disintegration, of collaboration and conflict which actually exist. I believe that it is possible for sociologists to turn their eyes away from the immediate problem of advising the Home Office or The Black Cause and to begin to argue about a typology of colonial situations, a typology of advanced capitalist industrial societies and a typology of the sorts of process which are generated by the migration of individuals from colonial situations to metropolitan capitalist countries.

16

Race as a social category

When the United Nations Organization was set up in 1945, one of its first intellectual tasks was to define the problem of racism which had been one of the major factors in Hitler's rise to power and the subsequent devastation of Europe. Hence UNESCO asked a group of biologists and social scientists to draw up a statement in 1949. The original statement and a further version in 1951 proved, however, to be ambiguous and unsatisfactory in certain respects and the Director-General of UNESCO therefore called upon biologists to meet separately in Moscow in 1964 and for their meeting to be followed by a meeting of biologists, social scientists and lawyers which would then address itself to the specific sociological problem of racism.

The question which the biologists in Moscow sought to answer was 'Are races biologically-based groups?' and to this they gave a complicated, detailed and technical answer. Implicit in that answer, however, was an answer to another question. This was 'Are the groups which have been called races in recent political debates distinguishable in biological terms?' and to it the biologists answered with a resounding negative. Hence the ball was thrown back into the politicians' and the social scientists' court. The question which was now asked was 'is race a social category?'

Sociologists taking up the challenge have not found the task of defining the sociological meaning of race an easy one, and some have given misleading or inadequate answers. Before offering my own views I would like to mention three of these.

The first is that the concept of race refers simply to ethnic differentiation. Men belong to different ethnic groups, it is said, not because of differences in biological heredity but solely because of culture differences. This is a widespread 'liberal' approach to the problem. Its inadequacy, however, lies simply in the fact that a far wider set of situations are based upon cultural differentiation of groups than those which are commonly called racial and that few of them have anything like the same conflictual consequences that racial situations do. The difficulty is this: one might decide to include relations between Catholics and Protestants in Northern Ireland in the same area of investigation as relations between black and white in English cities. But if one did this, would one have to go still further and include relations between Yorkshiremen and Lancastrians or between the middle- and working-class people of Leeds in the study of race relations? Obviously this would not do. Hence we must find some more restrictive criterion which will enable us to locate the peculiar and distinctive feature of race relations.

Another alternative which is tempting is merely to accept popular definitions and to categorize a situation as racial if the people whom we are studying think it to be so. This is a solution which commends itself to all those who adopt a subjective phenomenological approach to sociology. If society is not an objective fact but something which exists for the actor by virtue of his definitions of his situation, then races too would appear to have no claim to any other status than that of subjectively, and probably falsely, defined social objects.

The objection to this position is not, I believe, simply that it sells the pass to the racists, allowing them to define without regard to the findings of biological science what races are. It is that the subjectivist and phenomenological approach on which it is based is of the crudest kind. For to say that social facts are subjective by no means precludes the possibility of ideological distortion and rationalization as a legitimate objective for sociological inquiry. We may still see the observed actor's statements about the way in which he classifies the world as concealing from himself and from the sociologist the true bases on which he does so. Hence the defect of this approach is simply that it lacks a sufficiently developed theory of social interaction.

Before we proceed to develop such an approach, however, we must take note of another way of oversimplifying the problem. This is simply to confine the term racial to those situations in which groups are defined, rights and duties apportioned, different attitudes selected according to visible differences of physical characteristics. Differences of social position, so this view argues, are in the nature of human society, and some bases must be found for allocating men to one role or another. Age and sex are such bases in primitive society. Differences of physical characteristics such as skin colour are obviously amongst the most important in this modern world.

It is true that this approach is a fruitful and useful one in studying the conflicts which are to be found in the English-speaking world. They are above all problems of a colour bar. But there are, in fact, two difficulties about this position. One is that the physical differences referred to are in fact differences between the averages of overlapping groups, and that the actual distinctions are between groups which are thought of as mutually exclusive. The other is that there are many situations in which a racial difference has been imputed to a group even when there are no demonstrable physical differences. In short, the approach which defines race as a role sign confines the study of race relations somewhat arbitrarily to those situations where there is a clear colour difference, particularly between the members of European nations and groups of negroes.

What I want to suggest as a way of transcending these difficulties is a programme of sociological investigation which first defines the kinds of social differentiation in which subjective racial distinctions have been made and then, accepting that such situations need not always be defined in racial terms, look at the kind of definitions which are used in order to define them as racial. I propose to refer to a number of situations in our industrial and imperial world which have frequently been thought of as racial and then to consider whether the definition of differences as biologically determined is a sufficient criterion for distinguishing the forms of social differentiation which becomes racial.

The six situations to which I want to refer are these:

1 The situation of culture contact between peoples with an advanced industrial and military technology, and hunters, pastoralists and agriculturalists at lower levels of development.
2 The situation on a slave plantation.
3 Class situations in the classic Marxist or Weberian scene in which men within the same society have differing degrees of market power.

4   Status situations in which there is a concept of higher and lower but in which men are thought of as falling somewhere on a criterion of esteem rather than in mutually exclusive groups.

5   Situations of ethnic pluralism in which groups with differing cultures and/or physical characteristics work together in the same economy but retain their social and cultural identity.

6   Situations in which a minority group occupies a pariah or scapegoat role.

In each of these situations the differentiation may exist with or without being seen as a racial one. Each may exist with or without physical characteristics being used as a differentiating factor. Let us now consider each in turn.

In the first case there emerges what Toynbee has called an external proletariat. By virtue of its inferior technology the 'barbarian' culture at the gates of a great civilization is bound to give way and, even if the barbarians should conquer the civilized world, in the process they will become debarbarized. Before this happens, however, some definition of the roles of Greek or Roman or white settler on the one hand and barbarian or native on the other will be worked out. The distinction may not be seen as based upon biological heredity at all, let alone on skin colour. Thus for example, it is said that the earliest Dutch settlers at the Cape, distinguished not between Hottentot *qua* Hottentot and Dutchman *qua* Dutchman, but between uneducated heathen and the educated and baptized. On the other hand, Van Riebeck, the Dutch Governor, does categorize the Hottentots as a 'dull, stupid stinking people' and this kind of abuse could not go on long in a frontier situation without men arguing, following Aristotle, that the barbarians were not men at all, or more mildly that, though men, they were of a species biologically incapable of the intellectual standards necessary to achieve a high culture.

The same variability of rationalizations exists in the case of slave societies. Slavery does not necessarily imply a racial distinction. All that it does imply is a legal distinction between free and unfree. Transition from a free to an unfree status is readily possible through debt or capture in war, just as transition from an unfree to free status is possible by manumission. Moreover, slaves and freemen may often be of the same ethnic group and, if they are not, the slave will be gradually forced to adopt his master's culture. It is true, of course, that the Greeks rationalized slavery philosophically on the ground that the slave was a non-man, just as the European from the sixteenth to the eighteenth century often did so on theological and biological grounds. There are none the less, however, two separate things here. One is the slave economy and society, the other the rationalization on which it is based.

In advanced industrial societies, what matters more than men's legal status is their market situation and particularly, as Marx suggested, their relation to the means of production. Thus it is to be expected that there will always be a number of different social positions marked by varying degrees of economic power in any advanced economy. Such a situation might, however, sometimes take the form of a race rather than a class situation. This may happen if the system becomes hereditary so that mobility from one class position to another becomes impossible and, if this happens, members of the more powerful groups might come to regard those in weaker groups as socially inferior.

Oliver Cromwell Cox, the distinguished American negro Marxist sociologist, has in fact argued that race relations situations in the modern world are always of this type. Racial distinctions are relied upon systematically to ensure the continued exploitation of the proletariat. Hence he argues against the view of the American system of ethnic stratification as incipient caste and against the view that the relative openness of the Latin American race relations situation is due to the prevalence of the Roman Catholic religion. In the first case he points out that there is a degree of acceptance of the legitimacy of the situation by inferior castes in India which is not to be found in the case of the American negro. In the second he points out that Catholicism is associated with retardation of the growth of capitalism and that it is the latter factor which is responsible for the Latin American system.

Much of this is arguable. One case, however, which does seem to fit this kind of Marxian explanation is that of the colour bar in South Africa. True the distinction made is not between a white bourgeoisie owning industry, and a black proletariat being the only workers. But the distinction is none the less one which depends upon differential relations to the means of production.

The system of economic stratification depends upon the existence of a number of different relations to the means of production, and the most important distinction made is that between the worker who has industrial skills and whose rights are protected by trade unions and the essentially unfree and unprotected unskilled worker.

Separate from the social class system based upon differential distribution of market power is a system in which men are assigned to higher or lower positions in the social scale. Such status assignments sometimes lead to the emergence of hierarchically arranged corporate groups and the groups concerned tend to take the form of castes or estates. The significant thing about status systems in modern society, however, is that, as Cox puts it, the system operates with concepts rather than groups. Men are not either in one group or another. Rather they have more or less status on a kind of status-continuum which exists in the minds of the population at large. Clearly ethnic origins and colour will serve as a basis for assigning men to a system of closed status groups, but both degree of acculturation and colour will serve in the system based upon a status-continuum. Status systems of both kinds have existed at most times and in most parts of the world. They tend to develop a racial basis in those parts of the New World where slave-emancipation was followed by an elaborate status system. The caste or estate system is exemplified best in the United States Deep South, the status-continuum system in the Caribbean and Latin America.

Quite a different kind of situation, however, has occurred in certain societies which have been termed plural societies by J. S. Furnivall (1967) and which he saw to be exemplified most clearly in South-east Asia. Furnivall's focus is not upon the relation between the colonial power and the native people so much as between different ethnic groups which are involved in the same economy. Thus, for example, Chinese, Malay and Indian groups coexist in Indonesia. It would be wrong to describe that one is higher in the status scale than the other. Rather they meet, as Furnivall says 'only in the market place' and their social and cultural life at home remains relatively unaffected by culture contact. Clearly the groups involved here are from a biological point of view, distinct populations apart from their cultural distinctiveness. This does not mean, however, that the groups necessarily think of each other as races, unable by virtue of their biological ancestry to obtain the same standards of intellectual attainment. Racial beliefs of this kind may exist, but they do not necessarily do so.

The plural society concept, developed by Furnivall, does of course have some applicability in other kinds of colonial situations. Nearly every colonial territory has not merely a population of the descendants of European conquerors and the indigenous population, but a population of immigrant traders and of imported labourers as well. Thus one finds imported African slaves and indentured Indian and Chinese labourers in the Caribbean and one finds Indian, Syrian and Lebanese traders in Africa. Moreover inter-marriage may produce biologically distinct mixed populations who become ethnically distinct. In these cases the pluralism of the society might well be merged into some kind of stratification system.

Where such a system exists, the sixth kind of social differentiation to which I have referred might well be found. An ethnically or physically distinct group might assume an occupationally specialized role which is necessary for the proper economic and social functioning of the society, but which is nevertheless incompatible with its own value system. The classic case here is that of the Jews as usurers in mediaeval Europe, but Indian and other traders in colonial territories as well as immigrant landlords in metropolitan cities have played a similar role.

Distinct from the type of role which elicits fear and hostility is another group which is more likely to elicit contempt. This is the role of those ethnic groups who perform tasks which are thought to be beneath the dignity of, rather than incompatible with the values of the host society. It is well known in many African and Asian societies that the task of removing refuse and particularly human excreta are left to outsiders. Similarly Englishmen have shown an increasing unwillingness to work in foundries or mills where there is a lot of nightwork or to conduct buses, and immigrants have been called in to fill the gap.

Both kinds of groups mentioned here, the group which performs the inferior task and that which performs the ethically impermissible, are looked upon with suspicion by those who have a recognized position in the main society, and in the event of any threat to their society they become the obvious target for blame. Such was the fate of the Jews in Germany. Such it would appear is likely to be the fate of the coloured immigrants in Britain.

In the case of all six of the situations mentioned, it is possible to find instances in which the dominant group has explained the differences between its own privileged position and that of underprivileged groups as being due to a racial difference. So much is this the case that the definition of race relations problems has been stretched to include all these situations if there is a cultural or physical difference between the peoples involved. Indeed it is arguable that, given a combination of one of these situations and cultural or physical differences, it would be sensible to speak of a racial situation. I would like, however, to argue that another factor is essential to define the sociological category of race. It is important to understand this because this other factor is capable of further elaboration and provides the dynamics of true inter-racial conflict. I refer here to the kind of moral and intellectual justification which men offer for the differences of power and privilege which exist between them.

All social situations depend for their character upon the definitions of them which are given in the culture. We cannot see society, or a social institution, or a social relation. We simply learn to accept that the occurrence of certain forms of behaviour may be read as indicating the operation of a social institution or process. It is our capacity to do this which makes society itself possible. We do not, however, rest content with merely labelling the various forms of social interaction in which we engage, any more than we rest content with a world of discrete physical things. We grope after some kind of anchoring or validating principle which explains why things are as they are and why they should be so. Myth and theology, ideology, philosophy and science all provide us with systematic ways of meeting this need.

Some of the systematic ordering of belief systems tends to be deterministic and has the consequence of freezing the social systems which it explains. Hence if our religion holds that God has predestined ethnic groups to distinct destinies, we are unwilling to regard intermixture or mobility from one group to another as permissible or even possible. Thus theology can easily lend itself to the justification of rigid inter-group differences.

Characteristically, however, the advanced industrial societies have looked to science and ideology rather than to philosophy and theology to provide the necessary anchoring of their belief systems and it is in the nineteenth and twentieth centuries, above all, that the differences and conflicts mentioned above have been explained in biological terms. We rarely claim any more that God has predestined our nation to a superior destiny. To do so requires complicated interpretation of the Christian doctrine of predestination, beyond the capacity of most theologians outside the Dutch Reformed Church of South Africa. Far more commonly, we simply accept that our national characteristics and our good fortune derive inexorably from our genetic make-up.

Racism, the doctrine of racial differences between man, and racialism, the practice which derives from this doctrine is above all a nineteenth- or twentieth-century phenomenon because men in the nineteenth and twentieth centuries have looked to the natural sciences to provide an intellectual underpinning to their social behaviour. In the past they were perhaps more inclined to look to a deterministic theology and in the future may turn to a deterministic sociology. Both theological and sociological justifications will have much in common with biological and racist ones, in that they will be equally deterministic, but men who use them will not think of the world in terms of racial division. We are now in a position to define the kinds of social situations which the sociologist should recognize as racial. The term 'racial', we shall say, should be used to describe those situations of inter-group differentiation in which men explain the differences between them in terms of determinate biological theories. Such situations may, but need not necessarily, be associated with cultural and physical differences between the groups.

It is important, of course, to point out that the claim to scientific justification has no validity. Racism is based on pseudo-scientific myths. That is the point of the work done by the Moscow conference of biologists called by UNESCO. The task of the sociologist then becomes that of showing the real nature of the differences which exist and how pseudo-scientific belief systems undermine them. Rather than defining his field in terms of popular pseudo-scientific beliefs, he looks at these beliefs only to unmask them. The object of race relations studies should always be to show the true nature of the differences and conflicts which men describe as racial.

It remains, however, to point out a further crucial complexity of racialism in the contemporary world. This is that racial doctrines are no longer morally respectable in many countries, partly because of the work done by UNESCO and other bodies since 1945. This does not mean, however, that racism and the associated practice of racialism are dead. Men frequently act on racial assumptions but their public justifications make reference to non-racial criteria. Thus, for example, a city council may in fact discriminate systematically against a racial or ethnic minority in the sphere of housing, but argue that it does so on grounds of cultural standards. In this case the unmasking which sociological analysis necessarily involves is two-fold. First it must be shown that the practice is only understandable if one accepts that the council is acting on racial assumptions. Thereafter, however, it has still to be shown why it has turned in the first place to these racial assumptions. The ultimate part of the explanation must be to show the true nature of the differences and the relations between the two groups involved.

But the fact that the sociologist studying race relations finds himself unmasking racist beliefs by no means implies that there is no field of race relations studies. Social categories depend for their existence on the subjective definition given to them by social actors. Race is no exception. So long as it exists in the minds of men there will be race relations problems to study just as there will be men who can be helped to fight against the buttressing of injustice by the use of pseudo-scientific beliefs.

17 The problem of the sociology of race relations[1]

If there is any single problem which raises issues of social responsibility for sociologists it is the problem of race relations. This is not to say that sociologists must take responsibility for the crimes of Belsen or Buchenwald. What it does mean is that they should be able to make clear the kinds of social structures which are involved in race relations situations and the relationship between these structures and the belief systems which support them. This they have signally failed to do. Concerned as they have been, in their own insular way, with the particular practical problems of their own particular countries, they have usually sided earnestly with the liberals and addressed themselves to those petty problems which most disturb the liberal conscience. Only the raucous challenge of Black Power has gradually made it necessary for them to go beyond their restricted ideological standpoints and to bring these ideologies themselves into focus as a central part of their subject matter. Indeed, if a time comes when the problems of race relations recede into the past as no longer matters of significant controversy, a historical retrospect will probably regard the books which were written, and those which were not written, as a good indication of the place occupied by sociologists and other intellectuals in the social structure of racialism.

In such a historical retrospect it will be seen that the avoidance of the problem by the sociologist was not for want of a challenge. For no less a body than UNESCO called upon sociologists to define the problem in 1967 after biologists had made it clear that the notion of race as they used it has no relevance to the political differences amongst men (UNESCO, 1968).[2] By that stage it was

[1] This is a totally new version of a paper given to the annual conference of the British Sociological Association in 1968.
[2] These statements are best read in and for themselves, without the guidance offered by M. Banton who has written an introduction to them.

clear that there were problems in the world which were at least subjectively perceived as problems of race, that, where these problems existed, men died or were deprived of basic human rights in hundreds of thousands, and that there was a legitimate problem for sociologists in exhibiting the empirical correlates of these states of affairs. But those who then turned to the literature of sociology for guidance found that it was lacking even in the most basic definitions without which any serious attack on the problem was impossible.

Most of the literature of sociology dealt with race relations in one of three ways. Either it reduced the problem by a gross definition in terms of situations of contact between people with perceptibly different physical characteristics, especially skin colour; or it simply assimilated the problem into a wider one in which 'ethnic' difference was seen to be at the root of race problems; or finally, adopting a crude empiricist phenomenological approach, it was prepared to take into account any situation in which the 'actor's definition of the situation' (usually the discriminating or exploiting actor's definition of the situation) was taken as the sole empirical criterion for including or not including a problem within the orbit of race relations studies.

To some extent the first of these definitions of the situation is the most satisfactory, particularly if one confines oneself to the study of race in the English-speaking world, and to some extent the point is taken here that when one is faced with the kinds of colour situation which exist in the United States or in South Africa, worrying about definitions may seem like fiddling while the cities burn and the prisons and camps are already being built. But the fact of the matter is that the American and the South African situation are not universal. Colour is not always a salient factor, even in colonial and quasi-colonial situations, or, if it is, it is not salient in the same manner as in these parts of the world. A major part of our problem then, if we are to avoid insularity, is to show how and why these situations differ from others in which there is black-white contact.

The reduction of race relations problems to a wider category of ethnic problems again is one which has something to commend it. It used, for instance to be an important tactic of liberals to assimilate the two kinds of problems and thereby to demand the same sort of treatment, the same possibilities of assimilation for American negroes as existed for the European minorities who had been absorbed into the melting pot, or, in the case of South Africa the same rights as workers for goldminers and factory workers, be they black or white. But however valuable this might have been as a political tactic, it is not honest sociology, and can be used as a tactic with quite opposite intent by those who wish to play down the differences between the degree of freedom of one ethnic group and another. At the present day, those who are seeking to disguise discrimination against black people, therefore commonly use the term 'ethnic' and thereby imply that there is no difference between the situation of these people and that of other purely culturally distinguished minorities.

Finally, so far as the 'phenomenological' approach is concerned, the version mentioned above lacks one of the few valuable insights which has been generated by what is called 'labelling' theory in the sociology of deviance. This is that labels and definitions are relative things, and that what the respectable middle class call and punish as deviance, might not be regarded as meriting this label by the alleged deviant. In the field of race relations on the other hand there are many problems which are diagnosed as being due to race by those in power, which are seen simply as problems of exploitation and oppression by those who are on the receiving end of racial definitions.

In fact, so-called race relations sociology is far from being an adequate guide to an understanding of the problems of race which perplex the moral conscience of the world. Much more is to be gained from the literature which is concerned with stratification, that which is concerned with pluralism and that which is concerned with 'minorities'. And all of these in turn could be better understood if they were absorbed into a general literature of the sociology of imperialism and colonialism.

The debate about stratification and race relations emerged in the United States, where the concept of stratification was a general organizing one, and where the difficulty of fitting the situation of the American negro into the overall pattern posed something of an intellectual problem, was regarded as having been resolved in the work of W. Lloyd Warner (1936). This involved maintaining the overall stratification concept, as it was to be developed in Warner's Yankee City studies, but at the same time superimposing on it the concept of caste. The resulting theory was that of colour-caste. Both whites and negroes had their own class, or, what comes to the same thing in Warner's theory, status hierarchies, operating in terms of roughly the same value scales, but the essential principle of the whole structure was that the topmost negro was always thought of as separated from the lowest white, no matter what his achievement, and the barrier was impenetrable. To keep it impenetrable many of the avoidance mechanisms of the Indian caste system had to be adopted.

Warner's theory was far from satisfactory in many respects. For one thing it made no attempt to explain why negro-white relations were dealt with by one system, and relations amongst negroes or amongst whites by another. For another it failed to take note of those features of negro-white relations, such as the performance of intimate services relating to cooking and domestic work by negroes, which were quite incompatible with the anti-pollution logic of the Indian caste system. That these points were not adequately discussed in American sociological theory might have something to do with the fact that the principle issue was joined with Warner by the distinguished American Marxist, Oliver Cromwell Cox (1959). Thus the issue became one of whether the notion of caste had to be replaced by a more Marxist conception of class, and Warner's real insight that the class, caste or status position of the negro worker was different from that of the white worker tended to be lost.

The merit of Cox's approach, of course, lay in its apprehension of the fact that there was an element of sheer compulsion in white negro relations which was lacking in the Indian caste system, but which Cox took to be the characteristic of the relation between capitalist and worker. Moreover it seemed to explain in other than purely idealistic terms differences between the Latin American and North American colonies. It was not simply that the former were Catholic and the latter Protestant. Religious differences were the product of a third variable, namely the stage of capitalist development. Thus Brazilian Catholicism, and any lack of harshness in the patterns of race relations and slavery which might be detected, were simply to be understood in terms of the fact that the Portuguese settlers had not yet developed effective capitalist forms of production.

The application of such unmodified Marxist categories of analysis to the problem of black-white relations in America, however, raises more problems than it solves. It begins by misrepresenting the situation of the white American worker as based simply upon 'exploitation', but fails to note, as Marx or Weber would have done, that that exploitation is essentially the exploitation of free labour in a labour market, whereas the exploitation and the oppression of the negro has resort to many forms of compulsion other than purely market ones. Following from this it ignores the extent to which the increase in bargaining power of white workers has led to their relative incorporation within the framework of a welfare state, and that the negro worker is very often left out in this incorporation. Finally it fails to explain the actual motivation of poor-white racism and racialism, and avoids doing so by positing an entirely hypothetical future in which the workers of the world will indeed unite, not merely regardless of nation, but, equally, regardless of skin colour.

The more systematic models of social stratification employed recently in the United States by non-Marxist sociologists can, however, offer us little more guidance in solving our problems. Neither the simple form of functional theory stated in the commonsense language of Princeton by Davis and Moore (1945), nor the more sophisticated theories of Parsons (1954) stated in the language of Heidelberg and Harvard, get us any further. For both, the stratification system of a society depends upon its value system, and, though there may be different value systems superimposed in any given society, so that the current American pattern which rewards effective performance of adaptive roles may be overlaid in other societies by an emphasis upon goal-attainment, upon pattern-maintenance and tension-management or upon integration, these systems of roles are themselves to be regarded as hierarchically ordered as between themselves so that, by and large, if everyone does not accept his place, at least he knows it; that is to say he knows the position to which other people in general assign him. But, as Parsons himself admits, this scheme of things will not serve to explain ethnicity, let alone the persistently bottom-dog position of the American negro. 'In spite of the dispersion of members of given ethnic groups through different levels of the main class-structure,' he tells us, 'ethnicity to some degree tends to preserve relatively independent pyramids in the more general system.' (*ibid.*)

So we are back with Lloyd Warner or worse, since now not even the nicest Waspish immigrants can be fully explained in terms of the stratification model. How much less then can the model be extended even to America's Caribbean neighbours, where some of the inhabitants are white and some black, some Christian and some Hindu, some the descendants of slaves and others of indentured labourers and where, even though the slaves' descendants have had most of their own culture destroyed and can do little more than produce their own variant of the masters' culture, there can be said to be no overall shared value system in terms of which stratification can take place. It is this that has given some plausibility, and a certain theoretical centrality to the theory of cultural and social pluralism which has been taken to new levels of sophistication by writers such as M. G. Smith (1965; Kuper and Smith, 1969).

It is perhaps unfortunate that the theories of stratification and of pluralism have been so sharply opposed, and that Marxists have seen the very concept of pluralism as an attempt to escape from facing up to the exploitative and conflictual elements involved in stratification. For far from its being the case that pluralism directs attention away from conflict and exploitation in a way which stratification theory does not, the opposite appears to be so; for pluralist theory always brings in the factor of power at some point, and it begins by rejecting the whole notion of cultural consensus.

The notion of a plural society first became important in colonial sociology as a result of the work of Furnivall (1967), who used the concept in his study of Indonesian society. According to his account, the main unifying factor in an ethnically plural colony was the market place, and this market place, moreover, was marked by a kind of ruthlessness of exploitation not to be found in European industrial societies, where even market relations were governed, as Durkheim had pointed out, by some sort of common will. Moreover such a common will could not be expected to develop because the cultural basis for it did not exist in a society in which, apart from their market dealings, men retreated at nights to their separate ethnic worlds.

These ideas were taken up and applied in many other parts of the world in the late fifties, but especially in East Africa (Morris, 1968), in South Africa (Kuper and Smith, 1969) and in the Caribbean. Each regional area, of course, cried out for variations on Furnivall's main theme but there would have been a great deal of theoretical consensus at that time that the notion of pluralism was a better starting point for societies of a colonial sort than that of stratification.

The main criticism which might be made of M. G. Smith's earliest formulations was that they leaned too heavily on simple cultural anthropology and, particularly on Malinowski's essays in *A Scientific Theory of Culture* (1944) rather than on his more politically conscious work *The Dynamics of Culture Change* (1945), and that they left out any careful study of the relations of the market place which had had centrality in Furnivall. The result of this is that the various ethnic groups to be found in a multi-ethnic colony like what was British Guiana are seen as primarily culturally distinct. Each has the general attributes of a society and a cultural system as Malinowski defines these and, hence there is some uncertainty as to why we should refer to this as a society at all, were it not for the fact that there is one unifying institution which stretches through all ethnic groups, namely the state.

There are many difficulties about this theory. One is to explain why, according to Smith, American society is to be thought of as heterogeneous rather than plural. Apparently it is because the American negroes share most of the institutions of white society. But do not most of Professor Smith's fellow Jamaicans also? Surely he must mean something more than that the Caribbean colonies went on to employ Indian indentured labourers! In fact the difficulties over this issue are never finally resolved in Smith's work, although in a later major theoretical essay he offers new formulations about the relations between the Deep South and the North, and about the relations of American Indians in reservations which suggest that in a complex model of American society some attention would have to be given to pluralist features (Smith; Kuper and Smith, *op. cit.*).

More important, however is the problem of why colonial societies do not break up after 'independence'. According to Smith's early theory it was of the essence of such a society that the several plural elements should be dominated by one of them.

The only alternative to break-up, therefore, after the withdrawal of the governing colonizer, is the transfer of power to one of the other segments. This may be what happens in some cases and in all cases in some degree, but what it overlooks is the extent to which there are institutions other than the political one, which assign roles across the segments, and which exist in pre- and post-independence situations. So far as the Caribbean is concerned, the plantation, or its ghostly physical and social remains, linger on after independence, and in so far as they are productive, they remain governed by boardrooms in London or elsewhere long after the governor and his entourage have taken their boat back to the metropolis. Malinowski seems to have been aware of this in his *Dynamics of Culture Change* when he refers to the emergence of institutions of the 'third column' which belong to neither parent culture, but which are purely products of the contact situation, and instances migrant labour in South Africa as such a third column institution (see Rex, 1959).

Probably, for all Smith's theoretical brilliance, it must be admitted that his theoretical formulations are tied too closely to the empirical material with which he is most familiar. They have nothing of the comparative grasp of the principle variants of the plantation as an institution which are to be found in the work of Genovese and his school (Genovese, 1965, 1969, 1971; Foner and Genovese, 1969), and it is probably in the sociological development of some of Genovese's comparative historical ideas that the future of the study of plural societies even of the New World variety must be found. Not least, there is sufficient 'Marxism' in Genovese's thinking, coupled with a critical attitude towards crude economic determinism, to make one hopeful that analyses of the plantation and its surrounding institutions in different places, in different market conditions and in different times might be produced which might be helpful to a genuine sociology of race relations.

It should perhaps be noted that Smith wishes to reduce the study of race relations to the study of pluralism. He seeks to do this by concentrating on the fact that as between people of African and European descent in the Caribbean a man's actual placement in the status hierarchy really turns, not so much on the measurable darkness or lightness of his skin colour, but upon whom he mixes with and how close he is to the centre of things. Under this system any high status man is thought of as relatively white although the physical fact of his appearance might belie this.

The inadequacy of Smith's approach to the question of race relations has recently produced something of a reaction and there are many scholars who would want to claim that there is some ultimate and irreducible element in the perception of physical differences even though there may as yet be few who agree with Hoetink's concept of differences in the somatic norm-image which are embedded in different cultures (Hoetink, 1967). For our part we would say that, although in the long run we may have to admit that there is some such factor, there are still many other sociological variables to be explored, which might serve to explain why one or other descent rule, one or other somatic norm-image operates in different cultures. Of greatest importance are the nature of productive institutions, the total ecology of a region, the state of the market for particular products at a particular time, the kinds of labour employed classified in terms of their degrees of freedom; where there is slavery, the kind of detail of slave law and practice which operates and ideological differences in religion and law which affect and are affected by this; where there has been emancipation, the actual political and economic factors which have affected the emancipation process. What has to be discovered is what effect various combinations of these variables might have on whether there is a colour-bar as between whites and non-whites, a colour gradient strongly associated with status, or a situation in which colour is not salient at all. Moreover it is necessary to generalize this beyond the New World countries on which Genovese's school have done such good work to take account of the plantation situation which developed in various colonies in the Indian Ocean, and of the social structure and economy and polity cased upon goldmining and manufacture which grew up in the country which before all others today exemplifies what is called the colour-bar, namely the Republic of South Africa.

Before we reduce race relations studies even to the study of colonialism, however, it is necessary to say something about the problem of immigration, colour, and race relations in the metropolitan countries themselves. For this we are more likely to gain help from those who have sought to develop a theory of

minorities than from any other source. Thus we agree with
Wagley and Harris when they write (1964):

> minorities are subordinate segments of complex state
> societies; (2) minorities have special physical or cultural
> traits which are held in low esteem by dominant segments
> of the society; (3) minorities are self-conscious units
> bound together by the special traits which their members
> share and by the special disabilities which these bring;
> (4) membership in a minority is transmitted by a rule of
> descent which is capable of affiliating succeeding
> generations even in the absence of readily apparent special
> cultural or physical traits; (5) minority peoples, by choice or
> necessity, tend to marry within the group.

Such is the situation of most colonial immigrants in a metropolitan country, though it is shared, as Wagley and Harris go
on to say, by poor immigrants and refugees. What we have to do
in the sociology of race relations, in fact, is to set up a framework
which includes an account of metropolitan as well as colonial
social structures, to note that the colonial worker is put to work
after some kind of military conquest, so that he is never a wholly
free worker exploited solely through the labour market, that there
grows up around the basic productive institutions a whole
colonial social order, with a set of roles and status positions not
wholly and finally determined by exigencies of production, and
that in the metropolitan societies there develops a set of unwanted
economic and social positions which can most readily be staffed
by colonial or immigrant workers. Within this context of power,
authority, status, oppression and exploitation, men work and
live their social lives.

The mere existence of harsh power, authority and exploitation,
however is not by itself sufficient to constitute a race relations
situation. Racial exploitation and conflict may only be said to
occur where there is exploitation of group by group, where
group membership is easily detected by external signs and where
there is a consequent closure on mobility. Moreover, within this
context of the exploitation of one group by another, there is a
still narrower group of situations where, within the overall belief
system, there is a set of beliefs which asserts not merely that it is
undesirable, but that it is in some sense contrary to the nature of

things, that an individual should be permitted to reclassify himself and, hence to move from one group to another.

The necessary and sufficient conditions of a situation's becoming a race relations situation, therefore are (*a*) that there should be a situation of harsh oppression and exploitation, (*b*) that this should be a situation as between groups recognizable by signs regarded as unalterable, or, to put this in another and Parsonian manner, that there should be ascriptive role allocation, and (*c*) that the pattern of exploitation and discrimination should be justified in terms of some kind of deterministic theory. We now pass to a discussion under each of these heads:

Social structures underlying race relations problems

The following are historical situations in which it is frequently the case that the problem of relations between men are defined as problems of race relations:

1 Frontier situations where a people with an advanced technology and a high level of technology begin to compete for limited resources, particularly land, and border wars ensue.

2 Various forms of the social relations of production employing unfree labour. The slave plantation in the Southern United States is one central social form of this kind. The compound system for migrant labours in mining developments in Africa another, and various types of production employing indentured labour, a third.

3 Situations of class conflict in the Marxist sense of that term, in which one group is obliged to sell its labour to another under unusually harsh and exploitative terms.

4 Estate and caste systems in which groups enjoying differing degrees of prestige and sometimes of legal rights coexist and sometimes take on a corporate character and fulfil distinct occupational roles.

5 Situations in which stratification in the sense in which that term is often used to refer to a differential distribution of economic rights of status and of power is continuous and conceptual[1] rather than referring to corporate groups of any kind.

[1] This is the notion of social, as distinct from political, class, as it is employed by O. C. Cox (1959).

6 Situations of cultural pluralism, such that a number of distinguished groups interact for limited purposes only but to live separate social and cultural lives.

All of the above occur in colonial territories, but the process of contact between occupants of colonial roles and the colonizers is not confined to the colonial territories themselves. Colonial migrants may settle in metropolitan countries together with poor and politically persecuted refugees from non-colonial countries and find themselves in any of the following further situations:

7 Urban systems of stratification of a variety of different kinds in which the migrants add to the system at the bottom, forming some kind of new 'underclass' element.

8 Situations in which a particular group of outsiders is called upon to perform a role which, although essential to the social and economic life of a society, is in conflict with its value system, or is thought of as being beneath the dignity of the society's own members.

9 Situations in which in times of crisis a group which is culturally or physically distinguishable is blamed for the existence of a threat to the society's wellbeing. This is the process known as scapegoating. It is often connected with the structural situation outlined in 8 above.

The first type of situation is one which Toynbee refers to as characterized by the existence of an external proletariat (Toynbee, 1953). It existed when the barbarians were pressing at the edges of the Roman Empire, and it existed in a reverse form as the European countries extended their colonial frontiers. Toynbee's term is a good one, because it suggests two groups locked together in some kind of social dependence and struggle even though they are territorially distinct. When a border society exists, the main energies of the two peoples concerned is likely to be devoted to their frontier problem, and the frontier problem may in fact be the problem through the resolution of which a new inclusive society is being constituted.

Situations such as these do not necessarily come to be defined as racial ones, but certain factors in them are conducive to their being so defined. The first and most important of these is that, although the new inclusive society may be partially constituted, it is still possible to think of the outgroup as consisting of non-men. Secondly, in the continuing border wars the two groups define each other as, militarily speaking, enemies. And, thirdly, the existence of a differential in levels of cultural and political advancement enables the superior group to stigmatize its enemy as inferior.

It is hard to underestimate the effect of the frontier experience on relations between colonialists and settlers on the one hand and 'natives' on the other, not only upon immediate definitions of the situation, but upon long term images which the people of the industrially advanced countries have of people in the territories which they have exploited. In fact, the second period of European expansion overseas, marked at its outset by the so-called scramble for Africa, did not last very long, and it was possible within a three-generation family to call upon memories ranging from the first generation's involvement in colonial conquest to the third generation's battle with terrorists and rural and urban guerillas as empires crumbled.

One particularly interesting feature of the frontier situation is the ideological argument which ensues about the terms under which the conquered are to be incorporated into the new society. The problem is a particularly acute one when the conquering society is itself relatively democratic and finds difficulty in inventing new roles and statuses without doing violence to its own internal structure (see MacMillan, 1963). One of the consequences of this has been that the democratic conquerors have sometimes produced harsher conditions for those whom they have conquered because they could only define them residually, whereas in less democratic societies there were inferior but well-defined roles into which the conquered could be incorporated (see Elkins, 1963). These observations are relevant of course to the comparison between North and South American slavery, but they apply also to the relations of American settlers with the natives of the Americas—the Indians—and very clearly to the problem involved in defining the position of the Bantu people in the emergent society of the Cape Colony in Africa in the 1830s.

The setting up of a colonial society means, of course, the setting up of new forms of the social relations of production, unless the colony concerned was established merely for strategic purposes. Given that the colony almost always arises as a result of military conquest, it is unlikely that the workers within these productive systems will enjoy the rights of free labour. They may be enslaved, they may be indentured, they may be forced to make deliveries of crops, or they may be kept in reserves so that they can maintain a bare existence unless they are required for specific services to their masters.

This is not the place to review the vast literature on the variety of types of slavery which have existed in the world, both in the ancient world and in European-created colonies of the last four or five centuries. All one need to do is note that there are varia- tions in the actual harshness of the relation between master and man as well as in the possibility of manumission, but that what- ever variation there may be the field-slave in particular has a status quite different from that of any free worker. What some- times confuses the issue is that certain societies are said to have more lenient slave systems because they exist in market condi- tions which make intensive exploitation of labour impossible or because attention is shifted from the field-slave to the house- slave or craftsman. Undoubtedly there are some societies which allow greater flexibility in these matters than others and often have the appearance of manorial and estate systems rather than plantation and slave systems. We shall return to this possibility below.

The Western world, or, as it likes to call itself, the free world, lives with a grandiose historic myth about is own relationship to slavery. This is that, after a regrettable period of aberrance, the inherent humanism of Christianity asserted itself, and slavery gave way to free labour. This was in fact very far from being the case. Slavery was abandoned when it was no longer profitable to those who could give it its necessary military guarantee. But there were still parts of the world where other forms of com- pulsion were necessary to the colonialist. Not merely had there to be a military presence to guarantee the delivery of crops by peasants, but peoples had to be moved from one continent to another so that labour was available in the right places at the right time. Thus, if the first great invention of European colonial- ism was the field-slave, the second was the coolie, that is to say the Indian or Chinese labourer who would undertake to live and work abroad for a period of years under highly unfree conditions in return for a specific legal undertaking that at the end of that period he might either return home or settle down as a smallholder or tradesman in the colony of settlement. Under this system the British plantations of Mauritius, Natal, Guiana and Fiji were created and similar systems operated in the colonial territories of the other European colonizing powers. The existence of this new unfree form of labour created a problem of defining the relation not merely between it and its employers, but also between it and earlier forms which it has rendered redundant and also the native population, whoever they might be.

Indentures, however, provided the basis for a form of labour which did not require the shipment of large numbers of Indian or Chinese coolies. So far as Africa was concerned, there was a labour supply of conquered natives to hand and their conquest had been so complete that, while the form of indentures might be adhered to, the actual practice often approximated and still approximates to that which prevailed in the heyday of the slave trade. This was and is characteristic of Portuguese agricultural development in Africa. But a more characteristic form, and one with far greater potential for development is that which has been worked out in the Republic of South Africa (see Duffy, 1960).

The basic institutions for the organization of labour in South Africa are the reserve, the mining compound and the urban location (see chapter 21 below). The reserve was established by confining the African population to less than fifteen per cent of the available African land, breaking up traditional communal landholding systems and imposing taxation so as to force the landholding peasant and his landless brother alike to make at least temporary sorties into the wage-earning economy. Given this rural background, the mines could rely upon a supply of short-term migrant labour consisting of young men without their families, who would live in something like prison conditions for the period of their contract, and then be returned without benefits of unemployment assistance or pensions to their imagined rural homes. And, in so far as this system was not flexible enough to accommodate the variety of labour needs of the white population, there had also to be 'locations' i.e. segregated areas where a controlled number of natives could live in highly insecure conditions with their families, the husbands

going out to work in the factories and their wives offering themselves as domestic workers. The system as a whole has much to
commend it from an employer's point of view when compared
with slavery. The essential conditions of unfreedom which
pertain to slavery are preserved, while, at the same time, the
encumbrance of wives and children and the obligation to
support workers for long periods of unemployment are avoided.

One feature of this situation is the emergence of a very large
class of domestic servants. Such servants may, of course, be
treated with more or less paternalistic benevolence, but the
maintenance of the system whereby domestic servants are ever-
lastingly available can never be benevolent. Servants must not
decamp. They must not run off to better conditions of industrial
employment. They must receive part at least of their keep in kind,
so that they participate in the wider market only indirectly
through their masters' oikos. And they must be deemed, in myth
at least, to be incapable of skills other than those which it suits
their masters that they should have.

It is necessary to draw attention to the fact that most of these
unfree labour situations which we have mentioned depend upon
the existence of sanctions of a non-economic kind. Thus they are
to be distinguished from situations of class-struggle. To say this
is not to pretend that the free labour of capitalist societies is
universally well treated. This is very far from being the case. It is,
however, to insist, in a way which is consistent with Marx's
own approach to the class question, that exploitation in 'free'
capitalist societies is exploitation through the market. The
problem is whether there are some situations where such
market forces operate which are conducive to the emergence of
'racial' conflict. What we would suggest is that this is sometimes
the case, particularly where an economy based upon unfree
labour achieves an economic take-off. In these circumstances the
workers who find themselves able to bargain may begin to move
towards that situation which Marx described as becoming a class-
for-itself.

Race relations problems are most likely to be perceived when
a group which has been unfree and is only partially free by
comparison with settler labour does begin to exercise some
leverage in the labour-market situation. Here a particular kind of
class-for-itself, partially unfree in the market and therefore

compelled from the first to fight a political struggle, emerges.[1]
It might be suggested, on the other hand, that there is a theoretical
possibility that a class-for-itself might lose some of its rights to
the point at which it approximates to the condition of the
group which is moving in the opposite direction. Such a situation
might emerge as a result of a massive defeat of labour in countries
with fascist regimes, but it is arguable whether this has ever
happened in a pure form.

We must now turn to the case of those societies with ethnically
plural populations which have features suggestive of estate and
caste systems. Such a distinction can well be made, but it is
grossly confused by trying to make a distinction between
paternalistic and competitive systems. Before we can begin to
understand the problem it is necessary that we should say something about the kind of social structures which are likely to be
involved in the allegedly 'paternalistic' type of system.

So far in this discussion we have concentrated on structures of
production and particularly on structures of production for the
market. We must now consider what happens to a society when a
plantation system operates for subsistence purposes and also
what kind of society grows up around the institutions of
production.

With regard to the first of these, it is interesting to notice
that Max Weber in his *General Economic History*, chapter 6,
introduces the notion of the plantation under the heading of
'The capitalistic development of the manor' (1961). This draws
attention to the close relationship between the two types of
productive structure. Some Portuguese settlers in Brazil may
have seen their Big Houses primarily as manors. But these same
settlers or their successors might, at a later point, when there
was a wide market for their products, have turned their manors
into something more like capitalist plantations. On the other
hand there will have been some plantations which in times of
market decline were likely to develop in a manorial direction.

Both the manor and the plantation may coexist with, and be
defined in terms of, the legal institution of slavery. But along
with the particular legal or religious definitions of slavery, and

[1] Presumably this is one way in which Pierre van den Berghe's category
of 'competitive' race relations situations might be understood (see Van
den Berghe, 1967a).

the kindness or otherwise of the master, whether or not the agricultural enterprise is oriented to a strong market or not might have profound implications for the relations between master and man. What we wish to notice here is that in certain circumstances a slave colony might begin to develop manorial features. This is one of the features which no doubt some scholars wish to draw to our attention when they refer to these systems as paternalistic.

Of course it may be argued that the North American plantation system could never have become completely manorial and paternalistic in this sense, and it is on this fact that the strength of the argument for the crucially differentiating role of ideology as between North and South America rests (see Tannenbaum, 1946; Hanke, 1949; Freyre, 1956; Elkins, 1963). Even in the North, however, there are many 'irrational' features of the plantation system at certain times in its history which would justify one in saying that, in terms of what was possible within a Protestant and capitalist ethos, the system developed manorial features. We are, after all, talking about ideal types, and do not suggest that any particular historical case must coincide with our type.

Much of what is said in general terms about slave societies, however, is misleading, because it posits a society in which there are two roles and two roles only, namely those of slave and slavemaster. In fact the true sense of what such societies were like can only be gained when one takes into account all of the other roles which make the total social system possible. Amongst the other roles which should be brought into consideration are those of the house-slave, the slave-craftsman who hired out his services or has them hired out for him, the freed slave and the free person of colour born to a concubine, indentured labourers, who brought their own status and their own way of life into the society; and, after the formal fact of emancipation, white settlers, ranging from plantation managers to workers, traders of varying nationalities coming in partly to service a particular group (e.g. East Indian workers) and partly to play the role of a shop-keeping caste; the missionaries, who had a peculiarly important role in redefining the Christian gospel so as to adapt it to local conditions; and, finally, administrators who lived in the colony for a term of duty and then returned home without necessarly developing any close identification with settler interests (see Rex, 1970).

The colour and distinctiveness of colonial life varies enormously from society to society, but it is by no means the case that the most complex cultural elaborations are to be found where the economy is strongest. Indeed the opposite may be the case. When considerations of profit are paramount, a cultural system is likely to be rationalized and streamlined so that cultural frills are eliminated. It is on the whole in sleepier precapitalist times that rich and complex cultures are developed. Freyre has given us his own evocative description of Brazilian culture, and other such portraits could be drawn of the many-faceted cultures of some of the less productive Caribbean islands, or of the Cape before the encounter with the Bantu and the subsequent discovery of gold and diamonds.

There can of course be no single description of all of these sub-capitalist social formations, but each in its own way assigns roles to different groups, each group brings to a society its own culture and each society develops its own sense of a system of estates or castes. Of course it would be wrong to apply these terms too literally. We do not wish in any way to suggest that multi-ethnic colonies operating on a sub-capitalist level reproduce the main features of the European estate system or the Indian caste system. But there is inequality of legal and other rights between different groups, there is occupational specialization and, as a culture becomes established, there may not be that sense of perpetual conflict between groups which is evident when fully capitalist conditions occur.

In what we have just said, we have, of course, noted the fact of emancipation of slaves and have implied that it is possible to develop a morphology of colonial situations and colonial societies which applies both before and after emancipation. We should now note however that there is one very important difference between societies after emancipation. This is that in some a line is drawn between all white on the one hand and all men of colour on the other, whereas in other societies men are seen as being capable of being placed on some sort of colour continuum. Just why there are two such sharply different descent rules is a matter of continuing scholarly debate and we cannot hope to resolve the problem here (see Harris, 1964; Hoetink, 1967).

What we can do however is to note that whereas it is a familiar point that a clear demarcation of the ruling group is useful for purposes of economic exploitation and imperative co-ordination, colour may also play some part in helping to facilitate *status* differentiation, not simply in terms of either-or but in terms of more-or-less. Thus there are some societies after slave emancipation in which colour is not as closely related to social differentiation on economic and political dimensions, as it is on the status dimension. It is important for us to notice, therefore, that a system of status differentiation may, by itself, be a social structure supportive of race conflict.

One interesting historical point is whether in any of the Latin American countries which becomes industrialized the colour continuum will give way to a colour bar, just as the economic power of the capitalist class supersedes an earlier social order in which status considerations were all-important. Unfortunately this sort of question is unlikely to be answered until comparative history and sociology gets beyond arguing about whether the Brazilians are more or less wicked than the Americans. What is at issue is simply what the relative importance in the two societies is of the process of class struggle on the one hand and status ordering on the other and what role skin colour plays in facilitating these processes.

Finally we should notice the residual fact of pluralism. In our account of social structures so far, we have shown that there are many types of relationship that can hold between groups in a colonial society other than that of sheer cultural difference. In fact, we doubt whether Smith's early ideal type of a society of culturally distinct segments, which are held together by a state solely because they are ethnically different, and would otherwise fall apart, has any empirical referent at all. But it could well be that none of the factors of conquest and forced labour of class, caste, estate and status can by themselves explain the complexity of any society. In this sense it is not only possible but probable that pluralism might be a separate and quite important dimension.

In discussing these various types of social structure we have necessarily in our discussion referred to problems of race relations. It is important therefore, before we pass to a brief discussion of social structures in metropolitan countries to emphasize that in principle each of these situations—the frontier and conquest, the establishment of unfree forms of labour, the harsher forms of Marxian class-struggle, colonial-type caste and estate systems—status ordering and cultural pluralism can exist without their being defined as race relations problems or without producing race relations problems. But so far as colonial societies are concerned, one or other of these situations seems to be a necessary constituent of a race relations problem.

We must now turn to the basic structural forms of metropolitan societies to see what factors in them may produce race relations problems. Before we do, however, it might be as well to notice that the distinction between colonial and metropolitan societies is primarily of analytic importance. In some cases, most notably in the United States and in the Republic of South Africa, a metropolitan society and a colonial society have been established within the framework of a single nation state. Thus a migration from the Deep South to Chicago for a black American is akin to a migration from Jamaica to London or Birmingham, while on the other hand the board-rooms of Johannesburg are much like those of London or New York, a metropolitan economy and society having been established in this latter case as close as possible to the colonial productive system. What we are concerned with here, however, is the role of the immigrant from a colonial world to a situation in which he has to play a role in a metropolitan society. The problem is to show what the structural features of such societies are which make possible the incorporation of colonial immigrants.

The first fact about these metropolitan societies which is coming increasingly to be recognized is that they do not consist simply of a unitary class of citizens, as liberal theory would have us believe, nor of a unitary working class as suggested by both Marxist and social democratic theory. In the case of the United States, as industry developed, it was staffed by successive waves of immigrants, while in Europe itself, much less obviously, the labour force included a considerable immigrant component. If one looks even more closely at the statistics of occupational distribution of the immigrant labour force in the advanced industrial countries, one finds that in certain industries like engineering and construction the immigrants might constitute an actual majority of the labour force (see Castles and Castles, 1971).

Trade unionists are inclined to argue that the mere fact that such workers are immigrant does not make any difference to their social class position and status, if they are protected by trade unions and working-class parties. But the plain fact is that they are not. The immigrant workers are very often harassed by police and Labour Department officials and tend to be concentrated in sectors of industry, be they technologically backward or advanced, where conditions are unacceptable to native metropolitan workers and where employment itself is significantly less secure than it is for established workers. In such circumstances the immigrant workers become more isolated and can rely less and less on trade union protection. There is a significant body of evidence now available for the major European industrial societies which suggests that in any important industrial dispute in which immigrant rights alone are at stake the immigrant worker is forced to fight without the support of his native working-class 'comrade'.

The situation in industry is reproduced, if anything in a more severe form, in the matter of gaining the benefit of social welfare rights. Crucial here is the question of housing. European working-class parties have won for their members the right to cheap housing either by way of central or local government provision of rented housing or through the work of housing associations and co-operatives. These rights however are in short supply and when priorities are being calculated it is always the immigrant who is at the back of the queue. He will live in employers' or government camps, or, where these do not exist, will adapt whatever is the least desired form of housing to his own use. Thus there emerge the bidonvilles of Paris and the so-called twilight zones of British cities. And, given the segregation of immigrant workers in these areas, a whole range of further deprivations follows.

Whether this situation is to be thought of as a more or less conscious tactic of the employers and their parties to weaken working-class solidarity or whether it results merely from the ambivalence of native workers to certain occupational or other positions, the consequence is the same. One of the permanent features of these industrial societies is that they develop an underclass (see Baran and Sweezy, 1966), and the characteristic of this underclass position is that it does not share in any incorporation such as the 'end of ideology' theorists suggest. Immigrants share this underclass position with other contingents of the new poor, but the fact remains that the underclass itself remains a structurally distinct element from the established native working class. What the long-term dynamic consequences of the existence of this class are likely to be is not clear. Since its existence is a standing rebuke to the parties and ideologies of the working class, it may be expected that in due course organizational forms of a political alliance will be worked out. But this is by no means the only possibility, and the articulation of the needs of this class may take any one of a variety of forms ranging from community action programmes of a social-work type to urban riot.

More specific than this general notion of an underclass position is that of a pariah group. This is a group of outsiders who are called upon to perform some task which is either contrary to the values of or beneath the dignity of the host society, even though it is essential to the functioning of that society. The notion of the alien moneylender, or of the assignment of trading functions to outsiders and non-citizens is familiar enough and is, of course, exemplified, above all, in position of the Jews in European society. In this case the outsider performs commercial functions which are quite essential to the operation of important social mechanisms and are yet at odds with the values of the society. Another and less familiar pariah role is that of the slum landlord, a role which becomes more important as the notion of the values of the welfare state gains acceptance.

Apart from all these roles, which might be thought of as contrary to the values of, rather than beneath the dignity of, members of a host society, there are other roles like the removal of sewage buckets which are clearly unclean roles and which in many backward societies may be performed by outsiders. But this same notion of a job being too dirty or too degrading gains in importance in a society where general standards of the cleanliness and the ease of work rise. Domestic service comes increasingly to be performed by outsiders, so do many tasks connected with cleaning and catering, and so, too, do the dirtiest and most arduous industrial jobs.

Of course pariah roles exist in colonial as well as in metropolitan societies. What we would suggest, however, is that, in the colonial case, the system of occupational distribution tends as a whole to be organized in a caste or estate form, as we have indicated above. In the case of the metropolitan society, the roles concerned have a special character due to the invidious comparison between them and the incorporated roles which are covered by the welfare and trade union bargain.

Another feature of advanced industrial societies is their inherent economic, political and psychological instability. As a result of this it becomes functionally necessary from a sociological as well as a psychological point of view that there should be some individual or group who can be blamed for the economic crises, political tensions and anomie which are experienced from time to time by large sections of the population. In the simplest case one has the explanation of economic crisis as being due to the existence and activities of a small group of individuals or a minority group. The quotation which we made from a leading British trade unionist at the beginning of chapter 9 may serve to exemplify this (see p. 104). But this classic type of scapegoating with which social science became familiar in the 1930s in Europe may not be the only type. It could well be that the experience of social dislocation resulting from the loss of empire or the general industrial dislocation caused by technological advance might also lead to scapegoating. Such scapegoating will quite commonly apply to groups performing a pariah role, or to the whole underclass which we mentioned above, or to any group of distinguishable outsiders, or, for that matter, insiders. None the less, scapegoating is a separate process and a scapegoat group may be structurally distinct from any of the other groups mentioned.

One other possibility should be mentioned before we leave the question of the underlying social structures which may be defined in the public mind as racial. This is the emergence in the advanced industrial societies of a new type of revolution, namely a revolution of the colonial peoples and of their representatives in the metropolitan underclass and other minority groups against the rules of the whole imperial society. What the long-term destiny of this revolution is, whether it will be a race war, a movement based upon the concept of black power, the revolt of the underclass, or something which can be brought under the wing of the Marxist-Leninist revolution, remains uncertain. We return to discussing some of these possibilities in our final chapter. What we have to note here is that this revolution and some of its correlated phenomena, like the loss of faith in the goals of the advanced societies by their most educated members, are structural facts with considerable dynamic potential and that race relations situations may emerge from such structures.

Group exploitation and oppression and ascriptive role allocation

Although many, or perhaps all, of the structures mentioned above may be associated with racialism and racism, they need not necessarily be so. They are of themselves simply social structures marked by harsh exploitation and oppression and severe conflict, in which the participants may be defined simply in terms of the roles they occupy. It is necessary therefore to indicate what additional features are necessary to turn such situations into race relations situations.

One simple alternative here is to say that a situation becomes a race relations one if inequality is defined in terms of racist theory. This, however, is inadequate in that quite often the practice of racialism may exist without its theoretical correlate of racist theory, and the mere fact of the existence of racist theories would not of itself make a race relations situation were it not related to specific types of structures. What we are concerned with here is what is sometimes called institutionalized racialism, although we would point out that this phenomenon is not confined to cases in which originally there was a racist doctrine which led to the setting up of institutions which made the public confession of the doctrine unnecessary. We wish to emphasize that in some cases discrimination, exploitation or oppression might be suffered by a group without there being any explicit theory for their being subject to this fate.

What is important about the social structures which we wish to differentiate from the larger class of structures involving exploitation, oppression and conflict, which we have discussed, is that there should be a closure on mobility from one group to another, so that if a man has certain characteristics, he is thought to be incapable of altering those characteristics, and, therefore, incapable of altering his situation in life. In the language of structural-functional theory or the theory of social systems, this would mean that roles were allocated ascriptively.

The characteristic which is most useful as a basis for ascription or as a means of closing the possibility of mobility is that of physical appearance and of skin colour in particular. But to say this is by no means to say that differences of skin colour must always produce a closure of mobility or that they only are the signs which may perform this function. Religious and cultural differences might equally serve as a means of classifying men into groups so that they can receive differential treatment. Thus the difference between Hindu and Muslim, between Jew and Arab or between Irish Catholic and Irish Protestant clearly do not rest upon differences of physical appearance, for the two groups may be physically indistinguishable. What is the case, however, is that cultural and religious differences involved here are sufficiently visible for them to act as criteria for role ascription and to facilitate, not simply individual exploitation of man by man, but the more important structural fact of the exploitation of group by group.

The question may be raised about religious and cultural divisions in a community whether they do not exist as things in themselves as basic and independent sources of conflict regardless of other structural factors. This is sometimes said in the case of the six counties of Northern Ireland where many of the workers are Protestant, and, *prima facie*, this cannot be classified as a situation in which Protestants are engaged in the economic exploitation of Catholics. The weakness of this argument, however, is its oversimplified and ahistorical view of structures of economic exploitation and political oppression, for Northern Ireland is a colony of settlement, sharing many features of the situation in South Africa or Algeria, in both of which countries many settlers were workers.

While we do want to make the sociological point that any adequate race relations theory must draw attention to that which is in common between situations of colour conflict and situations in which differences are primarily cultural, we do not, however, want to draw attention away from the fact that the prime locus of race relations problems, especially in the English-speaking world, is that which concerns the relations between black and white. It is this factor more than any other which has facilitated the establishment of situations of group exploitation and distorted the simple pattern of class conflict or stratification which might be expected in terms of Marxist or functionalist theory.

The role of racist theory

Group conflict, particularly in situations of war and conquest, may have little in the way of intellectually argued theory to support it. Ultimately it is possible with little more in the way of verbal expression than a hostile grunt. But sustained relations of opposition, exploitation or oppression, particularly in the absence of warfare, require some measure of codification and rationalization. What we wish to assert here is that, while in the advanced industrial countries this codification and rationalization has been effected on a systematic and scientific basis, there are many other possibilities, both parallel to scientific justifications, prior to them, and in different social positions. Thus one can imagine a society which lays more emphasis upon cultural and historical theories than it does on scientific ones, even amongst the more technologically advanced countries. One knows that before the figures of Newton and Darwin came to play the dominant role which they have done in the last few centuries men turned to other sorts of theories such as theological ones to rationalize their social behaviour. And one knows that, while intellectuals may debate ultimate and systematic justifications, the man in the street has little recourse to theories other than those which are implicit in folk-wisdom, in proverbs, in jokes, or in popular newspapers or political ideologies. What we need therefore, as a part of the systematic study of the sociology of race relations, is an adequate sociology of knowledge, both in the sense of one which classifies the kinds of belief systems, knowledge and theories which are to be found in a culture, and one which shows how the more systematic theories are connected through social mechanisms with less sophisticated ones.

There is no space here to develop this sociology of knowledge here in a thorough and systematic way. A general outline of the problem may, however, be stated. If we start with the unsophisticated individual who finds himself in a situation of group opposition, his day to day rationalizations of his conduct may be found in such things as radio programmes, popular newspaper articles or even in the jokes which form part of the entertainment in a working-men's club. Some of these rationalizations arise spontaneously as means of bridging the gap between more generally accepted ideals and practice, as Myrdal has pointed out in an important essay (1958, ch. 5). Some are informed by theories which are held and argued verbally and in print at more sophisticated levels. There is undoubtedly a two-way relationship between the more and the less sophisticated rationalizations here. To some extent those who write in the popular newspapers are themselves informed by ideas from the more serious ones. On the other hand they also reflect that which their readers are saying. Not without interest, though, is the permissive function of public writing and utterance. There are many theories and rationalizations which are entertained guiltily and secretly in local areas, but when these are given expression in the respectable newspapers or television or radio broadcasts, or, when they are openly stated by populist politicians, they 'come out into the open' and become part of the public belief system. Thus it is important that in the late 1960s in Britain certain leading politicians began openly to retail stories of hostile behaviour directed against immigrants and to justify that behaviour. Again it has been known for some time that there was a groundswell of jokes with implications damaging to black people going on in working-men's clubs. The elevation of this type of joke to a top place in television entertainment radically alters the situation for the nation at large.

Very few men, of course, ever proceed to any complete and systematic discussion of their beliefs on either scientific, social scientific, theological, cultural or historical grounds. There is, however, an intermediate range of intellectual roles in a complex modern society, which are perhaps best exemplified in the leading articles of the quality newspapers and in the formulations of orthodox political parties. In many ways, the implicit science, social science, theology, or other such theory which informs these statements, is unsatisfactory from the point of view of the specialized intellectual, but it is practically far more important. Again there is a two-way process, whereby the journalist or politician is in some measure affected by his higher education but also reflects the view of the world which has come up to him from the less sophisticated social levels.

But finally we have to notice that the systematic statements of the intellectuals are themselves affected by the two-way process. If one looks for instance at the narrow question of the emergence and re-emergence of racial theories in biology one finds that this is only very loosely related to new scientific discovery or new forms of systematic reasoning. The notion that some men are intellectually inferior to others because of genetic factors, which are unalterable, is one which has recurred several times in European history, but most notably amongst British intellectuals in the mid-nineteenth century, when they were responding to the fact of empire and in Germany as a justification for anti-semitic policies.

In relatively recent times, genetic theories of racial inferiority have gone out of favour. They have been condemned as authoritatively as any intellectual theory could have been, by four expert statements by UNESCO. As a result the theories used to justify racial discrimination and exploitation have turned to other fields. This does not mean that racism and racialism do not exist. The structures of exploitation and discrimination are there. Groups are clearly enough distinguished for discrimination and exploitation to take a group form, and the unequal treatment which is meted out still receives its justification at an unsophisticated as well as a sophisticated level. Thus we dispute Michael Banton's contention that, because two leading British politicians did not use genetic arguments in their speeches during the 1960s, it was wrong to discuss what they said in the context of the theory of racism (Zubaida, 1970). True, if the term racism is confined by definition to the use of genetic theories, then Banton's point would have some validity. But this would trivialize the sociology of race relations almost beyond belief. What we are asserting here is that the problem of racist theory and racist ideas can only be fully formulated in terms of the relation which holds between ideas and social structures.

With this said, however, it should be noted that the unpopularity of racist theories in the field of genetics is no longer as complete as it was. Of recent times the work of the Harvard educationist Jensen has received an enormous amount of publicity from politicians, publishers and scientists, and in a general climate of biological opinion which has revived a number of primitive Darwinist notions, it is to be expected that theories at the less sophisticated level will lean more heavily than they have respectably been able to in recent years on straight biological theories of racial difference (see Eysenck, 1971; Richardson, Spears and Richards, 1972).

Of course biological theories are extremely useful as justifications of racial inequality. For they have to a supreme degree the quality of deterministic theories. There are of course other such theories, e.g. the nationalistic form of Calvinism professed by the Afrikaner population of South Africa and various sorts of sociological and cultural theories which one would predict are likely to have increasing currency in the ensuing few decades. But none of these can ever carry the same conviction with the layman who is more likely to believe in a deterministic theory if it has a tangible chemical base.

The question may now be put as to how those who wish to act against racism and racialism can best proceed. If the analysis which is presented here is correct, a number of things may be said. First there *is* some point in attacking theories as such, because even if we were to take the extreme view that such theories are mere epiphenomena thrown up by existing practice, we should still be able to admit that, once such theories exist, they 'take on a life of their own', they escalate racial conflict and, by the intellectual permissions they give, they enable racialists to act with greater confidence. It is also important within this to guard especially against the attempted resurrection of the biology of the 1970s so long as we recognize that a biology purged of racism is likely to increase the pressure for racist theories elsewhere.

On the level of practice and structure, however, there are more fundamental things to be done. If we can eliminate the closure of mobility and ascriptive role allocation we should do much to undermine racism as well as racialism, and, of course, if it were possible to eliminate the kinds of structure based upon inequality and exploitation which get put on to a group basis and foster racialism, we should be making the most fundamental of all attacks on racialism. It should be noted that in Britain in the 1960s racial discrimination was firmly institutionalized and that then the liberal conscience asserted itself to attack the simpler forms of racist theory. Clearly the sociology of race relations has much to offer those who want to pursue the fight against racialism and racism on more fundamental levels.

Briefly to recapitulate, our theory of race relations is this. First, race relations problems are primarily linked with the phenomenon of colonialism. Colonialism produces, in colonial and metropolitan countries alike, certain situations of a particularly harsh and exploitative kind, usually marked by a degree of physical compulsion which is unusual in the liberal-democratic and social democratic countries. Secondly, within this, racialism is marked by a closure on mobility and the allocation of roles according to the presence or absence of some external sign thought to be unalterable. Thirdly, such situations throw up, and are subsequently sustained by, racist theories of a more or less systematic, more or less sophisticated, but always implicitly deterministic kind.

No doubt there is much that can be said to round out and perfect this theory. But it is clear that it is a comprehensive theory whereas most of what passes as theory in the sociology of race relations is not. What is left out almost universally is any discussion of the political element. And, if this is true of academic sociology, it is all the more true of the policy-oriented study of race relations which has dominated the field as we have already shown in chapter 15. What we have suggested here is one way of getting beyond both the trivializations of academic sociology and the political evasions of policy-oriented research.

Appendix

Letter to Professor M. Banton

Dear Michael,
The problem which I have had as I have turned more and more to reading empirical accounts of race relations situations by sociologists, historians and others, is that I have a sense of total uncertainty as to what they are talking about. I don't think there is any real hope of posing problems for empirical investigation until we have more agreement than there is on theory and on terminology. Even a book like your own [Banton, 1968] based as it was on such very wide and deep reading of empirical material drawn from many countries, suffers from this. The general theoretical statement made in chapters 4 and 5 simply does not pose the kinds of questions which the empirical material could

throw light on, and the result is that in some chapters (particularly in those on British Africa) you either raise new theoretical issues *ad hoc* or leave out whole areas of discussion. (To say this does not mean that I do not think highly of the book, simply that I look forward to the day when we can all make a more systematic approach to the material and feel sure that the crucial questions are being discussed.)

I had not thought of role theory and the stranger hypothesis as occurring only in your own work. In fact I was first impressed by their inadequacy in dealing with British race relations problems when I read Sheila Patterson's work. What I did want to emphasize is the point which is implicit in what you call Little's 'class-colour-consciousness hypothesis'. This opens up a whole area of discussion, though, which has hardly begun. If we say that Englishmen think of coloured people as belonging to the lowest social class, what do we mean by class in this context? To make such a statement do we not have to have some model of an imperial and colonial stratification system to supplement that which we use in analysing British society. But then we also have to face the question whether or not terms like class and stratification are not better abandoned in favour of others derived from the theory of pluralism. Clearly M. G. Smith has raised these issues more than anyone else, but what we need, and what I myself am concerned to do, is to carry on the argument which he started. In the meanwhile I think that there is danger of over-simplifying the study of race relations, even in metropolitan societies, if we use concepts as empty as 'social distance', 'stranger', etc. I am glad, however, to have your own references to places in which you suggest that these concepts have restricted use.

Coming back to wider theoretical and methodological issues, I think that we probably have different views of the degree to which social systems have a determinate existence. Let me take an example from your book [*op. cit.*]. On page 222 you say 'Southern Rhodesia provides the clearest example among the British African colonies of a society in which there was a definite colour line from the beginning'. Clearly you don't mean 'from the beginning' in the sense in which the book of Genesis speaks of 'the beginning', but it has the same eternal ring. What I would want to emphasize here is that the definite colour line to which you refer was imposed by military force, and that force, together with attempts to obtain some kind of normative compliance, is central to this system, as to all others in colonial situations. In other words I am saying that a sociologist should never merely ask 'What system operates here?' without referring to the balance of power which underlies it. To fail to do this too often results in the representation of ruling-class ideologies as though they were simply unquestionable social facts.

My own position here is very close to that of Myrdal (1962) as I quote him on page 6 of *Race, Community and Conflict*. I see all social systems to some degree, but colonial social systems in particular, as the outcome of a struggle to impose an overall social order by a number of different groups, with differing goals, and, as Myrdal says, (p. 1056) 'differing value premises'. It is in this context that I believe we should look at questions about the function of beliefs. I don't see this as a simple empirical question, or as one which can be settled simply, by looking at a particular range of facts, and saying, 'this belief system has a function (or doesn't have a function) here'. What we are dealing with very often is a situation in which ruling groups with varying degrees of success are trying to ensure compliance with a particular order of production, of political rights and of stratification through the use of coercive, utilitarian and normative sanctions. Against this background we have to judge the ways in which the beliefs which men are found to profess actually fit. I would have thought that although, of course, the total range of beliefs professed is confused and equivocal, there could be little doubt that beliefs about the biological inferiority of the negro existed in the aftermath of slavery, and that they could be shown not merely to 'fit', with the attempt to maintain the political subordination of the ex-slaves, but that they were actually used in this way. I am really puzzled to know what you mean when you say that the evidence on the function of racist beliefs is equivocal.

Very important in this respect is the distinction which Weber makes between the two levels of sociological explanation. When we are talking about the sociology of knowledge, clearly one of the first things that we have to do is to consider relationships of meaning and to give meaningfully adequate explanations. Thus it is important to consider whether or not there is some compatibility or incompatibility of meaning between religious doctrines of various kinds and racist theories. With this done, it is possible to go on to consider whether or not there is the expected empirical association between compatible beliefs. It is, however, the duty of sociologists, as Weber has said, to try to give explanations on both levels.

For my part I do not think that any final answer has been given to the problems of the relationship between Protestantism of various kinds and Catholicism, on the one hand, and policies of racialism, and theories of racism, on the other. I would certainly say, however, that to merely refer to the suggestion that there might be a relationship to be explored both on the meaningful and the causal level between Protestant religion and racism (or negatively an inhospitability on the part of Catholicism towards racism) as a 'chestnut' suggests that you have access to some piece of empirical evidence far more decisive than any that I have seen. My reading leads me to the view that within a framework of theological and political thinking which made the incorporation of colonial peoples into the same society as settlers possible, Catholicism also permitted the expression of a considerable amount of hostile sentiment towards, and the practice of very intense exploitation of, colonial peoples.

One of the things which I notice about this particular debate is that it is very hard to free it from ideology. There are American liberals and Hispanophiles (if that is the proper word), who are determined to show that the North American pattern is as bad as could be by comparison with that in Latin America. And there are those who wish to defend the record of the North by arguing that the Latin American picture is just as bad. I know you don't want to do this, and I am sure you would simply agree that this ideological element has entered the debate too much. I wonder though whether your all too ready dismissal of what I suggested about Catholicism and racism has not been affected by the weight of ideologically loaded scholarly opinion.

Now, finally, may I return to your paper to the British Sociological Association [see Zubaida, 1970], and the reasons why I disagreed with it far more sharply than anything else that you have written. I have some difficulty here, because, if I understand you aright, when you replied to me at the conference you said that it was a paper about the history of ideas and not a sociological paper at all. In what I say below, however, I am assuming that you did intend it in part at least as a contribution to the sociology of race relations.

The important question which the paper poses is that of the relationship between beliefs and social structure. I should have thought that it was shared ground amongst sociologists that the beliefs which men professed about the world were in part affected by the social structures in which they played parts and by the interests generated by those structures. To say this is by no means to say that values and beliefs do not affect the actions which men pursue and the structures which they create (even this states the problem only on a superficial level. I have made a much more complex statement in my new book) [Rex, 1970]. What one clearly cannot do, however, without committing oneself to the crudest kind of idealism, is to deny that beliefs professed have any relationship to interests.

You seem to me to do this and, indeed, to vilify all of those of your colleagues who disagree with you, by lumping them together as Marxists. For my part I find this kind of closure of the discussion by name-calling very irritating. I am a sociologist, and I think I am not merely entitled but required by my profession to consider the question of whether or not the kind of expressions which emanate from Enoch Powell do not have the same kind of relationship to social structures as did the theories of Goebbels, whatever Powell's intentions. I have in my book attempted to define the field of race relations studies and as I define it I would certainly see the speeches of Powell as material worthy of analysis. When you, on the other hand, merely dispose of the problem by saying that to call Powell a racist is exorcism you misrepresent what those of us who are concerned with the sociology of race relations in Britain are doing.

Briefly, the position which I will outline in my book is as follows: In attempting to differentiate the field of race relations studies from other fields of sociological enquiry we need to look at several different levels. Firstly there is the level of social structure. Secondly there is the level of beliefs and ideas and theories. Thirdly, there is an intermediate level where principles, which may or may not be explicitly stated, operate in practice.

So far as the first of these levels is concerned, I think that the range of structures which we have to consider is wider than can be contained under the term stratification, both because of the factor of cultural pluralism and because of the fact of military conquest. The kind of productive institutions which are set up after conquest are of especial importance, but we have to be concerned with the images of society-as-a-whole which men have as well as of the narrower institutions of production. Any form of 'economic determinism' in this area of investigation would be misleading, if it led those who believed in it to neglect the extent to which coercive sanctions and some sort of proposed normative order affected the social structure, along with strictly economic and market factors.

The structures which are of interest to the student of race relations are always marked by a relative absence of consensus. This is always a feature of colonial societies as well as of many post-colonial situations and of minority situations in metropolitan countries. But conflictful social structures of this kind are a necessary, without being a sufficient, means for differentiating the field of race relations studies.

The second level of analysis narrows the field of interest further. I argue that it is a mark of race relations situations that men are treated as groups and that roles or rights and duties are allocated ascriptively. Such classificatory and ascriptive orientations of men to each other are commonly justified by reference to theories on one level or another but need not be. I argue this feature of inter-group relations serves to narrow our field of interest down further and that it is a feature which is necessary to all race relations situations.

The sufficient differentiation of race relations studies from other sociological studies, however, requires not merely the two features mentioned, but also a third, namely the presence of beliefs of certain kinds. I do not believe that it is useful to confine the kinds of beliefs which should be present to justify our including a particular problem under the heading of race relations to purely biological or genetic theories. Nor do I believe that we should say that race relations problems do not exist, unless there is a highly articulate and self-consistent set of beliefs. We are dealing with a race relations situation wherever there are groups rather than merely individuals in conflict, and where one or more of those groups holds beliefs about the other of a deterministic kind (i.e. believes that a member of the other group could not be other than he is).

For purposes of analysis it is useful to separate three levels in this way. As I point out, however, there really is no such thing as a structure of social relations which does not assume the existence of beliefs which one party has of another, just as there is no such thing as a system of beliefs totally divorced from social structure.

I hope that when you see my book you will see that, whatever else, the theoretical perspective which I have is not to be dismissed as being akin to that of Oliver Cromwell Cox. I know that it is not your perspective and that you see the field of race relations studies as being more narrowly defined than I do. For my part I would leave the editorial commentary to the editor, but if I were commenting on my own paper I would say that it raises the question of whether it is possible to define a field of race relations studies at all, once it is not defined in terms of the presence of biological theories. What I believe I have tried to do, is to show that one can say that there is such a field, and that it cannot be reduced to the study of social stratification. Lockwood also appears to be making a contribution towards this discussion [see Zubaida, 1970].

With best wishes, etc.

18　Nature versus nurture: a sociologist's view of the significance of the recently revived debate

Quantitative methods in the social sciences have much to commend them. If used sensitively they ensure that the observations of any one scientist or observer may be replicated by another. The great danger, however, is that, if they are used insensitively, the social scientist may seek to quantify for the sake of quantification, and, if the issue under discussion is not capable of easy quantification, it is likely to be put on one side and replaced by another. Too often, quantitative social scientists give us exact but irrelevant answers to the questions we are asking.

When we speak of 'sensitivity' on the part of a social scientiest we refer to his awareness of the relationship of that which he measures to a body of theory and through this body of theory, to other measurable concepts. We also refer to the sensitivity of the social scientist to the meaning of human action for the participant actors whom he observes. In a word, it is a requirement of sensitive social science that the social scientist should be aware of the fundamental epistemological problem of the human studies, namely that, while natural science is an activity in which scientists have concepts about things, in the human sciences the scientist has concepts about things which themselves have concepts.

These observations have led in recent times to a revolution in the social sciences. It has been argued for instance in relation to criminal statistics that official statistics have not recorded the quantitative occurrences of an act of a certain kind, but rather the numbers of those acts which other people such as the officers of the law categorize in a certain way. Similarly, most demographic and ecological statistics, when they are probed, turn out to refer, not to simple attributes of persons and their behaviour, but rather to the way in which people are classified in practical situations.

The ideology of empiricism and operationalism seeks to avoid these problems by arguing that, since there are no 'essences' in the world to be measured, the measurable variables are definable simply in terms of the tests which are used to make a measurement. Thus, for example, a foot is that which is measured by a foot rule, intelligence is that which is measured by intelligence tests, and so on.

What is called psychometrics is perhaps the least and the brashest of the empirical human studies. On the matters just discussed, it seeks to get the best of both worlds. It claims, on the one hand, that it makes no assertions about essential intelligence and that what it refers to is simply measured intelligence. On the other hand, however, it pretends that this measured intelligence has no reference to practical, social and political contexts.

The first point which we need to make here, in asserting the need for a genuine sociology and psychology which is theoretically founded and aware that it is dealing with meaningful action, is that when the psychometrician pretends that what he says about measurable difference has no practical significance, but simply refers to facts which may be classified as true or false, the intelligence tests to which he refers, are as a matter of empirical fact, used in practical contexts to assign children to different forms of education, to choose between one individual and another in job placement and generally to set one man above another. It is, therefore, not possible for a psychometrician to say 'I am merely facing up to a scientific truth, albeit an uncomfortable one'. What he does when he rates individuals or groups of individuals on a scale of measured intelligence is to say and to predict that one group of individuals rather than another should have privileges. It is of little use, therefore, that a writer like Eysenck should protest that there is a total disjunction between his scientific observations and his moral views (Eysenck, 1971). Scientific observations have political implications and the scientist should beware that that which he reveals may contribute to, or ease, human suffering. This, of course, is not in itself an argument for not facing up to facts. It is, however, an argument for the human sciences to beware of jumping to rash conclusions on the basis of simplistic scales of measurement.

If we look at the popularizations of Jensen's ideas on racial differences (1969), we find no such circumspection. The problem, not merely of the nature of intelligence, but of its causes and correlates, is oversimplified to an almost incredible degree. According to Eysenck, for example, the issue is between 'inter-actionists' like himself, who believe that both nature and nurture contribute to test intelligence, and those whom he calls environmentalists who are supposed to hold that intellectual capacity is solely the product of a few easily measurable environmental factors, such as amount of income, type of residential neighbourhood and years of schooling. All that is necessary to disprove the 'environmental hypothesis', and thence, by implication, to prove its opposite, is to show that when these few environmental factors are held constant, observed differences between individuals or between groups are maintained.

The reply to this rests first of all upon the recognition that intellectual arguments which go on between social scientists on the matter of nature and nurture do not involve one side which is simply environmentalist in Eysenck's usage of that term. Those whom he specifically attacks, namely UNESCO, and a distinguished line of social scientists, who have worked since 1945 to expose fallacies of racism, have always recognized that there is ground for supposing that there is a genetic component in measured intelligence. Moreover, they have also recognized that the processes of selection and isolation do lead to groups of men having different gene pools. What they have disputed is that these differences are so great that manipulation of the environment is not capable of fundamentally altering them.

More important than this, however, is the naïve belief that environment can be reduced to an index based upon the few quantitative variables. Such as view naturally commends itself to those who refuse to accept that the relationship between the performance of acts and the events which precede and follow them may be meaningful rather than simply casual. But even if we take the assertions of psychometric empiricism in their own terms, it seems clear that the argument that any measured differences not assignable to size of income, type of residence or length of schooling, must be due to genetic factors, shows a remarkable over-eagerness to jump to conclusions. When such a method is applied to the comparison of negro and white intelligence in the United States, there are obviously a great many other variables which should be controlled. They cannot all be summed up under something as simple as 'motivation' (one of the factors discussed by Jensen and Eysenck). It matters that the negro group is continually exposed to a picture of American society in which, if it is not subject to racial exploitation, it is at least the object of benevolent paternalism. Moreover, if one looks at length of schooling, it is clear that negroes studying American history in which the heroes are all white, are bound to respond differently to their education from their white school-fellows.

Curiously, Eysenck asks that those who oppose him should offer 'experimental' evidence. Fortunately, neither he nor his opponents are able to undertake such experiments. Since, however, the crucial variable is the difference between white and negro history and the fact that negro history involves the fact of slavery, experiment would mean subjecting the group of negroes to white experience over several hundred years or subjecting a group of whites to negro experience. The empirical study which holds constant size of income, type of neighbourhood and length of schooling in the United States of the present day, therefore, should in theory be supplemented by an experiment in which the peoples of Africa conquer, capture and enslave some millions of European and American whites, under conditions in which a very large proportion of the white population dies, in which the white culture is systematically destroyed, and in which, finally, a group of emancipated whites living in 'good neighbourhoods' are then compared to their negro masters. It is not sufficient to brush aside this assertion, merely by saying that we should not draw conclusions from 'hypothetical experiments'. The fact is that the differences in the history of negroes and whites are a factor of immense significance, and that any statistical reasoning which leaves them out can reach no conclusions of any value whatever.

One of the difficulties which the empiricist has, of course, is that he deals only in the external attributes of individuals. He cannot concede that intelligence or any other attribute of the individual may be understandable in terms of the meaning of an individual's environment to him. What has happened to the negro over several hundred years is a process of Sambofication, as Elkins (1963) amongst others has pointed out, and the nearest comparable process, of which we had to have evidence, is what happened to the inmates of German concentration camps. Similarly, the environment of a young educated American negro today is apprehended as one in which he seeks politically for a new identity, and in which white education and the white police are equally agencies which undermine that identity.

This is only one aspect of the meaningful environment of minority groups in the United States. What is necessary before we can draw conclusions about the performance of one group or another is that we should understand, on a meaningful level, the type of relationship which a minority group has to American society. Thus, for example, one cannot regard the relationship of negroes, the descendants of slaves, to that society as qualitatively the same as that of American Indians, sidetracked from absorption by their life on reservations, or Oriental immigrants who might be descended from indentured labourers, and who are very often engaged in one or other minor commercial occupation. Any acquaintance at all with the literature on the sociology of plural societies makes it clear that, given the very different relationships to a social system which minorities might have, it is quite meaningless to compare them as though the only environmental differences between them are those of socio-economic status.

It should, of course, be noticed that Jensen and his supporters do not claim that they have reached final conclusions. At best they say that it is important that certain hypotheses should still be regarded as open to test. None the less, the mere assertion that these hypotheses are important in a scientific sense is taken by many to mean that the notion that there are genetically based differences in intelligence between the races is no longer simply a notion of racists. A view of racial inequality is then revived which common in the early nineteen-thirties, but which was discredited in democratic countries after the defeat of Hitler. The main problem which we have to face then is one in the sociology of knowledge as it affects race relations. What difference does it make to our total political situation that scientists appear to be unconvinced that racial differences in intelligence are not innate?

In one sense it may be argued that this fact is not particularly important. After all, there have been long periods of history in which nations and other groups have exploited each other without seeking any scientific validation for their views. Moreover, it is true, particularly since 1945, that very few politicians indeed have claimed that discrimination is justifiable because of inherited differences in intelligence. None the less, what we shall argue here is that, given our culture and the set of beliefs in that culture about the nature of science, the basing of racial inequality on a scientific proof of differences in intelligence, makes that inequality far more permanent and durable than it otherwise would be.

At the lowest level, individuals find themselves in competition with or opposed to members of ethnic groups and come to express hostile sentiments towards other groups. Action in these matters usually precedes that of rationalization. It is only as the individual seeks validation and justification for his views amongst his fellows that the process of rationalization begins. Very often the highest level of such rationalization is reached in the sharing of an anecdote about an out-group amongst members of an in-group. Yet the process whereby such low-level rationalizations are achieved connects with rationalizations at a higher level which are provided by the definitions of social reality contained in media-messages, and in the statements of influential local leaders, such as ministers of religion and political leaders.

All individuals finding themselves in new situations seek to arrive at a shared definition of these situations with their fellows. Most of us do not really feel that we know what the world, and particularly the social world, is like until we have corroborated our views by checking them with those of our intimates, but more systematic rationalizations occur when individuals are affected in their definitions of reality by what the newspapers or television programmes have to say. In a quite different and more trivial field than that of race relations for instance it is interesting to notice how the judgement of the followers of the main spectator sports are limited and shaped by the picture of the sporting world which is provided by sports journalists.

The level at which the popular press, radio and television provide rationalizations for action is, of course, itself fairly unsystematic. In the field of race relations, one does not expect to find systematic argument about the nature versus nurtue controversy in the columns of, say, the *News of the World*. What one does expect to find there are anecdotes, yet such anecdotes may be of great importance. To give an example, on the Sunday evening which followed the first of Mr Enoch Powell's speeches on the subject of race, BBC television presented a programme in a story series about a local councillor, in which an outbreak of stomach trouble in the town was traced to an Indian restaurateur who offered his customers cat food instead of fresh meat. Such a programme may be expected to have had the effect of reinforcing one of the best known myths about Asian immigrant communities. The belief referred to here is widely held but its inclusion in a serious BBC programme gives it a kind of legitimacy, which it could not otherwise hope to have.

Those who control the popular mass media may or may not be aware of the extent to which they help to define social reality for their readers. There may, on the one hand, be cases of sheer manipulation of public opinion, but on the other, there will be cases in which the media merely reflect what are known to be popularly held beliefs. In either case, however, popular mass media do have some sociological significance.

Just as the images of reality which result from face-to-face sharing of experiences are influenced and reinforced by the messages of the popular media, however, so these latter are affected by more systematic formulations to be found in other 'more serious' publications. What is said in a loose language of sentiment in the popular papers and programmes is said more systematically and intellectually at a higher level in the quality papers and quality television and radio programmes. Such programmes attempt to deal with problems of current affairs in terms of relatively consistent and coherent sets of beliefs, even though the set of positions which they occupy falls far short of a systematic scientific statement.

On the whole, the quality media have not been entirely useful in promoting racism. They represent the public face of a culture and society and must adhere to a minimal standard of political beliefs from which those which foster racialism tend to be excluded. Such a situation, however, might still change if those occupying positions of authority and moral respect bypass the quality newspapers and other media and lend their support directly to reinforce the racist definitions of social reality which are to be found at the grass roots.

One of the features of most advanced industrial societies is the down-to-earth outspoken politician who is willing to say things which are believed, but which have become taboo in quality discussion. We sometimes say that such politicians produce a gut reaction rather than an intellectual response, but for all that, their political speeches are of the greatest importance in that they raise the level of respect which is to be accorded to racist myths and anecdotes. Neither the quality papers nor the populist politician's utterances, however, have anything like the systematic deterministic nature of scientific statements. Indeed they do not form any kind of coherent theory at all. It is only when they in turn are subject to rationalization that the higher forms of systematic knowledge become related to political action. At this level we find political intellectuals who write books and argue in public places, defending their beliefs in a systematic way. They may argue from a cultural, historical, sociological or religious standpoint, or they may argue from the point of view of science.

While the big taboo on scientific theories of race was maintained between 1945 and 1967, individuals seeking to rationalize racial discrimination would refer to the differences in history and culture between groups, or occasionally to religious-belief systems. In most cases the picture of the world which they were able to draw was not a deterministic one. Man may, after all, change his culture or his religion, even though there have been cases, as in South Africa, where doctrine like that of predestination have been used to suggest that there are immutable differences between groups which are ordained by God. While, however, religious beliefs usually involve some possibility of the individual's transformation through a process of salvation, it is a feature of scientific theories about human nature that they tend to be deterministic. Increasingly, in our culture, we are encouraged to believe that what we can do depends upon scientific possibilities and those scientific possibilities are held to be determinate. Thus, when it is said that negroes are genetically inferior in their intelligence to whites, the differences which exist between them are thought to be entirely immutable. Undoubtedly it is the consciousness of many scientists that this would be the effect of their talking loosely about racial differences which has led them to be very careful and cautious about what they say.

If, then, there is nothing like a conclusive case for the genetic determination of racial differences in intelligence, why is it that at this moment in our history theories which have remained dormant for thirty years, are suddenly revived? The answer to this must surely be that the enunciation of such theories fulfils a political and social need. It may be suggested that it is precisely when there is a gap between theory and practice in matters of race relations that the support of science is sought in order to bridge this gap. Thus, in the United States, the arguments of Jensen have been used against the acceptance of various aspects of poverty programmes. The popularization of his ideas by C. P. Snow and Eysenck may also serve to provide rationalizations for racial inequality in contemporary Britain.

Interestingly enough, these are not the only scientific theories which help to validate racialism and inequality. One interesting phenomenon in our recent scientific history has been the revival of biological explanations of criminality (e.g. the 2-Y chromosome theory). Another is the body of ideas associated with the words ecology, conservation, pollution, etc. In this latter case human political judgement is no longer considered, even as an intervening variable. The ills of the world are simply explained as being due to inexorable scientific laws.

The crux of the sociological argument about racist biological theories, therefore, is this. On the political level, societies may pass through periods in which there is no great need for any kind of theory which emphasizes the differences and incompatibilities between different ethnic or religious or 'racial' groups. In such periods popular maxims and anecdotes will affirm the essential similarities between men, and informed opinion will deplore the political behaviour of the small minority of disturbed persons at home who are 'prejudiced' and of governments abroad which work on a basis of racial supremacy. As strains in such a society develop, however, there is a ground-swell of opinion in which popular maxims and anecdotes guiltily and uneasily spotlight racial differences. Thus in Britain, for example, towards the end of the nineteen-fifties, racist jokes began to be heard in working-men's clubs.

This first guilty snigger of racism however, gained a new significance when leading politicians of both parties began to include hostile references to immigrant minorities in their speeches. Some like the late Lord Carron included ambiguous references to immigrants in the course of general attacks on government policy. Others, like the labour leader Robert Mellish, found themselves drawing attention to the contrast between political ideals and the realities of the situation with which they were forced to deal (at the level of local government).

In the next stage, however, the diagnosis of the problem became more systematic. Mr Enoch Powell, widely recognized as an intellectual in British politics, argued that basic issues were being suppressed, and set out his own arguments as to the way in which the presence of a large proportion of immigrants in the population of British cities must undermine British culture.

Although Mr Powell's speeches produced widespread public support, they neither claimed that immigrants were in any sense inferior or that the differences between them and their British hosts were innate. The effect of world scientific opinion and the work of UNESCO since 1945 was such that responsible politicians were wary of committing themselves to such views. Mr Powell therefore based his case on the inadequacies of official statistics which, he argued, underestimated the number of immigrants, and upon the clear cultural differences between immigrants, particularly Asian immigrants and the British.

The possibility always existed, however, that the immigrant population of Britain would become something of an underclass, deprived of normal welfare and trade union rights, particularly in the sphere of housing and employment. Mr Powell's speeches gave only marginal help in fostering this situation. True, his insistence on the impossibility of assimilation gave some kind of basis to those who wished to discriminate. But the argument was never as watertight as it could have been, had it been based upon a theory of the biological basis of racial differences.

Whether they have intended it or not, the popularizers of Jensen in Great Britain have now fundamentally altered the situation. The politicians who favour discrimination may in future argue not merely that Indians, Pakistanis and West Indians should not be assimilated and given equality of opportunity. They will now point to Eysenck's or Jensen's work and argue that assimilation is impossible and that equality of opportunity can only guarantee that negroes at least will under such circumstances find their own level. There will, of course, be little hesitation about invalidly applying results from tests on American negroes to all blacks in Britain. But in all likelihood it will not be long before American experiments are replicated with Indian, Pakistani and West Indian subjects in Britain. The account of the structure of a society's belief systems which we have given here is, of course, speculative. It is a complex hypothesis about the way in which ideas are related to action and social structure in advanced industrial societies. The validation of such an hypothesis would have to take place through consultation of historical events. To the psychometrician whose approach to this problem would be based on the measurement of prejudiced attitudes and the correlation of these with other measurable attributes, such an hypothesis is too complex to be capable of testing. Unfortunately historical reality is complex and its truth is unlikely to be discovered by the techniques and methodology of dogmatic scientism. The function of such scientism is not to discover the truth but to prove the inevitability of the status quo.

Pluralism, colonial conflict and black revolution

Part IV

19

The plural society in sociological theory

To a very large extent post-war sociological theory has confined itself to dealing with integrated social systems. Thus, for example, functionalism, at least in the form in which Radcliffe-Brown presents it, revives the analogy between society and the organism, while Parsons in his *The Social System* confines his analysis to institutionalized roles, i.e. those roles in which the behaviour of 'ego' and 'alter' is governed by norms which they share, and each has a 'need-disposition' to act in accordance with the other's requirements. In political sociology, too, one finds the notion of balance and consensus concealed behind the question-begging term 'legitimate authority' in terms of which, following Weber, the state is defined.

Against this trend Merton, Coser, and others have, in varying ways, sought to emphasize that social relationships might be less than perfectly institutionalized, and that both at the microcosmic level of particular social relations and at the macrocosmic level of societies, conflict is endemic in social life. The object of this article is to draw attention to the great importance of the study of so-called plural societies as a field in which the validity of some of these theoretical models might be tested and their concepts refined. Far from this being simply one among many specialist fields of study it is a field of crucial and strategic importance for sociological theory. It may well be, also, that a clearer picture of the workings of plural societies might serve to illuminate some of the problems of Western industrial societies better than can be done by the model of an integrated social system.

The work of three contributors to the study of plural societies merits the special attention of sociologists. These are Furnivall, whose historical researches in Indonesia and Burma necessitated the formulation of crude sociological concepts, and who first introduced the term 'plural society'; Malinowski, who is more concerned with the interpenetration of culture-patterns in the culture-contact situation; and finally, Gunnar Myrdal for whom the 'pluralness' of American culture raised problems on a methodological level. Other names like those of Thurnwald (1935) and Westermann (1970) also come to mind, but the concepts used by these three will serve as the framework around which a picture of the workings of plural societies may be built up.

Furnivall was the first to emphasize, and has emphasized more strongly than any other writer, that the sort of society to be observed in Indonesia or Burma was of a different sociological type from any European Society (1948; 1967[1]). The essence of the difference was that in these 'plural societies' people of different ethnic origins do not meet each other except in the market place, where the members of each group must dispose of their goods and services to members of other groups. As a result no common 'social will' or 'social demand' develops. But 'social demand' is an essential fact in the liberal-capitalist West, where, although the laws of individual supply and demand would place no limits on the sorts of labour contract which were permissible, the 'social demand' condemns and outlaws 'sweated labour'.

Thus the plural society is, according to Furnivall, Adam Smith's ideal given literal expression. The social consensus for which Adam Smith made no allowance, but which, as Durkheim pointed out, was essential to laissez-faire societies, is missing in the Asian market-place. The main point about the 'pluralness' of a society, according to this view, lies solely in the fact that it leads to the occurrence of economic or market relations in the raw. The problem then becomes that of trying to discover how such a society can continue to exist, or, if it cannot, in what directions it is likely to change. This is not quite what Parsons calls 'the Hobbesian problem of order', for the basic socio-economic institutions are taken for granted. Rather it is the 'market problem of order', the problem of why life in the market-place is not poor, nasty, solitary, brutish and short, and, if not, why not.

A major point on which Furnivall is unclear in his exposition is whether he sees the absence of social demand to be a feature of relations within each ethnic group or only of relations between groups. On the one hand he does suggest the existence of in-

[1] Furnivall's *Netherlands India* first appeared in 1944, but I refer throughout to the 1967 edition.

group solidarity in each group outside market-hours. On the other, he is very insistent on emphasizing the development of individualistic attitudes in other than market relations. A good example of the latter is the development of certificate-hunting attitudes in the sphere of education, coupled with a lack of interest in government suggestions that the group should receive education along the lines of its own culture. Perhaps the truth is that, once the Western market system has become established, nearly every aspect of an individual's social relations and activities become dependent upon the market situation, and that only domestic and residential community institutions remain relatively unaffected, so that a matter like education tends to be considered in terms of its market value, although something like baptism may be seen in terms of its integration value for the particular group. Unfortunately Furnivall is insufficient of an anthropologist to pursue this sort of question. His major emphasis appears to be upon the effect on the market situation of cultural heterogenity among the participants.

Furnivall's first attempt to answer the question of how a plural society could continue to exist is given in his *Netherlands India* (1967). There he mentions what he calls four 'resolutions' of the plural society which are to be found in the long span of Indonesian history. These appear to be the ways in which intergroup relations might be structured other than by market processes. First, there is the way of caste, by means of which Indonesia's conquerors resolved their race relations problem; second, the rule of law by means of which Raffles sought to reorganize Indonesian society, giving equal access to the same courts but otherwise letting market processes operate; third, nationalism, whose solution of democracy and self-government Furnivall at this time thought impracticable because it would put economic and political power in different hands; and, finally, the Dutch solution of federalism. In his later work *Colonial Policy and Practice* (1948), Furnivall seems to have moved towards accepting the feasibility of the nationalist 'resolution'.

To sum up Furnivall's account of the plural society:

1   He sees such a society as arising as a result of the extension of commerce and trade, so that a market situation of a new type emerges in which those who participate do

not share common values, customs and social institutions, but live for other than economic activities, apart from one another in separate groups.

2   The market society which emerges, therefore, lacks the social buttresses which are normal in Western capitalist society. To a much greater extent than in European markets people will be inclined to pursue their own individual self-interest and to exploit others, especially if the others are from another ethnic group.

3   To avoid a sort of market anarchy some sort of social framework has to be imposed. The four historic systems which have been tried or proposed are those of Caste, The Rule of Law, Nationalist Democracy, and Federalism.

The great merit of Furnivall's theory is that it raises in a sharp form the question of the relation between market systems on the one hand and culture and community on the other. In fact it is in the separation of these two, as much as in the separation of ethnic groups, that the 'pluralness' of Furnivall's models appears to reside. There is no doubt that this is one of the central questions in colonial sociology. The point which Furnivall fails to make sufficiently clearly, however, is the extent to which the market system itself produces new group affiliations and gives new meaning to old ones. Such a conception, emphasizing the conflict of aspirations between natives, settlers and imperial government, is implicit in Furnivall's later book, but its implications for the general theory of the plural society which forms the book's central chapter are not fully worked out. What is needed on the theoretical level to systematize Furnivall's most important insights is an explicit statement, both of the way in which pre-existing cultures are brought into relation through the market, and of the way in which the market, which draws people together into a single social system, also divides them into new dynamically related groupings.[1]

Turning from Furnivall to Malinowski (1945), the most obvious thing which we notice is the absence of any references to

[1] So far as Indonesia is concerned, the historical material from which such theoretical hypotheses could be drawn is very clearly set out in Wertheim's *Indonesian Society in Transition*, The Hague: Van Hoeve, 1956, 2nd ed. 1959.

relations of the market kind. What Malinowski is concerned with is the interpenetration of culture patterns in a situation of culture contact. Undoubtedly Malinowski's failure to emphasize the economic circumstances which lead to culture contact prevents him from giving a clear account of the dynamics of culture change, and is a major weakness of his analysis. Yet on the other hand he has what Furnivall lacks, a lively sense of the way in which culture patterns interpenetrate and conflict. Culture is not merely something carried on in a segregated home after the market closes. It is something in which people are continually engaged and which brings them into contact with other groups both in the market place and elsewhere.

The first and most essential thesis which Malinowski advances is that, in the culture contact situation, institutions come into existence which cannot be attributed to either parent culture, but which are wholly new (Malinowski calls this 'the three column approach' to culture contact). But Malinowski is not very clear as to which institutions belong in his third column. At one point he tells us that mining and plantation enterprise or indirect rule obey laws which cannot be deduced from either culture, but on the very same page he tells us that they are the effective influences of the Western world.

The reason for this confusion appears to be that the dominant culture produces new institutions in the contact situation (Furnivall's market without a social demand is such a new institution born of the contact situation) but that these institutions are not stable because they clash with emergent native patterns. According to this view there would not be only three columns as Malinowski suggests, but five, and their headings would be:

I	2	3	4	5
European domestic patterns	European emergent contact patterns	The out-come of conflict	Native emergent contact patterns	Traditional native patterns

Malinowski himself recognizes that more 'columns' are necessary, but his view of what columns there should be differs from that suggested here in a significant way. He suggests the five headings:

I	2	3	4	5
White influences interests, intentions	Processes of culture contact and change	Surviving forms of tradition	Reconstructed past	New forms of spontaneous native reintegration and reaction

The most striking difference between the second list and the first is that although there are three columns for the native culture and only one for the European in Malinowski's table, it is the European culture which is assigned the determining role. There is no column for native intentions or interests. Natives simply react.

There are a number of reasons for this difference. Malinowski is an anthropologist primarily interested in primitive cultures and the adaptations which they make in the contact situation. Moreover, in the pre-war situation, when colonial nationalism was less obvious a factor, European rather than native intentions determined native culture change. (On this point, however, it may be noted that some other writers of the thirties, notably Westermann, gave far greater recognition to the role which nationalism was likely to play.) A sociologist interested in the total situation of contact would be as much concerned with race relations as with the modification of primitive culture, and, the later he wrote, the more weight he would have to give to the emergent patterns of behaviour of native populations and to the aspirations of colonial nationalism.

We should distinguish here between two different things. One is the discovery of the principles of social and cultural change, in order to predict what is likely to happen next. The other is the giving of practical advice to one or other of the groups engaged in the contact situation. So far as the first is concerned, the problem is to assess the extent to which either of the groups is able, by mobilizing sanctions, to realize its intentions, and, if the outcome of the conflict is seen to be likely to be indecisive, to suggest what sort of compromise will be arrived at. The second problem is merely that of clarifying the picture of the intentions and aspirations of the various parties and suggesting to the one whom one is supporting the most economical way of achieving at least some of its aims.

Malinowski does not clearly distinguish between these two tasks when he puts forward what he calls 'the principle of common measure'. The adoption of this principle means that the anthropologist must 'collate European intentions or policy with the corresponding African institution and assess whether in the process of change the interests of the two sides clash or dovetail (*op. cit.*, p. 272). Giving a specific example he says:

> The principle of common measure declares that only what is effectively useful both to him (i.e. the African) and the European community should be administered to him educationally and that in a form directly compatible with his future functions. (*ibid.*)

If this is thought of as a scientific theory of culture change, or even as advice about how best to co-operate with the trend of history, it has some puzzling features. Why should one not ask of any European activity whether it accords with African intentions and then say that only this should be 'administered' to the European. The puzzle disappears if we recognize that Malinowski is merely offering advice to Europeans on how best their intentions might be realized. Thus Malinowski's principle of common measure was frequently quoted in support of the South African plan for Bantu education which avowedly aimed at the preservation of white supremacy.

These facts, however, should not blind us to the real merit of Malinowski's theory. There is no reason why an anthropologist should not put his findings at the disposal of practical men for the better realization of their purposes. Malinowski did make a real contribution to our understanding of the workings of the culture contact process by recognizing that there were emergent patterns arising in the contact situation different from those of the parent cultures. This is a real advance beyond Furnivall, for whom patterns of culture seem to be somewhat inert and divorced from the rough and tumble of the market-place. But Malinowski fails to give us any theory of change. After having shown a conflict of patterns he passes to giving practical political advice.

This is a very convenient point at which to pass on to a consideration of the work of our third theorist, Gunnar Myrdal

(1958, 1962), for Myrdal's great theoretical contribution to sociology arises out of his consideration of the relation between sociological research and deliberate social change planned by practical politicians.

Myrdal doubts the possibility of achieving complete objectivity in any sociological investigation and prefers to regard objectivity as a goal towards which sociologists must strive. We are so much a part of our culture that it is very difficult indeed to imagine anyone ridding himself of presuppositions of an evaluative kind. But nowhere is this more so than in dealing with racial questions, because race questions immediately raise emotional tensions which make it impossible for us to preserve a value-free attitude. In America, Myrdal suggested that the degree of racial tension was such, and power so firmly in the hands of the whites, that even those who spoke on behalf of the negroes very often tacitly accepted valuations made by the dominant whites.

Some sociologists have attempted to overcome this problem by confining themselves strictly to the facts. Myrdal suggests that the notion of a sociological fact is more complex than those who hold this naïve view suppose. There are no facts without hypotheses, and hypotheses in sociology inevitably involve the assertion of a relationship between some institution, custom, or activity, and someone's purpose. Usually those who claim that they are sticking to the facts have tacitly assumed that the fulfilment of the purposes of a particular party is something necessary and beyond question. In Myrdal's view the purposes or values to which social facts are being related should be explicitly stated by the sociologist. In this way the truly scientific questions can be kept separate from questions of value. Myrdal then goes on to base his own analysis upon the evaluative standpoint that it is desirable that the aims of what he calls the American Creed should be realized.

These are, of course, methodological issues, but they reflect important problems of social organization. There are a number of different evaluative viewpoints for the analysis of American society because American society consists of ethnic and other groups which make conflicting value judgements, or which have conflicting aspirations. This is Malinowski's problem once again, with the extreme columns referring to the domestic culture of the imperial country and the traditional culture of the natives left out.

Here we have simply two patterns emerging in the market and in other race-contact situations of American life. They could each be looked at in terms of their 'functional' value for either group (this is the only sense in which Myrdal is prepared to admit the term 'function'), or in terms of the contribution which they make towards the attainment of any other state of affairs which someone may deem desirable.

But if sociology is to be more than merely a practical technique, it should also deal with the question of how a situation develops if there is no intervention from outside. That is to say that, in addition to saying what must be done to implement this or that set of values, the sociologist should be able to predict what will happen if things go on as they are doing. Clearly Myrdal has this very much in mind, for he writes (1958, pp. 157–8):

> In a scientific treatment of practical aspects of social problems, alternative sets of hypothetical value premises should not be chosen arbitrarily. The principle of selection should be their relevance. Relevance is determined by the interests and ideals of actual persons and groups of persons. There is thus no need of introducing value premises which are not held by anybody.

> Within the circle of relevance so determined a still more narrow circle of significance may be taken to denote such valuations as are held by substantial groups of people or by small groups with substantial social power. Realistic social research on practical problems will have to concentrate its attention on value premises corresponding to valuations which have high social significance. On the other hand it is certainly not necessary to adopt only those valuations which are held by a majority of the population or by a potentially dominant group.

Here it is apparent that Myrdal has attained the same perspective on social change in American society, as we suggested was the logical development of Malinowski's account of culture change in the contact situation. Malinowski does not reach this level of clarity, precisely because he fails to make the value judgements guiding his investigations explicit, concealing them under the so-called 'principle of the common measure'.

It seems clear that, though his subject of investigation was not one of those societies which are commonly thought of as 'plural', Myrdal has made a contribution of the first importance to the analysis of plural societies. In Furnivall, a plural society is regarded as being one in which originally separate cultures remain separate, and so fail to provide a social buttress for the market situation in which people of different ethnic origins meet. In Malinowski, the culture patterns themselves are seen as interpenetrating and conflicting, leading to the emergence of new forms. In Myrdal the interpenetrating and conflicting patterns are not 'culture patterns' in the usual sense of the term, but value patterns made up of sets of valued activities, which further both the interests and the ideals of groups brought together by economic, political and socio-cultural forces. The notion of interests and ideals which develops Malinowski's category of European 'intentions' and the notion of the 'social power' possessed by conflicting groups together provide the dynamic element in Myrdal's theory, which is missing in both the work of Furnivall and that of Malinowski.

In the light of this review of theoretical contributions to the theory of plural societies it becomes possible to suggest a programme in terms of which plural societies might be studied. The following conclusions appear to emerge from our review:

I Malinowski and Furnivall rightly draw our attention to the importance of the culture patterns which existed prior to the contact situation, and Malinowski makes an important distinction between those elements which survive and those which we have to reconstruct as they existed before contact. A study of these patterns is essential to the understanding of plural societies, since there are many important social and cultural features of such societies, which defy explanation simply in terms of the market situation, or in terms of the contact situation. This appears to involve a kind of historical explanation, which functional anthropology commonly avoids, but since there is no integral whole in the market situation in terms of which they can be explained, it seems essential to accept some such historical explanations here.

2   But Malinowski argues that the only reason for the
survival of culture patterns from the past is that they do
serve a function in relation to the existing situation
(*op. cit.*, p. 272). There is not in Malinowski's theory
the same radical divorce that there is in Furnivall's
between the market and culture patterns, and this
should lead to a much greater understanding of the
living elements in a group's culture. Furnivall, on the
other hand, by dissociating market and culture emphasizes the non-normative aspects of the market situation.
What we have is a conflict, not of culture patterns, but
of interests. Finally, Myrdal looks on the conflict
situation in American society as one between differing
ideals as well as between differing interests. These ideals
are to be distinguished from culture patterns and from
interests.

Actually the views of the three theorists on this point
are complementary rather than conflicting. In analysing
the market situation or any other aspect of the contact
situation (it might be through, say, religious missions or
through war) we should have to consider the traditional
patterns, the interests and the ideals and aspirations of
each of the participant groups.

3   Such an analysis would involve the unmasking of
concealed value judgements in the conclusions drawn
about the 'facts' of their society by participating groups.
Usually such conclusions will point to the objective
necessity of the performance of certain duties for the
society as a whole, or to some consensus which is
alleged to prevail among members of different groups.
Of course, if the society has ceased to be a plural
society and has become an integrated one, certain
activities would be necessary to preserve its equilibrium,
and there might well develop something of a consensus.
Myrdal has performed a useful service, however, in
drawing our attention to the fact that very often an
alleged social consensus refers to nothing more than the
consensus of the dominant group. If this is so we should
in the analysis of plural societies also be concerned with

the ideologies (or in Mannheim's terminology 'ideologies and Utopias') or the various groups in terms of which they rationalize their cause.

4   When we have exposed the nature of the conflicts in the contact situation, our next aim should be to explore its dynamics. This is a more complex problem than it would at first appear. Myrdal's view seems to be that the realization of the aspirations of a group depends upon the size and social power of the group and the size and power of the groups deployed against it. But this does not help us to predict what sort of compromise or other outcome might emerge from any particular conflict and any particular balance of power. And, as Myrdal recognizes, account must be taken of the extent to which the aspirations and valuations of a formerly oppressed group might be, in the common usage of the term, 'Utopian'. At the present stage of development of sociology we should be compelled simply to proceed empirically and historically to try to discover the sort of outcome which might be expected to follow a particular type of conflict in a particular situation. Systematic comparative studies in a limited field (say, among plural societies in Africa) might then lead us to formulate limited generalizations of a dynamic kind. We should be able to say that, given the existence of a particular conflict of culture patterns, interests and ideals, and given a certain balance of sanctions, it was to be expected that a particular type of readjustment might occur.

It should perhaps be noted, however, that the mere existence of a conflict of culture, interests, and ideals by no means implies that the structure of the society will change. What may happen is that the nature of the sanctions employed by the dominant group might change. Whereas previously they had employed ideological sanctions supporting their claim to dominance with a 'myth of authority', they might under pressure be compelled to abandon this and to fall back on more obvious physical sanctions. If an opinion might be ventured on this point it is that the true significance of

'passive resistance' movements is that by challenging the
'myth of authority' they expose the conflict situation
and the nature of the dominant group's authority.

To clarify this outline we might consider the task facing the
sociologist of plural societies in contemporary Africa. If we may
assume that some knowledge of traditional cultures has already
been obtained the principal steps for the investigator appear to
be the following:

1 To study the economic interests as well as the expressed
intentions of representative members of each group in a
territory.

2 To study the roles which members of one group assign
to members of the other as a result of having these
interests and intentions and to compare these with the
other group's self-assigned role. Thus, to take one of
Malinowski's examples, we should note any variance
between the sort of education which the European
settler wishes the African to receive, and the sort of
education desired by Africans. Or we might compare
the European's view of the rights of a native workman
with the rights which the workman seeks for himself.

3 To study the power situation, including not only the
more obvious and more important factors such as the
control of weapons and of market-opportunities, but also
the more intangible factors such as control of ideas and
communications, access to governmental authorities, etc.
Which of these less tangible factors were important
would have, of course, to be decided from case to case.
The ultimate test of their importance would be the
possibility of demonstrating their causal importance in a
sequence of social change. But at this earlier empirical
stage the sociologist would be compelled to select for
study those types of power which appeared to him
important on the basis of working hypotheses.

4 To study the society over a period of time in order to
discover what changes it undergoes, both in the relations
and the role-expectations between groups and in the sort
of sanctions employed by either group in the pursuit of
its purposes.

5 To compare different sequences of development in order to discover whether any limited generalization about development could be made.

Such a programme would provide a useful framework for studying contemporary developments in African and other plural societies. It represents an attempt to combine the insights of Furnivall, Malinowski and Myrdal derived from the study of different areas.

We may now return to the question posed at the beginning of this essay: To what extent is the application of this theoretical model limited to colonial situations?

It should be noted that some of its key problems were suggested not by a colonial situation at all, but by Myrdal's study of contemporary America. Could not a similar plan of study be employed in the analysis of British society? For myself I am prepared to accept that the scheme is less applicable in a society like our own than in the colonial situation. Class divisions in Britain are certainly not as far-reaching as are the differences between race groups in the colonies. None the less I think that our analysis of our own society would be enriched by studies which started by assuming conflicting valuations rather than some sort of social consensus. We should always look on the idea of a social consensus with suspicion. Very often it represents nothing more than the ideology of the ruling group. The study of plural societies is important for sociology generally because the explicit recognition that they are plural draws attention to the fact that social systems do exist in which conflict is more obvious than consensus. The model of the plural society, when its workings are more fully understood, is one which is just as essential to the sociologist as is, say, Parsons's model of an integrated social system. The process of social and political change currently going on in Britain's multi-racial colonies provides us with the sort of empirical material against which such a model can be tested and refined.

20

South African society in comparative perspective

It is very difficult to adopt a detached and objective sociological approach to South African society. Indeed, few people attempt to do so. Usually what is discussed is the simple and straightforward question of how far South Africa deviates from the ideal type (using that notion to refer to what is ideal in the common-sense use of the term, as well as to a Weberian methodological device) of a democratic society. Such discussion is, of course, important, but it draws attention away from the primary question which should be faced by students of South African society: what sort of society is it, and to what laws of development is it likely to conform?

When this question is faced, it becomes clear that the conceptual tools which we have for dealing with it are inadequate. What has happened too often is the simple application to South Africa of models derived from the political sociology of European society, without any recognition that this might be a new sociological type which, if it is not compounded of entirely new elements, at least combines the old ones in entirely new ways.

I have not been concerned in my own recent research with the study of South Africa. What has concerned me, however, may be relevant, for I have been trying on a more general international and comparative scale to see what it is which distinguishes race relations situations, structures and problems from other categories of situation, structure and problem in sociology (Rex, 1970). I hope, therefore, that what I am doing will throw light on the problems of a society whose members define their major preoccupations as racial ones.

At the risk of oversimplifying grossly, I would suggest that the major areas of argument in the comparative study of race relations boil down to two. The first concerns the kinds of social structure which are present when there is thought to be a conflict of a racial kind. The second is about the relationship between ideas and theories on the one hand, and social structures on the other.

Under the first heading of structural studies there are two kinds of argument. One is that race relations problems may be reduced to problems of social stratification, albeit of a special kind. The other is that concepts derived from stratification theory do not adequately cover crucial cases of race relations and that a different set of concepts, namely, that derived from the theory of pluralism, has to be introduced.

As a starting-point for the consideration of stratification theory, we may take the functional theory advanced in a simple form by Davis and Moore in 1945 and, in a much more sophisticated form, by Talcott Parsons (1954). What is common to these theories is the view that stratification follows from the existence in a society of a common value system. Given that values are shared, certain qualities and performances of individuals are likely to be rewarded in order to encourage such qualities and performances in the future.

Quite clearly this theory of stratification is not dealing with the same sort of sociological material as Marxist theory is or, when he talks about 'class', the sort of structure Weber (1967) discusses. It will be important, therefore, to return to their type of theory later. What is of immediate importance, however, is that theories of stratification of the functionalist kind break down when applied to black-white relations in the United States.

Lloyd Warner (1936) suggested dealing with the problem by his theory of class and caste. According to this view there was an upper, middle, and lower class in the negro as well as the white community, but a caste-like barrier marked by taboos on inter-racial eating and marrying. As more negroes entered the higher social classes the caste-line would swing round from a horizontal to something nearer a vertical position. But it would not, as Warner saw it, break down. According to this view, it should be noted there is still thought to be a value-system common to whites and negroes in terms of which each community ranks its own members. Its main deviation from functionalist theory is simply its inclusion of the notion of a caste-barrier cutting across the status-stratification system. The exact nature of this caste-barrier remains unclear and its origin is unexplained.

We shall have to deal in a moment with criticisms of the notion of a common value system in colonial societies, but before we do so we must notice the Marxist criticism by O. C. Cox of the notion of the caste-barrier (1959). Cox argues that the barrier between black and white bears no relationship at all to, say, the Indian caste system (which, curiously, Cox represents in a somewhat un-Marxist way as being based upon a shared value system and the consent of the lower castes). Rather it is seen as being simply the line between contending classes brought into being by colonial capitalism. The difficulty with this theory, however, is to explain why the white working-class does not fall on the same side of the line as its negro equivalent. For my own part, I find valuable insights in all three of the types of theory mentioned. I would not, of course, want to accept an over-simplistic functionalist or Marxist view of the nature of the colour-line. What I would suggest, however, is a formulation somewhat as follows.

Advanced industrial societies in the capitalist world do not have a simple and unitary value system. Rather they are historical products, which have arisen from the attempt by a ruling group to impose values and institutions which accord with its own interests on the population at large. In opposition to this set of values and institutions, those who are most conscious of exploitation in the society have created their own defensive institutions and values. In so far as the society stabilizes itself, however, these two sets of values have been able to coexist, and members of all classes have come to value the state of stability itself. This is what Lipset seems to be getting at when he talks of advanced capitalist societies having solved their political problems.

All of this occurs within a population which shares a common history, language and culture. But members of such a population also enter into economic relations with outside groups and these relations may be of a less peaceful kind and lead to the establishment of economic institutions quite different from those which exist within the first-mentioned population. Hence, if one looks at the total social system which includes a metropolitan society and its colonies or its colonial immigrants, one finds an absence of a shared value system and not one class struggle, but two. In the case of the 'colonial' class struggle, at first there may be less overt conflict than there is in the metropolitan one, simply because the colonial people are lacking in power. But in the long run the colonial people might be active in their resistance at the very time that the metropolitan working class are becoming 'incorporated'.

The failure of both functionalist and Marxist theories to explain the differences of value and interest between differing colour and ethnic groups, however, has led to the exploration of an alternative theory, namely that of the plural society. As Furnivall, the first author of this concept, described what it meant (1948, p. 304):

> probably the first thing that strikes the visitor is the
> medley of peoples—European, Chinese, Indian and native.
> It is in the strictest sense a medley, for they mix but do not
> combine. Each group holds by its own religion, its own
> culture, its own ideas and ways. As individuals they meet
> but only in the market place, in buying and selling. . . .
> There is a plural society, with different sections of the
> community living side by side, but separately within the
> same political unit. Even in the economic sphere there is a
> division of labour on racial lines.

Smith (1965), who has elaborated the concept and applied it to the Caribbean, argues (p. 82) that plural societies are marked by the fact that institutional systems including 'kinship, education, religion, property and economy, recreation and certain sodalities' are not shared. Instead each segment of the society has its own institutional set. The sole factor holding the segments together is political power (Smith, 1965, p. 86):

> Given the fundamental differences of belief, value and
> organization that connote pluralism, the monopoly of power
> by one cultural section is the essential precondition for the
> maintenance of the total society in its current form.

Finally the concept of stratification has to be thought of as applying within the segments rather than between them. It will be noticed that, relatively speaking, pluralist theory seems to accept a certain looseness in the relationship of one segment to another while at the same time attaching a crucial significance to cultural differences. By contrast, functionalist and Marxist stratification theories both seem to point to a much closer involvement of one group with another. Functionalism emphasizes the ultimate value system, Marxism the activity within the social relations of production as the central issue in men's lives. Pluralist theory seems to imply that involvement in the polity and in production is less important for men, as a central life-interest, than is the culture which governs their relations outside of their working lives.

For myself, I would certainly want to criticize Smith for his failure to see that one cannot, in the former slave society of the Caribbean, speak of each 'segment' as having its own institutions relating to 'property and economy', and that the dynamics of the society turn upon the involvement of men of differing ethnic backgrounds in the same social institution, viz., the slave plantation. But, for all this, the emphasis of pluralist theory does draw attention to some central features of colonial social structure, which Marxism, for instance does not.

Marxism of course, points out that all societies with capitalist institutions must become internally differentiated and that, in the more advanced stage of their development, the revolutionary working class will move from being a class-in-itself to being a class-for-itself. This change in the consciousness of the working class seems to imply the development of structures, organizations and programmes of action, if not institutions in the sense in which Smith uses the term. For the Marxist there is a certain state of organization and awareness which constitutes true consciousness, and, in the long run, economic events are likely to sweep away any form of false consciousness. But one such form of false consciousness would be the feeling of the plantation worker in Guyana that before being a worker he was an East Indian. The Marxist theory would appear to imply that such segmentary culture consciousness must give way to true working-class consciousness.

One of the difficulties of Marxist theory in European contexts has been to show that the working-class does become a class-for-itself, does become, that is, a collective actor in history. In fact, in the hundred post-Marxian years, working men have given their loyalty to many groups other than merely revolutionary classes. How much more likely is it then that colonial workers who already have the capacity for collective actions through their ethnic organizations will prefer these organizations to the classes and parties which seek to recruit them.

This is not, however, merely a matter of ideas and culture, of consciousness and ideology. For the groups of men who feel themselves to be united in colonial contexts are in fact united by their history and their destiny. They are not groups which were differentiated from one another by developing economic institutions. They are the descendants of distinct groups, who were compelled to live together and operate the same economic institutions together, by that group which possessed the necessary military force. Hence what we are witnessing is not simply the class struggle engendered by capitalist development, but the 'race war' engendered by colonial conquest. This is why normal stratification models do not appear to apply, and why colonial societies seem so recalcitrantly plural in character.

There remains the question of the influence of ideology. For Cox this is purely a question of the 'superstructure'. Racial conflict is less acute in Brazil than in the USA, not because of its Catholic religion, but because of its relative backwardness of economic development (Catholicism is merely another consequence of its backwardness). On the other hand others have suggested that, along with Catholicism, there went the shaping of a wholly different set of legal and economic institutions than that which was to be found in the United States or, for that matter, in South Africa (Cox, *op. cit.*).

I am not sure of my own position on this, since I am insufficiently expert in the evaluation of the historical data. I am inclined to feel, however, that the Catholic countries of Latin America had, at the turn of the century, a set of institutions of a semi-feudal kind, which made their social structures sharply different from that of the USA, most crucially, of course, in that graduations of colour were recognized rather than an absolute division into white and coloured, or white, coloured and black. These differences were so great that I do not believe that any amount of industrialization is going to cause Brazilian society to converge with the social system of the USA or South Africa.

Rather unsystematically I would like also to mention three other variable elements in these colonial situations before I turn to South Africa.

1   The extent to which the subjugated colonial people retain the culture of their ancestors in the pre-conquest period.
2   The relative differentiation of a mixed-race group and the nature of its cultural affiliation (i.e. to the ruling or the subjugated group's culture).
3   The extent to which status differentiation develops within subjugated groups and to which the upper strata within these groups affiliate culturally with the ruling group.

With this background we are now perhaps in a better situation to see what the major problems are in delineating the South African social type. Obviously I do not propose to solve these problems in a few paragraphs, but hope that what I have to say may stimulate further thought and research.

In the first place South Africa is an advanced capitalist country whose religion is basically Protestant. That is to say that there is no ideological obstacle to development of the institutions of an advanced capitalist society, and the country has now passed beyond the stage of economic take-off and generates capital for its own economic development. It is of some interest, perhaps, to note that the purest form of Calvinism was located in the rural areas and in white working-class areas in the towns, and that it was associated with what some might see as pre-capitalist institutions, whereas business enterprise was the work of other Protestant and Jewish entrepreneurs. However, there was always the world of difference between the economic life of the Afrikaner farmer and that of the Portuguese settler in Brazil, and in the last twenty years the various Dutch Reformed Church and Afrikaner nationalist organizations have helped to put the Afrikaner into business. Given the importance of this variable from a sociological point of view, the study of changes in ideology amongst Afrikaner nationalists becomes a crucial area of research.

It would be wrong, however, to approach South African society and its economic institutions purely in terms of ideologies. The fact is that its economic development was able to take the course which it did, because of the fact of the military conquest of the Bantu peoples and their availability as a reservoir of cheap and rightless labour. Rhodes's taxes, the Glen Grey Act and the activities of the labour-recruiting companies laid the foundations of a kind of socio-economic structure quite unlike those of other advanced capitalist countries. Yet, just as it is worth noticing that, whereas Max Weber sees slavery as incompatible with pure capitalism, Elkins speaks of the American plantations as operating according to the logic of unopposed capitalism, so in the South African case the military situation post-conquest makes possible the use of unfree labour as part of an efficient capitalist system of production. There is a central need in the sociological study of South Africa for a study of migrant and compound labour, not in its effect on tribal life, but as one of the possible types of labour organizations and exploitation. The problem would be to investigate the fit between this type of labour and the other institutions of a capitalist society.

Given that South Africa is an advanced capitalist society, the question arises as to how far it can be understood in terms of Marxist models intelligently applied. I say 'intelligently applied' because I do not believe that we can get very far by insisting that the important 'class' difference in South Africa is between those who own and those who don't own the means of production, whereas the difference between black and white workers is only a difference between strata. Surely the point is that there are a number of different relationships to the means of production more subtle than can be comprehended in terms of a distinction between owners and non-owners and that each of these gives rise to a specific class-situation, or, as Marxists might say, to distinct classes-in-themselves.

The basic distinction which has to be made and which makes it necessary to distinguish South African society from, say, Australian society, is that between free and unionized labour on the one hand and labour which is subject to a variety of restrictions on the other. Further, there is the distinction between compound and other forms of unfree labour and the distinction between labour in mining and manufacture on the one hand, and farm labour, domestic service and subsistence farming on the other.

Some might argue that to extend the Marxist notion of 'class-in-itself' to cover all these cases is to rob it of its distinctiveness. Perhaps this is so, but in the opinion of the author, the notion of a whole range of class situations such as we have mentioned here is an illuminating one. There might be some case for speaking of 'estates', since the group concerned is affected by the degree to which it has or lacks political rights. But if that term or the term

caste is taken to imply consent to the overall pattern of apportionment of rights, its use would be misleading.

The next question which arises is the capacity of the free and
unfree workers (including one or more of the groups mentioned
above) to become classes-for-themselves, i.e. to achieve a degree
of autonomy in their culture, their organization and capacity for
collective action in pursuit of their interests. Here we would have
to see the class-for-itself possibility as only one of several possibilities. The others are the control of the organizations and
culture of the working-class group by the ruling or property-
owning class, the 'incorporation' of the working-class groups
through the development of shared goals between labour and
capital, and, thirdly, tribalism and nationalism in which ethnic
rather than class identity is given precedence.

The free unionized white working class has, of course, like the
working classes of the advanced capitalist societies of Europe,
been largely 'incorporated', and though the history of white
labour's relations with capital is a bitter and even a bloody one,
the free white worker today enjoys rights and privileges in the
economic sphere which, together with his political and social
privileges, put him firmly on the opposite side to his fellow-
workers. This is not to say that South African white workers,
particularly poor-whites, do not experience class bitterness and
hostility. This is, of course, an underlying theme in all nationalist
politics. But it is to say that on balance reformist rather than
revolutionary ideologies prevail.

So far as the African workers are concerned, the possibility of
incorporation in this sense is not even open. What the government's labour legislation has done is to seek to establish *control*
by government officials and to prevent any spontaneous organization of a class-for-itself kind. In the nature of the case it is
unlikely that there will be much research into this question to
show whether or not the possibility of control has been successful.
What is, perhaps, more interesting, is the fact that the group
structure and consciousness on which resistance to control is based
might have nationalistic or even a tribal form.

It is interesting to compare the situation of the North American
slave with that of the South African worker in this respect. The
slave had his own culture completely destroyed, and his master
saw to it that he was both deprived of the possibility of any

cultural or political autonomy and educated to accept his servile status. The African worker in South Africa can look to his own culture and social organization as a base for the establishment of a measure of autonomy.

This situation, however, has much greater complexity than has been suggested hitherto. From the point of view taken here, the distinction made by Mayer between 'red' and 'school' people is of considerable significance (1963). The 'reds' provide the African worker with a 'reference-group' which seems to offer autonomy, if not the capacity to pursue economic interests more effectively. The 'school-people' on the other hand offer a number of alternative social strategies ranging from complete acceptance of white authority and white values to political and trade union-based resistance to those values. Here, however, we are forced to pass beyond a narrow focus on the social relations of production as the basis for our studies of South Africa. For cross-cutting any distinction between groups of workers possessing varying degrees of freedom is the distinction between individuals according to the degree in which they accept 'white' or 'western' values. Clearly the proportion of the African population who become 'detribalized' increases every year. What the policy of 'apartheid' has meant here is a dual policy of restricting the rate of inflow into the detribalized sectors, and ensuring that those who do make the transition do so on the Europeans' own terms. Bantu education implies a unitary value system but one which consigns even those Africans who accept it to a position of inferiority.

On another level, too, a narrow Marxist approach must break down. In what we have said so far we have spoken as though there was some kind of ruling class marked by its control of the means of production. It would be gravely misleading, however, to sketch any outline of a sociology of South Africa which did not draw attention to the implications of the separation of political and economic power. The incorporation of the white working class takes place, not through trade union bargaining, but through white control of political power, which means control of that power by privileged white workers and farmers. Thus, instead of a welfare and trade union bargain such as forms the basis of a political contract in Western Europe, the bargain sought and won by the white voters is a guarantee of privilege in the labour market for workers and in the market for labour by farmers. This bargain may, of course, be more precarious than that between labour and capital in Europe, but it has held since Smuts's pro-capitalist policies were defeated in the twenties.

Finally we must give some consideration to three other groups, the 'African middle class', the Cape coloureds, and the Indians. How far can one detect in South Africa what may be called the tipping of the Lloyd Warner caste line? If one can, should this be interpreted simply as the growth of a service-group within African society, or should it be seen as the basis on which an African élite or class will emerge either to change or to stabilize South African society. For myself I do not see this group as playing any role independent of a wider African nationalist movement, though it might, it is true, affect the goals of that movement. However, apartheid, by depriving the African community of the advantages and disadvantages of being serviced by Indian, Chinese and other traders, certainly increases the numbers of this group and the Nationalist party hopefully looks to it as a source of potential allies, while others see in it the seeds of political change: All one can really say at the moment, therefore, is that we need more studies of such strata, élite or classes.

The Cape coloureds represent a different kind of problem. They are non-whites who have a variant of white culture. More-over they are recognized politically, culturally and socially as a distinct group. There is no equivalent group in the United States, though there does seem to be, on the social and cultural level, in the Latin American countries. What are the implications for the stability of the system of this group in South Africa being placed at an intermediate point on the scale of rightlessness, and what views, in the long run, are to be found amongst Cape coloureds as to their ultimate affiliation? Clearly in recent years the ambiguity of their political status has been resolved in the direction of their being separated from the Europeans, but is it not possible that in the long run political power will be shared with them? Much will depend on how far the racism of the South African whites has taken on a life of its own. In so far as it is a factor which is related to economic self-interest, the likelihood would seem to be that the white group (opposed of course by those poor-white factory workers and artisans who are in compe-tition with the coloureds) will eventually want Cape coloured allies more than it wants to preserve its racial purity.

So far as the Indians are concerned, it would seem at first that apartheid, pressed to its logical conclusion, might endanger the fabric of South African society. For the Indians are both a pariah group (i.e. a group of outsiders who perform essential roles, such as those of traders in African areas, which are beneath the dignity of white society) and a scapegoat group (who are blamed for the manifest evils in the society). To remove them from their organic relation with the multi-racial society as a whole would seem to raise the question of how their role as pariahs and scapegoats will be fulfilled. One possibility is, of course, that their occupations will be adequately fulfilled by others, and that the resentment of the society will be so effectively dealt with that there will be no need for a scapegoat group. The other alternative, however, is that while the hue and cry of the policy of segregating Indians will itself be part of the scapegoating ritual, the policy will itself be modified so that the Indian trader of the stereotype does not finally disappear.

There are, of course, a number of other themes, some of which I have not discussed and some which arise in the course of detailing the areas of investigation which I have outlined here. None the less, I hope what I have said might provide a starting point. For those who are interested in social morphology for its own sake it might be useful to discover what sort of social species we are dealing with in South Africa. For those who wish to stabilize or overthrow it, it will be important in showing how sociologically viable the system is.

21

The plural society—the South African case

The attempt to extend the theory of the plural society to the study of South African sociology raises immediate difficulties. It is a theory which has been evolved to deal with certain types of colonial situations in which the theories of class conflict and of social stratification manifestly do not work and in which the main emphasis is upon culturally distinguished segments rather than 'classes'. Probably this follows from the fact that none of the other societies to which the theory has been applied, e.g. Indonesia, the Caribbean, or East Africa, have been industrializing societies, and that they therefore, lack the tight political and economic framework which a society which is industrializing or has industrialized must have. South Africa, on the other hand, is an industrial society, there is such a framework, and concepts like those of class conflict derived from European and North American industrial experience do seem to have some relevance.

At first sight Marxist concepts would appear to be important in this way, since this is clearly a capitalist society and the conflicts which one observes are rooted in the exploitation of the different ethnic groups as labour. Such concepts, however, also prove difficult to apply, in that there does appear to be a division of economic and political power and a capacity of those who possess political power to influence the development of the economy in directions that would seem to be, from a rational capitalist point of view, 'irrational' and 'ideological'; and in that there is clearly a division of the working class on racial lines which is altogether too systematic and structurally based to be accommodated even by the most flexible use of the Marxist concept of class consciousness. Moreover there does remain a rural and traditional element in the society amongst whites as well as blacks which constitutes an extra dimension in all South Africa's problems.

In the debate which has opened up about these problems, the parties to the argument have tended to simply point to the deficiences of each other's position and to assume that by so doing they therefore defend their own. Thus writers who emphasize the pluralist racial and ethnic features of the situation are attacked for failing to relate 'prejudice' to the dynamic structure of the society, and this criticism is then used as a justification in itself for falling back on simplistically applied Marxist categories. On the other hand the discovery that the polity has a directing influence over the economy, that capitalism sometimes works against the application of the colour bar, if only because it prevents effective exploitation of labour, or the fact that white workers fight *for* the colour bar, are all taken as sufficient proof in themselves that race is an independent factor, not reducible to any other which has to do with the economic structure of the society.

In fact, what these difficulties point to is not the necessity of adopting one theory or another, but of looking again at existing theories of social structure and asking whether the specific contexts in which they have been applied have not led to their being stated in too specific a form. What we should then do is to see whether a restatement of the theories in a more general form, in terms of more fundamental variables, does not lead to the possibility of their extension to new situations like the South African one. Thus, for example, if one looks at the general rather than the specific importance of M. G. Smith's notion that the 'political institution' must be shared in a plural society if it is to remain a society, one is forced into a restatement of his theory which pushes it beyond its own cultural anthropological limitations (Smith, 1965). Equally if one looks beyond Marx's definition of the kinds of class conflict which were likely to occur in advanced European and industrial society to the more general point that class formation and class membership are dependent upon the relations which men have to the means of production, whatever the factors which affect those relations, one is likely to have a theory of much more general significance (see Wolpe, 1970). In these terms, ineed, it might well be possible to work towards a general theory which combines some of the advantages of pluralist theory with those of Marxism. It will be convenient in trying to state such a theory to begin from the statement of pluralism as it was developed by M. G. Smith in 1959.

Smith distinguishes between cultural heterogeneity, which occurs in all complex societies, and pluralism, which does not, but which indicates a different genus of societies, as follows:

> It is obvious that modern societies are culturally heterogeneous in many ways. They contain a wide range of occupational specialities, they exhibit stratification and class differences, they often contain ethnic minorities and their rural and urban populations have somewhat different ways of life. Some writers describe modern society as pluralistic because of its occupational diversity. I prefer to say that it is culturally heterogeneous, and to reserve the term pluralism for that condition in which there is a formal diversity in the basic system of compulsory institutions. The basic institutional system embraces kinship, education, religion, property and economy, recreation, and certain sodalities. It does not normally include government.
> (Smith, *op. cit.*)

What does Smith mean by saying that the various groups or segments of the plural society have diversity in their compulsory institutions, *including property and economy*, and what are the consequences of his exempting government, and government only, from his list? The obvious criticism which springs to mind is that in the Caribbean, where the institution of the plantation is a basic institution, and where the whole social order once rested in its foundation upon slavery, it seems a little strange to refer to the various ethnic groups as having diverse institutions of property and economy. Slavery, it is true, is a different institution looked at from the point of view of the slave from what it is, looked at from the point of view of the slave-holder, but that raises different points of theoretical interest.

Clearly it makes no sense at all to speak of the slaves' ethnic group as having its own institution of property and economy, when no slave can live outside the slave plantation or at least outside the institution of slavery. Surely then it would be appropriate to recognize, as Malinowski did, that along with the institutions of each group in a situation of culture contact, there were certain wholly new institutions, which had to be recorded in a (third column', and which grew up out of the situation of contact 'Malinowski, 1945). It seems strange that Smith, whose theory draws heavily upon Malinowski's concepts of institution and culture, should have so little to say about this 'third column'. Had he considered it more thoroughly, he would surely have had to say something about shared economic institutions.

There are probably several different reasons for Smith's adopting the position which he did. For one thing, he did not feel that slavery could be explained satisfactorily as an economic institution and considered that it was better understood as part of the cultural norms or ideals of the slave-owning group. For another he had the anthropologist's disposition to study all institutions within the concept of kinship and the domestic order, so that 'economic institutions' could be taken to refer primarily to such questions as the inheritance of domestic property. Probably, however, it is even more important that Smith's own starting point for his study of the Caribbean was the study of 'the social history of certain colonies during the period between the abolition of the slave trade and the abolition of slavery itself' (Smith, *op. cit.*). Given that this was also a period during which the sugar plantations ceased to be viable economic propositions, it was perhaps natural that he should have concentrated on the fact of institutional diversity between the various segments, and that he should have seen such unity as the society had as depending much more upon its forms of government than upon its economy.

These limitations of theory, arising from the specific circumstances of its development, have to be borne in mind in any attempt to apply the Smith theory to South Africa. In the latter case, we are not talking of a social system which has ceased to function around its basic institution for the exploitation of labour. What is happening instead is that the full implications of the system for the exploitation of native labour are only now being realized. Far from there having been any historical equivalent of slave emancipation in the case of this labour system, and far from the economic system in which it is embedded being in decline, the definition of the native workers' position within the system has become sharper and sharper, and the economy has remained in good heart.

There are, of course, those who would argue that the present system of exploiting African labour is, in fact, a traditional and irrational historical legacy and that, were it not for the doctrinaire ideological pressures on the economy arising from the polity, the system would be swept away. Such writers would argue that this is, therefore, not simply an economic institution, just as Smith did in the case of slavery. This, however, is to confuse two positions. One is that which argues that what capitalist entrepreneurs come to accept as the context of their operation does not accord with an ideal of maximizing the rationality of the enterprise in all respects simultaneously. The other is that the acceptance of this context must lead to economic disaster and that the whole system must, therefore, be swept away.

The first of these propositions may be true without implying the second. What needs to be disputed here is Max Weber's contention that free wage labour was the only form of labour compatible in the long run with the logic of rational capitalism (Weber, 1961, p. 208). In fact it can be shown that in their heyday many West Indian plantations were managed with a high degree of capitalist rationality, even though their owners had to accept such limitations as having to keep their slaves alive during periods of unemployment and under-employment. And they were highly profitable. Equally, South African employers may have had to accept an industrial colour bar, when it was in their interest to employ cheap black labour in skilled work. But this by no means implies that they were condemning themselves to financial ruin by accepting this restraint. What we see, in fact, from the case of plantation slavery, as we do from the case of African labour in South Africa, both of which are what we might call world historical systems to be set alongside of free wage labour as alternatives, is that capitalism is compatible with a variety of forms of labour. Comparative and historical sociology has the task of outlining the main features of those forms and of showing their functional interrelations with other institutions in the larger society.

A useful distinction can be made at this point between three alternative forms of ensuring compliance by their workers which may be used by employers. These are the use of normative, utilitarian and coercive sanctions. Industrial societies can rarely make use of the first. Still less is it possible for employers of native labour in capitalist colonies to do so. The choice, therefore, is between offering financial rewards sufficient to attract a labour supply or the use of force. The former of these methods has the disadvantage that the worker may bargain over the price of his labour, but has the advantage from the employer's point of view that he may easily be dispensed with, since his labour is bought for limited periods only. The use of force, on the other hand, has marked advantages, in that the worker can be made to do his master's will without the possibility of bargaining about the terms, but, if it leads to slavery, it involves the disadvantage that the worker must be supported and kept alive in times of economic depression when there is no market for the product of his labour. What is interesting about some of the forms of labour used in South Africa is that they enable the employer to control a variety of forms of legitimate violence, which he may use against his workers, but, at the same time, do not require that he should buy the worker for life and be responsible for the worker for life. The achievement of this state of affairs represents a considerable advance in rationality over the slave system. Indeed it might be said to be the theoretically most perfect system of labour exploitation yet devised.

The position to which this leads also enables us to understand more fully one argument which arises between pluralists and Marxists. The pluralist insists that what we are dealing with in colonial labour situations are not so much rational-economic as traditional normatively oriented institutions. The Marxist argues that such situations are economic and that they involve a high degree of rationality from the employers' point of view. What we can now see is that the pluralists are wrong in imagining that if an institution is not economic in character it must be based upon normative and traditional factors, and Marxists are wrong in so far as they argue that labour exploitation is purely economic. The fact of the matter is that there is a non-normative factor at work which sets economic factors in a definite context. This is the capacity of the employers to command the use of coercive violence during and after colonial conquest. If Smith had argued, therefore, that the political bonds of plantation society extended into the employer-employee relation itself, he might have found a more satisfactory answer to the question of why plural societies do not break up. Similarly it should not come as any surprise to find that, in the South African context, political factors affect economic behaviour. It is of the essence of this kind of labour situation that they should. The world of politics is the continuation of the world of violence initiated during the period of colonial conquest.

With this background we may turn to giving a schematic account of the main features of pluralism, stratification, and conflict in South African society. Rather than do so either by recording systematically all the forms of labour which are to be found, or historically by relating the present to earlier forms of labour and society, I shall proceed instead by outlining in ideal typical form the central institution of labour, around which other forms may be seen clustering as variants, and introduce other structural and historical elements as secondary factors, which provide the context of the labour system, and which might also serve to enrich the detail of our account of the operation of the total system. I do so in the belief that starting this way can explain more of the total pattern of South African pluralism than by beginning at any other point.

The central labour institution to which I refer is the institution of migrant labour in its most unfree form, namely that which is to be found in the compounds of the gold and diamond mines. In this institution one sees the way in which political and economic factors, the world of the employer and employee, the world of black and white, and the world of town and country, are in fact a single world. It is only when this is understood, therefore, that one can go on to note the diversity, heterogeneity, and pluralism which such a politico-economic institution may still permit.

Essential to the institution of migrant labour living in compounds are the rural reserves, from which the workers come, and in which their dependants continue to live. They are reserves not merely in the sense in which that term was originally used, namely as places where land is reserved for native as against settler occupation, but reserves of labour on which the industrial complex based upon mining depends. No industrial system has ever had such plentiful reserves so readily on tap.

South Africa's Bantu population were confined to the reserves after conquest and after a land settlement which gave four-fifths of the land to the 15–20 per cent of the population who were settlers. When it is added to this that most of the best land was excluded from the Bantu portion, it is clear that, from the outset, the Bantu were placed in a position of what Roux has called, following Toynbee, an external proletariat (Roux, 1949), i.e. a people who lacked the necessary means to perpetuate their own economy, society, and culture, and were therefore forced into *de facto* dependence on those who had placed them in this position. Yet they were not even given the chance of sticking together and doing what they could to satisfy their own subsistence needs and survive. Cecil Rhodes, translated from the boardrooms of the mining industry to the premiership of the Cape Colony, imposed upon them a so-called poll tax (its most important feature being that it had to be paid by every adult male) thus forcing all families to some extent out of the subsistence and into the cash economy, and also pioneered the break-up of communal land-owning systems with a system of individual tenure in certain areas with the full intention of creating a supply of landless workers. These measures were sufficient to ensure that the peasant population would be responsive when the agents of the recruiting company arrived in the village.

The worker recruited in this way was about as open to intensive exploitation as any worker could be. In the first place, he was literally kept behind barbed wire in prison conditions, even though these conditions could be represented by the employers as being of a paternalistic kind designed to ensure his welfare. Second, his basic wage remained small and unfluctuating, since his keep was provided in kind and the employers worked on the assumption that the worker was a target worker, only concerned to accumulate during the period of his contract enough to pay his tax and to invest small sums in a family holding in the reserves. Third, no form of insurance, or welfare, or old age pension needed to be provided since any particular worker ceased to be the employer's responsibility after the end of his contract. Finally the compound was built and run on the assumption that the worker was not entitled, during that period of his life which he had contracted to give to his employer, to any of the comforts of family, kinship and community. Max Weber's bureaucrats may have been motivated to divide their lives between their office and their home by ideal factors. The native worker in South Africa was forced to do so, and the proportion left to his home after nine months out of twelve spent wholly with the employer was insignificantly small. No system of plantation slavery ever guaranteed exploitation of this degree.

The rationale of the system was that the native worker relied for his welfare on what was supposed to be a second source in the reserves. They were in fact sometimes spoken of as though they were the welfare state of the migrant labour economy. But the more the mines exploited rural labour, the more these bases were eroded. Already overcrowded, due to the land settlement, they lacked the essential labour force and moral and social leadership, necessary to keep them productive, so that each year the rural areas were capable of supporting a smaller population, or of supporting the same population only at a lower level.

The one way out of this situation was for some of those who had encountered urban society during their stay in the mines and others who, while not having been there, had heard of it, to look for more permanent prospects of urban settlement and employment. This meant employment outside the mines and other compound-based industries on a permanent wage-earning basis, and it meant the settlement in the urban areas, along with the adult male workers, of women, children, and elderly dependants. Thus there emerges, along with the compound and the reserve, the third element in the migrant labour system, the urban native location.

Before we can understand what the location means, it is essential to understand both that urban labour outside the compound poses the possibility of the emergence of a class of free wage workers amongst the natives, and that the settler population, employers and workers alike, will unite to resist this possibility. The employers are concerned to ensure that there is sufficient compulsion brought to bear on the native immigrant to the city to ensure that he works at a high level of profitability to his employer, even though they may also be more concerned, in some cases, than the mine-owners are, to ensure that their workers develop a permanent loyalty. The free white workers will use all the means available to them, especially through their trade unions and political parties, to ensure that natives do not compete with them for a livelihood.

Not surprisingly, the ideal for all employers is the compound situation, but another model is provided by the situation of the domestic servant. Just as the system of plantation slavery was accompanied by a growth of the domestic institution, so is the South African labour system accompanied by an elaborate development of the institution of domestic service. In South Africa, of course, as in any other country, domestic service is one of the least free forms of labour, in that the servant is thought of as participating only indirectly in the market, relying for his income and welfare, to some extent at least, on the benevolence with which his master administers his private household. But, whether the servant is a man or a woman, there is a move towards an additional feature of the situation. The servant, like the compound worker, is assumed to have no kin, and the breaking of his contract with his employer is deemed to be a criminal offence.

Nearly all African labour partakes in some measure of the characteristics of the compound worker and the domestic worker's status. All are liable to masters and servants legislation, and none are completely free, even though the development of secondary manufacturing industry may lead to greater flexibility of wages, greater permanence of the labour force and hence greater recognition of the needs of the worker for kinship and community life. Being a servant implies that a man is unfree. He may not have trade unions to negotiate on his behalf, and he may not be allowed to form organizations which give him the chance of sharing in political power. It is surely a noteworthy fact, but also it is by no means surprising, given what has been said before, that the direction of change in South Africa has been towards the removal of such political and trade union rights as native workers possessed, rather than their gradual acquisition, as has been the case amongst the European working class. The long-term trend in this change is a sure indication that the native workers of South Africa are not becoming a class in the European Marxist sense.

But the deprivation of freedom to which the worker is subject does not cease at the factory gates. If he does have a family with him in town, if he is not completely a factory hand, he and his family must be subjected to restrictions and harassment which prevent their attaining the kind of bargaining power which comes from living in a stable and permanent community setting. So in urban areas legislation and pass-laws ensure that the right to live permanently in town is restricted to only a privileged few, and that dependants always remain unsure that they have security of tenure. All of this demands that the worker and his family should be segregated and contained in order that they should be administered, and the logic of this is that their homes shall be so tightly fenced and policed that their locations become a kind of compound for families.

So far we have concentrated on the employer-native worker relation, mentioning the existence of a free white labour force only in passing. What has now to be noticed is that although the employers may find themselves in conflict with this labour force and see it as too powerful and therefore 'irrational', the actual behaviour of the white worker serves in the long run to intensify the exploitation of the native labour force. What happens is that, in order to guarantee its own freedom, the white working class demands the restriction of the native's freedom and thereby makes possible his increased exploitation. Thus it is the white worker, as much as anyone, who demands the exclusion of the native worker from the towns and from competing freely in the labour market, but this exclusion *incompletely achieved* means that the native worker *does* enter the labour market but *under inferior conditions only*.

The crucial conflict about the role of native labour comes over the question of the kind of tasks that such cheap and unfree labour should be allowed to perform. This issue took white South Africa to the verge of revolution in the nineteen-twenties. What has happened since, however, is a workable compromise. In the main, native workers are confined to unskilled roles, but when there is an obvious labour shortage (i.e. when there is a category of jobs which white workers will not undertake) what has been regarded as skilled or semi-skilled is redefined and the job is undertaken by cheap black labour. At the same time the employers and their political allies no longer contemplate the wholesale removal of the industrial colour bar. The long-term result of all this is that the white workers come to form an aristocracy of labour consisting of skilled and supervisory workers, most of whom enjoy a high degree of privilege and join with their employers in policing the exploitation of the natives.

Clearly the analysis just presented justifies neither wholly pluralist nor wholly Marxist conclusions. The crucial thing to note about the native labour force is that it *is* a labour force and that what happens to it and what it does is determined, not by its separate culture, but by the needs of the economic system. And what is true for the workers themselves extends to their dependants in the reserves as well as in the towns. On the other hand, the relationship to the means of production of the native workers is quite different from that of the white working class. The latter have the means to defend their liberties and their job security as well as negotiating over the price of their labour. The former have none of these things. Hence it is not sufficient to dismiss the difference between white settler and native workers as status differences only. Both actually and potentially, as class-in-itself and class-for-itself, the native workers are distinct from working-class settlers.

Another question which pluralist theory raises in the South African context is the role of a shared value system as between the various ethnic groups. *Prima facie*, it might seem that the urban native worker, exposed as he is to all the formal and informal influences of the city, and less and less subject as he is to traditional influences, must be regarded as having been incorporated into settler society, in a way which would not permit one to go on using the term pluralist. But here the cultural emphasis of pluralism may be misleading, for there *is* a sense in which this is a plural society, namely the sense which derives from its having not one working class but two. Yet there is a pluralism on the value level too, and it is to be found to some extent amongst the white settlers as well as among the native workers and peasants. By this we refer not merely to the obvious division of the English- and Afrikaans-speaking settlers, or the tribal and linguistic differences amongst the natives. These are understandable in terms of the heterogeneity which Smith refers to as being different from pluralism. What is more important is the distinction between rural and urban life, which also means participation in a different socio-economic system and one whose roots are to be found in earlier periods of South African history.

What one would expect amongst the Bantu peoples, of course, is some kind of cultural continuum, from complete participation both culturally and socially in their native tribal system to complete allegiance to European or settler values; and for some analytic purposes it might be useful to retain the notion of such a continuum. What is interesting, however, is the appearance of whole new cultural groupings which, although they emerge only amongst the native populations, have the character of what might be called, in Malinowski's terms, 'third column' cultures. That is to say they belong neither wholly to white nor to settler culture but result purely from the fact of culture contact itself. Thus according to Mayer (1963) there are at least three such groupings in East London. There are the 'red' people who wear European clothes only for work, but who normally wear red blankets and ochre as a symbol of their allegiance to traditional culture. There are the 'school' people who have accepted mission-school values and wear mission-style clothing now dated and unresponsive to fashion. Finally there are the people who are wholly the children of the urban native slums. The existence of these different groupings and life-styles suggests *both* cultural pluralism *and* a range of attitudes towards the legitimacy of the society's existing form of government.

The rural settler also has his own culture and life-style. His interests lie in retaining control over as much of the best land as he can and in winning out in the competition for labour in which he is forced to engage with urban employers. He works to prevent native labour going to the city and allies himself politically with the settler workers to form the most powerful conceivable alliance of settler interests. Yet the values which govern his life, including its economic aspects, are derived from an earlier phase of history when the Trekboers of the eighteenth century and the Trekkers of the nineteenth sought continually to escape from the influence of central government of any kind. Such anarchistic values conflict with those derived from another aspect of the Trekker myth, which equates the Trekkers with the Children of Israel and acts as a solidarity myth for the Afrikaner political alliance as a whole.

Another feature of the South African situation which is sometimes referred to as pluralistic is the distribution of functions as between the native settler groups which we have mentioned, and the Cape coloured and Asiatic populations. The Cape coloureds, however, have clearly been divided from the Afrikaner worker, not by their language and culture, but by the difference in the economic functions assigned to them and the rights which they enjoy. In economic terms the coloureds have established themselves in a range of skilled trades, in factory work and other minor roles, and have succeeded in defending some of these positions against white competition. At the same time the fact of this competition has led to a continuous process of deprivation of political and social rights and to increasing segregation so that a niche has been found for the coloured population, which, while it is a state of almost complete rightlessness compared with the white settler population, is none the less a position of great privilege when compared with that of the African.

'Indians' were recruited as indentured labourers for the South African sugar industry in the latter half of the nineteenth century. As indentured workers they occupied a legal and economic position different both from slaves and African servants and workers. It was, however, a position of greater economic and political strength than either of these, and when the former indentured labourers were joined by traders entering the society as secondary colonialists to take up trading opportunities, they came to have their own recognized occupational specializations and consequent social rights within the system. The ascendancy of the Afrikaner political alliance, however, has meant that the Indians have appeared as powerful competitors and, therefore, a prime target for the restrictions of opportunity which characterize the Nationalist segregation policy. Many Indians now stand to be impoverished by this policy, so that despite the adaptiveness which has enabled them to live within a context of white South African social values, while still maintaining an internal life apart, the Indians have been forced into a segregated and inferior position.

Thus whether we look at rural or urban Bantu, white urban employers or workers, urban or rural whites, Cape coloureds or Indians, what is evident is certainly not the pluralism of cultural segments which either Furnivall's analysis of Indonesia (1948; 1967) or Smith's of the Caribbean suggests. If there is division, the divisions can be seen to be functionally interrelated within an overall pattern of political conflict generated by the capitalist development of the country since the mineral discoveries of 1867 and 1886. Clearly what we have is not something which can be adequately interpreted in terms of some universal Marxist law of class struggle, but a specific kind of class struggle there undoubtedly is, namely one in which the classes are groups of varying histories and ethnic origins who enter the modern society with varying rights and degrees of rightlessness, according to the kind of conquest or unfreedom which was imposed on them in an earlier period. The history, the structure, the forms of social differentiation which South Africa presents are, as in the case of any former colonial society, the product of such conquest and unfreedom. In South Africa they combine in a unique way but do so in terms of the economic and social processes inherent in one of the few examples of a capitalist economic take-off which is to be found outside Europe and North America.

Finally it should be mentioned that, over and above all that we have said, there are present in South African culture survivals from two earlier social and economic and political situations.[1] Thus we should note that South Africa was in the first place a Dutch colonial society and produced in the Western Cape Province particularly a society variant of the Dutch colonial pattern which was developed in Batavia. Not unnaturally therefore we should expect that any sensitive analysis of Cape society even today would yield evidence of the same kind of cultural pluralism as Furnivall described. Or again we should note that another way of life and another social order was produced in the Eastern Cape border between 1800 and 1850, as the farmers of the frontier encountered for the first time the military power of the Bantu and had for the first time to deal with a border situation. These are important facts and they add a richness to the total cultural complexity which is South Africa. But they by no means refute our main contention here, which is that all the various groups and segments in this society are held locked together, albeit in a bitter conflict, not solely by the institution of government, but by a rapidly expanding economy and the exploitative labour system on which it depends. Whether it is valuable to refer to such a society as a plural society may be a mere matter of terminology but, if the term is meant to imply a society in which there is no involvement of all the different groups in a single political economy, or if it is taken to imply an absence of economically based class conflict, then South Africa certainly does not present us with a case of the plural society.

[1] I am grateful to Marcus Balintulo for extended discussion of this idea of the pre-existing pluralistic forms in South Africa.

22

The structure of 'black revolutions'

Poverty is safe when it is unaware and alone. The poverty in today's world is increasingly aware. And it no longer needs a still uncommon literacy to inform it. The air is full of pictures and sounds, from advertising posters, television and cinema screens, radio sets. The most ragged of the workless in the cities of Brazil can catch sight of television and the cinema glares in a thousand small Indian towns, within reach of other forsaken villages around. The cheap radio set, pouring unsuspected desires and demands in a cataract of local languages, finds an audience in stretches of Africa or Andean America which have never seen a book. And disaffection is just the other side of discovery.

Nor is poverty alone. The villagers who crouch around their radio sets in Kenya hear of the world in Swahili from Moscow and Peking as well as—if rather more sedately— from Nairobi and London, and they find soon enough how numerous and similar are the poor. And they find if they do not know it already, a new division too—that, by and large, the rich of this world are white and the poor are coloured. It is a powerful discovery.

In their poverty and their weakness the coloured nations cannot but be impressed by the one amongst their number which has acquired power, and, if not yet a white standard for all its citizens, at least a capacity for independent economic advance. . . . China is . . . the . . . impressive example.

Thus Ronald Segal in his boldly named book *The Race War* (pp. 11–12). Surely this projection of the revolution of the Third World is now so obvious a fact that it merits serious sociological analysis. The notion of 'race war' replaces the notion of 'class war', but what exactly does this mean?

In 1848, the political ideologies available to man in Europe were those of the liberal bourgeoisie, the descendants of the outcast merchants who settled within mediaeval European civilizations, created their own social order within those civilizations and, having consolidated their position, went on to impose on the rest of the world what Marx was to call their political and economic sway. Yet as the bourgeoisie struggled with the resurgent forces of absolutism, Marx and Engels detected the rise of a new class within bourgeois society, rising by a 'similar movement' to that which had produced the bourgeoisie. But this class could form and rise to power with a rapidity which had not been available to the bourgeoisie; 'that union, to attain which the burghers of the Middle Ages, with their miserable highways, required centuries, the modern proletariat, thanks to railways, achieved in a few years'.

It is not, however, merely the hope which Marx and Segal entertained of the effect of the revolution in communications which leads one to search for parallels between the projected proletarian revolution and that of the Third World. In both cases there are those who own and those who do not own, there are organizations which mobilize power and revolutionary organizations which defy that power and, beyond what exists in the way of organization, with executive committees, there is in both cases a consciousness stretching worldwide, so that each particular struggle is in a separate part of one great war of man against man, waged in the name of justice and equality.

Whether Marx was right or not in his projection of a revolution of the urban industrial proletariat in the advanced industrial countries is of little account here. What does matter is that, in sketching the sociological outline of a revolutionary class rising to power, he suggests some central sociological questions which have to be asked about the structural and ideological conditions of such revolutions. If we understand these questions, we shall be in a better position to see whether the revolutionary forces of the Third World are in a better or worse position to realize their revolution than was the European proletariat. Marx's picture of the rise of the proletariat follows his account of the rise of the bourgeoisie. It begins with the words 'a similar movement is now going on before our very eyes'. What then is the structure of this movement? For the bourgeoisie it went through various stages, in Marx's words, as follows (1962, p. 36):

> An oppressed class under the sway of the feudal nobility, it became an armed and self-governing association in the mediaeval commune: here independent urban republic (as in Italy and Germany); there taxable third estate of the monarchy (as in France); afterwards in the period of manufacture proper, serving either the semi-feudal or the absolute monarchy as a counter-poise against the nobility, and, in fact, the cornerstone of the great monarchies in general—the bourgeoisie has at last, since the establishment of modern industry and of the world market, created for itself in the modern representative state exclusive political sway. The executive of the modern state is but a committee for managing the common affairs of the whole bourgeoisie.
>
> The bourgeoisie, whenever it has the upper hand, has put an end to all feudal patriarchal idyllic relations. . . . It has drowned the most heavenly ecstasies of religious fervour, of chivalrous enthusiasm, of philistine sentimentalism, in the icy water of egotistical calculations . . . for exploitation veiled by religious and political illusions, it has, in fact, substituted naked, shameless, direct, brutal exploitation.

Now leaving aside the rhetoric, what Marx is saying here is that, in the growth of a class, there will be changes in its own internal structure, in the structure of its relations with society at large, in the ideology in terms of which it views its own internal structure and in the ideology in terms of which it interprets the whole social world.

For the proletariat, Marx saw a similar line of development, although here he is inclined from time to time to state his argument in an older Hegelian vocabulary. The structure of social relations of production first produces the group of people who, whether they are aware of it or not, have common market interests. At this stage, being largely unaware of their objective position, the individuals involved have the status only of a thing-in-itself or 'class-in-itself'. When, however, the individuals with the same market position become conscious of the fact, when they see themselves as being opposed to those with opposite interests and seek, by destroying their opponents, to destroy the whole social order and create a new one, the class-in-itself, regains control of the alien world and, as it does so, becomes a class-for-itself.

Now, with a hundred years hindsight, we must either admit for the advanced capitalist countries that no effective proletariat-for-itself has come into existence (neither the Russian case nor those of the East European countries constitute adequate examples, for either they had revolutions in conditions of relative economic backwardness or they had new regimes imposed during a phase of military conquest) or we must say that the typical development of the European proletariat leads to its incorporation into the bourgeois-capitalist order or some variant thereof.

The latter alternative is that which has been chosen by the sociologists of bourgeois complacency whose typical representatives in America in the sixties were S. M. Lipset and Daniel Bell, and on a rather more sophisticated plane in Britain, T. H. Marshall. According to all of these writers, the development of advanced industrial society has led to the development of a bundle of social rights and a consensus between employer and worker alike that there should be full employment and a welfare state, but only such socialization of property ownership as was necessary to guarantee these conditions.

It is possible to argue against the so-called end-of-ideology thesis that it represents so much wishful thinking on the part of the bourgeoisie and their personal managers. In fact, the welfare state and full employment are likely to be maintained if, and only if, it is clear that workers are prepared to fight to defend them; and in most of the advanced industrial countries at the same time it seems clear that, whether through economic necessity or simply taking advantage of temporary weakness of the working class, the political parties of the bourgeoisie have sought to undermine the welfare and trade union bargain and to fall back on an open class-rule.

This, however, is really a matter for argument. It is also at least possible to argue that, for twenty-five years after the Second World War, the politics of countries like Britain, France, Germany and the United States turned simply on the question of shares within the bargain. Conservatives would press the bargain one way, the forces of labour the other. What was more damaging, however, to the end-of-ideology thesis was something that can be quite sharply put. It might be pointed out that by the time Lipset or Bell were able to read the reviews of their books, they need only to have glanced out of the window to notice that the cities and the campus were burning. Our real problem here is to capture and understand the new politics which was on the streets, not merely in colonial towns in Latin America, Africa and Asia, but in the metropolitan countries themselves.

The first point to be noted is that the new situation need not necessarily be regarded as a refutation of Marxist theory. True, the new politics were not those of the proletariat as that class had been defined by European social democrats. But certainly it was the case that the new revolution on the streets was a revolution of those who were differentially placed in relation to the means of production—and differentially placed not merely in relation to those who owned them, but also, in relation to those who, through trade unionism, had gained some degree of control over their use. It was the revolution of the various contingents of the new black, and often immigrant, poor in the metropolitan countries, and the revolution of the unfree worker and the peasant in the colonial world.

To understand this we need to have a more comprehensive account of the social relations of production of the bourgeois countries than European Marxism made fashionable. As Eric Williams has pointed out (1966) there could have been no English industrial revolution, had it not been for the triangular trade and, before there could have been that small confrontation called Peterloo in St Peter's Fields in Manchester, there had to be a phase of primary accumulation of capital which made industrialism possible. That phase of primary accumulation meant the dispossession of Irish peasants, it meant slave ships and manacles, and it meant that whole American world which the white slave-masters made.

It is the custom in social science departments in British universities to offer students courses on the social structure of modern Britain. These courses show how, in a formerly Protestant but now largely secular society, industrialism flourishes to produce affluence for socially enfranchised workers who live in suburbia in small isolated conjugal families. Such courses leave out the whole colonial sub-structure on which the metropolitan social system rests. They say nothing, to mention only a small point, of the Catholic families of Ireland which continue to breed new recruits for the British proletariat at a rate well above the two and a half or so which British mothers think normal. Much more importantly, however, they say nothing at all about the range of types of unfreedom which colonial systems of production allow.

The first and clearest form of labour on which British and American growth have depended has been that of slave plantations in North America and the Caribbean. Thus there were men who were in law and in fact not truly men but things. Not merely did they lack trade unions, the mark of proletarian labour, they lacked any capacity to produce institutions and culture of their own. What the British and American plantation system produced was 'Sambo' who must, perforce, dance to his master's tune, because he had no tune of his own, and, with that political elegance of which the British were sometimes possible, Sambo was permitted to excel above all others in that most British of all institutions, the cricket test match.

But when the slave system yielded to historical necessity, and first the British and then the Americans found the ideological means to crusade for abolition, new forms of labour had yet to be found to man the sugar plantations and the rich mineral deposits which were being opened up in Africa. Mauritius and Guiana saw the emergence of that great new social invention, the coolie, an Indian or Chinaman forced by poverty or landlessness into indentures which, at best, offered him freedom in the remote future, but, with that freedom, a bleak choice of starving in his country of migration or repatriation to serve back at home.

Indian and Chinese coolies were, of course, somewhat more difficult to manage than African slaves. Prior to their forced migration as coolies, most of them had been exploited through crop-purchase which required little in the way of political control. Moreover, they showed a remarkable capacity for taking advantage of the opportunities with which colonialism presented them, to become secondary colonialists themselves and to go in for trade.

Coolie labour of the Chinese kind proved a spectacular failure in one case at least, namely in the South African gold mines. The British electorate, so the history books tell us, would not tolerate this form of slavery. They would not indeed, because surely and successfully guided by that genius of colonialism, Cecil John Rhodes, they had found a better and, in its effectiveness, alternative form of labour exploitation. The Bantu tribes of South Africa, after a series of border wars, were confined to lands which could not possibly support them, and then subjected to many taxes which could only be earned by the male head of the household forsaking his family in the reserves to go to live in an enclosed compound, and to work far underground digging out that essential symbol of all the world's exploitation—gold.

As has been pointed out in the previous chapter, this form of labour exploitation is more perfect and more satisfactory than any other known to man, the reserve, the compound and location ensure that the worker gives the maximum effort for the smallest reward, yet at the same time the system fails to develop that irritating feature of the slave plantation that the worker must be fed in good times as well as bad. After nine months he returns to his reserve.

Apart from the plantation workers and miners of colonial society, another force had to come into the reckoning, namely the peasantry. The peasant is a man who is outside the main structure of industrial society. He is poor perhaps, but he has and makes an economic and cultural world of his own. Yet the time comes when his right to remain remote from the centre of things is questioned, when the developing industry and the developing towns demand that he must yield up his crops at the price which the townsman is prepared to pay, or he could be sucked into the capitalist orbit by dealing with his poverty by resort to the merchant-usurer, as surely as did the domestic worker under the putting-out system in seventeenth- and eighteenth-century England.

Lastly, but by no means least, colonial society produced in great profusion that class for which Marx saw little long-term future, the fedual lackey and domestic retainer. Slavery had found a place for the 'house-nigger', but 'house-niggers' could be found even when slavery was no more. As the institutions of what Weber called 'booty-capitalism' and 'adventurer-capitalism' in his studies of the ancient world, took a new lease of life in the late nineteenth century, so the oikos, the big house, the manor, came back into being.

In some of the British settler territories in Africa, domestic service became the second largest form of employment for Africans, and the characteristic of the domestic servant was that he did not participate directly in the market to find his subsistence. His participation was indirect and he relied for food and board solely on his master's benevolence or lack thereof.

The question which must now be asked is how it could be possible for all these many contingents of what Fanon was to call 'the wretched of the earth' to unite for a single revolution. Manifestly at first they could not, at least on the organizational level. Peasants and buying agents, servants and masters, plantation labourers and plantation owners, miners and overseers, all fought their own individual struggles. Their interests were diverse, and only in conditions of nationalist revolt were they likely to be brought together, under leaders whose concern for their interests was in any case as calculating and hypocritical, as was that of the English political reforms of the 1820s for the interests of the working class.

The starting point of a revolutionary consciousness, which in this case preceded revolutionary organization, came within the world communist movement. It took the form, to use the phrase later taken up by one of the Third World's most effective intellectual spokesmen, Régis Debray, of a revolution in the revolution. Marx had argued that the urban proletariat was the only possible standard-bearer of the social revolution. The peasantry never could become a class-for-itself, because the peasant remained an isolated individual dealing in isolation with those who oppressed him and capable of taking political action only through a Caesarist figure like Louis Napoleon Bonaparte. Marx's pamphlet, 'The 18th Brumaire of Louis Napoleon Bonaparte', was to stand for nearly one hundred years as Marxist orthodoxy on the political potential of the peasantry.

Lenin was to face the problem of heading a revolution in a country in which there was a small and underdeveloped proletariat but a vast peasant nation. He dealt with the problem by creating a 'vanguard' party based upon the proletariat but led in effect by intellectuals. This 'vanguard' party then allied itself with the peasants but, in the long run, sought to impose the urban intellectual and proletariat will on the countryside. The story of Marxism outside Europe, is one of the abandonment of this, the essence of Marxism-Leninism. A nationalist revolution

in China was followed by a civil war in which the communist contenders for power created an army of peasants and workers,
which, after many years of bloody struggle, took power from the
nationalists. This was an experience which was to give meaning
and structure to other revolutions outside the communist world.
For all peasants who succeeded in overthrowing their urban
masters there was more to be learned from the thoughts of Mao
Tse Tung, however naïve they might seem to urban intellectuals,
than could be learned from *Das Kapital* and *The Communist
Manifesto* or the 1844 manuscripts. Crude though they may be,
these thoughts were thoughts that made sense to peasants
engaged in military struggle for liberation.

The next instance of this kind of revolutionary experience was
in Algeria, where a nationalist country-based armed revolution
was deliberately planned and conducted against the French, with
peasants, workers *and the native bourgeoisie* uniting in a single
movement, despite the protestations of Trotskyists that only a
working-class struggle could usher in a socialist revolution, and
despite the failure of the French communist party to offer other
material or moral support. Something had now to be said about
the political role of the colonial people as such, for it seemed clear
that, Marxist theories about sociological priority of relations to
the means of production notwithstanding, to be an Algerian
Freedom Fighter, fighting against French colons and the French
Army, was far more in the way of participating in a class struggle
than was being an Arab or colon trade unionist in Algiers. Also
here it was clear that deliberate planned armed revolution was
possible even without economic crises and the growth of trade
union consciousness. The spokesman of the new doctrine of
revolution was Frantz Fanon, a native of Martinique, and a one-
time pupil of Aimée Cesaire, who had resigned from the French
communist party after pointing out to Maurice Thorez that the
main aim of the people of Martinique was not necessarily the
liberation of the French proletariat. Fanon was to weld the ideas
which he gained from his experience of the Algerian revolution
into what was for many to become a Third World's alternative
to the communist manifesto.

Fanonism means before all else that the struggle for liberation
is not to be brushed aside simply because it is not the revolution
of Marxist theory. The 'wretched of the earth' are the people

called 'natives' who, in a thousand ways, have a different relationship to everything that matters (and not only the means of
production) from that of the settlers. It argues, too, against non-
violence, with even greater depth than Marx did against the True
Socialists, because Fanon made it one of his central themes that
the native lives in a world of delusion, fantasy and false-
consciousness, until he is prepared to act rationally to achieve his
aims by a violent confrontation with his masters. Far from it
being the case, as pacifists have always argued, that violence
corrupts those who use it, according to the Fanonist argument it
may actually serve to liberate the revolutionary not merely from
his masters but from his own sick fantasies. Finally, however, if
Fanon believes in the national revolution, he is also fully conscious
of the neo-colonialism to which people are likely to be led by
the native bourgeoisie. Hence the revolution of the Third World,
like that of Europe, has to be maintained in permanence.

Algeria has, in fact, not had a socialist revolution, though there
are some socialist elements within it. Perhaps some Marxists
might claim that Boumedienne's coup and those other coups
which will follow, only serve to make the point that the peasants
will always look for a Bonaparte or a Caesar.

But not long after the Algerian revolution, another leader at
the head of a peasant army led that army into his nation's capital
as a conqueror. The new leader, Fidel Castro, was able, whether
by good luck or good judgement, to withstand all the military and
economic threats that the United States was able to deploy.
After coming to power he called himself a communist and relied
increasingly on the communist party. If, in doing this, he changed
the nature of his regime, he also changed the nature of com-
munism. Another formula for revolution was worked out, and
Castro's lieutenant, Che Guevara, set off as a revolutionary-at-
large, to spread the message and sew the seeds of revolution
throughout Latin America. His death at the hands of the
Bolivian army served only to make him a legend and a rallying-
point for revolutionary forces in the new world and the old.

China, Algeria and Cuba had made the point: revolution was
not simply the task of the urban proletariat. Indeed it came to be
widely accepted in Latin America that, far from the organized
labour movement being a vanguard of the revolution, as the
Venezuelans sought to argue, it and its political allies were

ultimately part of the other side. They were amongst those in colonial society who had been bought off by some sort of welfare state deal, and represent the affluent world, which was precisely the world against which the wretched of the earth were fighting. To some extent too, though Cuba had to maintain friendly relations with Russia, Russia came to be seen no longer as the motherland of socialism and the revolution, but as part of the white affluent and oppressor's world. What appeared to many western liberals and socialists to be a welcome breathing space, the detente between Russia and America, was to the Third World merely an indication of Russia's collusion in capitalist imperialism.

While the above perspective was one which dominated the thinking of Latin American socialist revolutionaries, new developments in the revolution of the Third World arose from the exercise of United States power and the spread of United States influence in all parts of the world. In the world of 1970, most men who see themselves as fighting against capitalism see this as meaning fighting against the United States, for the United States is not merely the 'first new nation' as Lipset maintains, it is the world's first capitalist nation, in which the whole structure of the society and the style of its culture depend upon the operation of capitalist organization and enterprises, uncluttered by any other cultural or social legacy. Moreover, for most countries in the world, in a decreasingly powerful Europe, as well as in Latin America, Africa and Asia, a process of secularization and commercialism has been set in train which appears as one above all of growing Americanization. It is sometimes described as Cocacola Imperialism.

The real strength of Segal's argument, quoted at the beginning of this chapter, lies in the fact that China has resisted this progress of Americanization itself and has also successfully fought the Americans off in South Korea. Above all, the people of Vietnam have fought against American power for a period of more than six years, and appear to have created dissension and demoralization, not merely in the American people at home, but within the American army itself.

It is perhaps necessary to point out here that what is important in what we are saying does not really depend upon whether or not the United States is rightly described as a capitalist-imperialist power. That may be or it may be not. What matters, however, is that it is perceived as such, and that in the consciousness of revolutionaries in the Middle East, Africa and Latin America, the fight of the Vietcong and their allies in South-east Asia comes to be seen, before all others, as that in which the revolution of the Third World is being successfully fought and won.

The Fedayeen of Palestine, the guerillas of Latin America and of Southern Africa, increasingly come to model themselves on the Vietcong and appeal to models of guerilla warfare drawn from China, Algeria and Cuba. The typical unit of the Third World revolution, therefore, is not the trade union engaging in political action, but a secretly recruited guerilla army seeking to establish itself in the countryside, until it can starve out the cities. But a new dimension is added to the problem by the fact that in the turbulent summer of 1967 the young black American student leader, Stokeley Carmichael, called for the creation of another Vietnam in the United States itself.

On the structural as distinct from the ideological level, of course, the activities of guerillas and of revolutionaries vary enormously from country to country. Were anyone to suggest setting up a high command of the revolution in Peking, Havana or elsewhere, divisions and differences would soon open up. Moreover it is clear that wherever there is a revolutionary force in being, there are alternative contenders bidding for its control. None the less, in 1970, the apparent victory of the Vietcong, and the relative disintegration of normally established United States society, are events sufficiently striking to unite under a single banner the most diverse groups. And in this process the growth of the Black Power movement in the United States occupies a peculiar and central place.

The story of black militancy in the United States goes back to the days of Marcus Garvey and, in the United States, as in Garvey's native country, Jamaica, what black people have sought in what has appeared to them to be an alien land has been a return to an African Zion. By contrast with this, the liberal phase of negro politics, which runs from the NAACP to Martin Luther King, was essentially integrative in its aims. It could not survive King's assassination and today again black separatism is the order of the day. Some black leaders, as for instance the Black Panthers, aim at creating what they call a 'Marxist-Leninist party' which will carry through a socialist revolution. Some still hanker after an African Zion, some seek simply to establish an electoral force with which white politicians must bargain as their predecessors had to with Irish and Italian power but some, and they may not be the least important, are prepared, Samson-like, to tear down the temple of American civilization even on their own heads.

The internal black revolution in the United States, coupled with the Vietnam war, creates what is perhaps the most vital link in the chain of black revolution, for it brings into one movement the most sophisticated black colonial people and the most highly organized military power in the Third World. Moreover, it does not merely establish a continuing pattern of guerilla warfare in town and country alike in all parts of the colonial world, but opens up a structural fault in the metropolitan social systems of Europe and America.

What American experience of the late sixties showed was that there were, even within this affluent society, many groups who were left out of the welfare deal. The blacks were not the only such group, but their militancy opened up a new possibility which Marxism has not bargained for, namely, the revolt of the underclass. A revolt which, although it might not lead to the economic and political sway of that class, could at least, do much damage to the society's functioning. Similarly, in Britain and in European countries, an underclass of immigrant workers emerged, which was increasingly harassed and differentiated as a separate part of the labour force. Amongst these immigrants, and more particularly amongst their children, the slogans of Black Power had increasing appeal. In fact, however, the full implications of the revolt of the immigrant underclass may not yet be apparent.

Many people in Britain imagine that they have discussed what is politically outstanding between the British and their West Indian immigrants when they have discussed Black Power. Few have any idea of what political trends are stirring amongst the non-English speaking Asian communities.

The structural fault in the advanced metropolitan nations has shown itself, however, not merely in the overt revolt of the black and underprivileged. Significant numbers of the most educated members of these societies began to lose faith in their own nation and culture and created on an international level a counter-culture of a whole new kind. It is no accident that in California the convicted murderer, Manson, should become the object of a cult. Such a phenomenon may represent an extreme case but symbolizes, as completely as anything could, the society which has lost faith in itself. Amongst the latest exotic cultural blooms reported from California, is a new form of Christian-Hippie evangelicalism whose members appear to be known as 'Jesus-freaks', but young Californians interviewed about this pheno-menon assert themselves by saying openly that they prefer Satan.

To say all that we have done is by no means to say that what we have called 'the black revolution' is likely to succeed soon, either in America or on the various colonial battle-fronts. In fact, what is most likely to happen is that in the metropolitan coun-tries democracy itself will disappear, for it is through the use of democratic rights that the revolutionary movement has been able to build itself up. What may be expected in the future, how-ever, is a slow build-up of criminal and political violence of a kind which people will call anarchistic and meaningless. On the other hand, the guerillas who seek to establish bases in Rhodesia, South Africa, Palestine or the Latin American countries, are likely to find the going as difficult, if not more so, than Guevara did in Bolivia.

They will suffer and will have to bear the kind of crushing defeat that the Arab nations and the Palestinian guerillas in particular have suffered, but for all that, the ideal and the goal of the Third World or the black revolution will survive. The argument of this chapter is that it will be the determining factor in world history for many years to come. Compared to it, the revolution of European Marxism will appear sociologically as little more than a little local difficulty.

This appears to be an appropriate point to end a book on race relations. We cannot know what the ultimate outcome will be, but any discussion of race relations, whether in Birmingham or Chicago, in Johannesburg or Peking, will be meaningless unless the fact of the gathering forces of black and colonial revolution is taken into account. Our vision of the future can be none other than that which Segal attributes to one of the most significant leaders of a slave rebellion in the United States, Nat Turner (Segal, 1966, p. 181):

I had a vision and I saw white spirits and black spirits engaged in battle and the scene was darkened—the thunder rolled in the heavens and blood flowed in streams—and I heard a voice saying 'such is your luck, such you are called to see, and, let it come rough or smooth, you must surely bear it'.

It is not for the sociologist *qua* sociologist to comment further on the rights and wrongs of this struggle. But the state of affairs which Turner describes in his vision is, to use the slang of drop-out America 'just about where it's at'.

Bibliography

ALTHUSSER, LOUIS (1970) *For Marx*, trans. Ben Brewster, London: Allen Lane, the Penguin Press.

AMALGAMATED ENGINEERING UNION (1967) *Annual Conference Proceedings*.

BANTON, MICHAEL (1967) *Race Relations*, London: Tavistock.

BANTON, MICHAEL (1969) 'What do we mean by racism?', *New Society*, no. 341, 10 April, pp. 551–4.

BARAN, PAUL ALEXANDER and SWEEZY, PAUL MARLOR (1966) *Monopoly Capitalism: an essay on the American economic and social order*, New York: Monthly Review Press.

BELL, DANIEL (1960) *The End of Ideology*, New York: The Free Press.

BERGER, PETER L. and LUCKMANN, THOMAS (1967) *The Social Construction of Reality: a treatise in the sociology of knowledge*, London: Allen Lane, the Penguin Press.

BLACKSTONE, TESSA (1969) 'The problem of dispersal of coloured children'. Unpublished paper presented to the Race Relations Group of the British Sociological Association.

BOLT, CHRISTINE (1971) *Victorian Attitudes to Race*, London: Routledge & Kegan Paul.

BURNEY, E. (1967) *Housing on Trial*, London: Oxford University Press.

BUTTERWORTH, ERIC (ed.) (1967) *Coloured Immigrants in West Yorkshire: social conditions and the lives of Pakistanis, Indians and West Indians*. London: Institute of Race Relations.

CASTLES, STEPHEN and CASTLES, GODULA (1971) 'Immigrant workers and the class structure'. University of Sussex: unpublished Ph.D. thesis.

CORRIGAN, P. and MCGREAL, R. (1969) Unpublished paper presented to the Race Relations Group of the British Sociological Association.

COX, OLIVER CROMWELL (1959) *Caste, Class and Race: a study in social dynamics*, New York: Monthly Review Press.

DAVIDSON, BASIL (1966) *Black Africa*, London: Oxford University Press.

DAVIS, JON GOWER and JACKSON, JOHN (1970) 'Race, community and no conflict, *New Society*, 9 July, No. 406, pp. 67–9.

DAVIS, KINGSLEY and MOORE, WILBERT E. (1945) 'Some principles of stratification', *American Sociological Review*, vol. V, pp. 242–9.

DAVISON, R. B. (1966) *Black British*, London: Oxford University Press.

DEAKIN, NICHOLAS, COHEN, BRIAN and MCNEAL, JULIA (1970) *Colour, Citizenship and British Society*, London: Panther Books.

DE KIEWET, C. W. (1941) *A History of South Africa, Social and Economic*, London: Oxford University Press.

DESAI, R. (1962) *Indian Immigrants in Britain*, London: Oxford University Press.

DUFFY, JAMES (1960) *A Question of Slavery: labour policies in Portuguese Africa and the British protest, 1850–1920*, Oxford: Clarendon Press.

DURKHEIM, EMILE (1933) *The Division of Labor in Society*, trans. George Simpson, New York: The Free Press.

DURKHEIM, EMILE (1938) *The Rules of Sociological Method*, ed. George Catlin, trans. Sarah Soloway and John Mueller, New York: The Free Press.

ELKINS, STANLEY M. (1963) *Slavery: a Problem in American Institutional and Intellectual Life*, New York: Grosset and Dunlap. (2nd ed. 1968, Chicago: Chicago University Press.)

ETZIONI, AMITAI (1968) *The Active Society: a theory of societal and political processes*, New York: The Free Press.

EVERSLEY, DAVID and SUKDEO, FRED (1969) *The Dependants of the Coloured Commonwealth Population of England and Wales*, London: Institute of Race Relations.

EYSENCK, HANS J. (1971) *Race, Intelligence and Education*, London: Temple Smith.

FONER, LAURA and GENOVESE, EUGENE D. (eds) (1969) *Slavery in the New World: a reader in comparative history*, Englewood Cliffs, N.J.: Prentice-Hall.

FOOT, PAUL (1966) *Race and Immigration in British Politics*, Harmondsworth: Penguin.

FRANK, ANDRE GUNDAR, *The Sociology of Underdevelopment and the Underdevelopment of Sociology*, Copenhagen: Zenit Reprint, n.d.

FREYRE, GILBERTO (1956) *The Masters and the Slaves: a study in the development of Brazilian civilization*, trans. Samuel Putnam, New York: Knopf.

FURNIVALL, J. S. (1948) *Colonial Policy and Practice*, London: Cambridge University Press.

FURNIVALL, J. S. (1967) *Netherlands India: A Study of Plural Economy*, London: Cambridge University Press.

GARRARD, JOHN E. (1971) *The English and Immigration*, London: Oxford University Press.

GENOVESE, EUGENE D. (1965) *The Political Economy of Slavery: studies in the economy and society of the slave south*, New York: Pantheon.

GENOVESE, EUGENE D. (1969) *The World the Slaveholders Made: two essays in interpretation*, New York: Pantheon.

GENOVESE, EUGENE D. (1971) *In Red and Black: Marxian explorations in Southern and Afro-American history*, London: Allen Lane, the Penguin Press.

GOLDTHORPE, JOHN (1969) 'Social inequality and social integration in modern Britain'. Presidential address to the Sociology Section of the British Association for the Advancement of Science, Exeter.

HALSEY, A. H. (1970) 'Race relations—the lines to think on', *New Society*, no. 390, 19 March, pp. 472–4.

HANKE, LEWIS (1949) *The Spanish Struggle for Justice in the Conquest of America*, Philadelphia: University of Pennsylvania Press.

HARRIS, MARVIN (1964) *Patterns of Race in the Americas*, New York: Walker and Co.

HMSO (1962) *Commonwealth Immigrants Act 1962*, London: HMSO.

HMSO (1965a) *Report of the Committee on Housing in Greater London* (Cmd 2605), London: HMSO.

HMSO (1965b) *Immigration from the Commonwealth* (Cmd 2379), London: HMSO.

HMSO (1967) *Control of Immigrants Statistics 1966* (Cmd 3258), London: HMSO.

HMSO (1968) *Control of Immigrants Statistics 1967* (Cmd 3594), London: HMSO.

HMSO (1969) *Council Housing, Purposes, Procedures and Priorities* (Ministry of Housing, Local Government and Welsh Office), London: HMSO.

HOETINK, H. (1967) *The Two Variants in Caribbean Race Relations. A contribution to the sociology of segmented societies*, London: Oxford University Press.

JACOBS, JANE (1965) *The Death and Life of Great American Cities*, Harmondsworth: Penguin.

JENKINS, ROBIN (1970) 'The production of knowledge in the Institute of Race Relations'. Unpublished paper to the Race Relations Group of the British Sociological Association.

JENSEN, A. R. (1969) 'How can we boost I.Q. and scholastic achievement?', *Harvard Educational Review*, winter, 39, pp. 1–24.

JOHN, AUGUSTINE (1970) *Race in the Inner City: a report on Handsworth, Birmingham, with comments from Robert Holmar, John Lambert and Dipak Nandy*, London: Runnymede Trust, 2 Arundel Street, London.

JONES, K. (1961) 'Immigrants and the social services', *National Institute Economic Review*, no. 41, pp. 28–40.

KUPER, LEO and SMITH, M. G. (1969) *Pluralism in Africa*, Berkeley and Los Angeles: University of California Press.

LAMBERT, JOHN (1970) *Crime, Race Relations and the Police: a study in Birmingham*, London: Oxford University Press.

LAMBERT, JOHN and FILKIN, CAMILLA (1971) 'Race relations research', *Race*, vol. XII, pp. 329–35.

LEWIS, OSCAR (1965) 'The Folk-Urban Ideal Type' in Philip M. Hauser and Leo F. Schnore (eds), *The Study of Urbanisation*, New York: Wiley.

LIPSET, SEYMOUR MARTIN (1959) *Political Man: the social bases of politics*, London: Heinemann.

MACMILLAN, WILLIAM MILLER (1963) *Bantu, Boer and Briton: the making of the South African native problem*, Oxford: Clarendon Press (rev. ed.).

MALINOWSKI, BRONISLAW (1944) *A Scientific Theory of Culture and Other Essays*, Chapel Hill: University of North Carolina Press.

MALINOWSKI, BRONISLAW (1945) *The Dynamics of Culture Change: an enquiry into race relations in Africa*, New Haven: Yale University Press.

MARX, KARL and ENGELS, FREDERICK (1962) *Selected Works*, Moscow, Foreign Languages Publishing House.

MAYER, PHILIP (1963) *Townsmen or Tribesmen: conservation and the process of urbanization in a South African city*, Cape Town: Oxford University Press.

MEAD, GEORGE HERBERT (1934) *Mind, Self and Society*, Chicago: University of Chicago Press.

MISHAN, E. J. and NEEDLEMAN, L. (1966) 'Immigration: some economic effects', London: *Lloyds Bank Review*, July.

MORRIS, HAROLD STEPHEN (1968) *The Indians in Uganda*, London: Weidenfeld and Nicolson.

MYRDAL, GUNNAR (1958) *Value in Social Theory: a collection of essays on methodology*, London: Routledge & Kegan Paul.

MYRDAL, GUNNAR (1962) *An American Dilemma*, New York: Harper.

NIEBUHR, RICHARD H. (1957) *The Social Sources of Denominationalism*, New York: Meridian Books.

NISBET, ROBERT (1964) *Power and Community*, New York: Oxford University Press.

OPIE, R. G. (1968) 'Britain's immigrants. Do they help the economy?', *New Statesman*, 15 March, p. 323.

PAHL, RAY (ed.) (1968) *Readings in Urban Sociology*, Oxford: Pergamon Press.

PAHL, RAY (1970) *Whose City?*, London: Longman.

PARK, ROBERT E., BURGESS, ERNEST W. and MACKENZIE, RODERICK D. (1925) *The City*, Chicago: University of Chicago Press.

PARSONS, TALCOTT (1954) *Essays in Sociological Theory*, New York: The Free Press.

PATTERSON, SHEILA (1968) *Immigrants in Industry*, London: Oxford University Press.

PEACH, CERI (1968) *West Indian Migration to Britain: a social geography*, London: Oxford University Press.

POLITICAL AND ECONOMIC PLANNING (1968) *Racial Discrimination*, Harmondsworth: Penguin.

REDFIELD, ROBERT (1947) 'The folk society', *American Journal of Sociology*, vol. 41, pp. 293–308.

REX, JOHN (1959) 'The plural society in sociological theory', *British Journal of Sociology*, vol. 10, pp. 114–24.

REX, JOHN and MOORE, ROBERT (1967) *Race, Community and Conflict*, London: Oxford University Press.

REX, JOHN (1968a) 'The Sociology of the Urban Zone of Transition' in Ray Pahl (ed.), *Readings in Urban Sociology*, Oxford: Pergamon Press.

REX, JOHN (1968b) 'The Race Relations Catastrophe', in T. Burgess (ed.), *Matters of Principle: Labour's Last Chance*, Harmondsworth: Penguin.

REX, JOHN (1970) *Race Relations in Sociological Theory*, London: Weidenfeld & Nicolson.

RICHARDSON, KEN, SPEARS, DAVID and RICHARDS, MARTIN (1972) *Race, Culture and Intelligence*, Harmondsworth: Penguin.

RICHMOND, ANTHONY (1970) 'Housing and racial attitudes in Bristol', *Race*, vol. XII, no. 1, pp. 49–58.

ROSE, E. J. B. *et al.* (1969) *Colour and Citizenship: a report on British race relations*, London: Oxford University Press.

ROUX, E. (1949) *Time Longer Than Rope*, London: Gollancz.

SEGAL, RONALD (1966) *The Race War*, London: Cape.

SIMMEL, GEORG (1950) 'The Metropolis and Mental Life', in Kurt H. Wolff (ed.), *The Sociology of Georg Simmel*, New York: The Free Press.

SMITH, M. G. (1965) *The Plural Society in the British West Indies*, Berkeley and Los Angeles: University of California Press.

TANNENBAUM, FRANK (1946) *Slave and Citizen: the Negro in the Americas*, New York: Vintage Books.

THURNWALD, RICHARD (1935) *Black and White in East Africa: The fabric of a new civilisation—a study of social contact and adaptation of life in East Africa*, London: Routledge and Sons.

TÖNNIES, F. (1955) *Community and Association*, London: Routledge & Kegan Paul.

TOYNBEE, ARNOLD J. (1953) *A Study of History*, London: Oxford University Press.

UNESCO (1968) *Four Statements on the Race Question*, Paris: UNESCO.

VAN DEN BERGHE, PIERRE L. (1967a) *Race and Racism: comparative perspectives*, New York: Wiley.

VAN DEN BERGHE, PIERRE L. (1967b) *South Africa, A Study in Conflict*, Berkeley and Los Angeles: University of California Press.

WAGLEY, CHARLES and HARRIS, MARVIN (1964) *Minorities in the New World*, New York: Columbia University Press.

WARNER, W. LLOYD (1936) 'American class and caste', *American Journal of Sociology*, vol. XLII, pp. 234–7.

WATERHOUSE, J. A. H. and BRABBAN, D. H. (1964) 'Inquiry into fertility of immigrants: preliminary report', *Eugenics Review*, vol. 56, pp. 7–18.

WEBER, MAX (1958) *The Religion of India: the sociology of Hinduism and Buddhism*, ed. and trans. Hans Gerth and Don Martindale, New York: The Free Press.

WEBER, MAX (1961) *General Economic History*, trans. Frank H. Knight, New York: Collier Books.

WEBER, MAX (1967) 'Class, Status and Party', in Reinhard Bendix and Seymour Martin Lipset (eds), *Class, Status and Power: social stratification in comparative perspective*, London: Routledge & Kegan Paul, 2nd ed.

WEBER, MAX (1968) *Economy and Society: an outline of interpretive sociology*, ed. Guenther Roth and Claus Wittich, New York: Bedminster Press.

WERTHEIM, WILLEM FREDERIK (1959) *Indonesian Society in Transition: a study of social change*, The Hague, Van Hoeve, 2nd ed.

WESTERMANN, DIEDRICH (1970) *The African Today and Tomorrow*, New York: Humanities Press, 3rd ed.

WILLIAMS, ERIC (1966) *Capitalism and Slavery*, Chapel Hill: University of North Carolina Press.

WIRTH, LOUIS (1964) *On Cities and Social Life*, Chicago: University of Chicago Press.

WOLPE, HAROLD (1970) 'Industrialism and Race in South Africa', in Sami Zubaida (ed.), *Race and Racialism*. London: Tavistock.

WRIGHT, PETER (1968) *The Coloured Worker in British Industry with special reference to the Midlands and North of England*, London: Oxford University Press.

ZUBAIDA, SAMI (ed.) (1970) *Race and Racialism*, London: Tavistock.

Index

305